College Reading

with the

Active Critical Thinking Method

BOOK 1

Fifth Edition

JANET MAKER

Los Angeles Trade-Technical College

MINNETTE LENIER

Los Angeles Pierce College

 **Wadsworth**
Thomson Learning™

Australia • Canada • Denmark • Japan • Mexico • New Zealand • Philippines • Puerto Rico
Singapore • Spain • United Kingdom • United States

Executive Manager	Elana Dolberg
Senior Development Editor	Kimberly Johnson
Editorial Assistant	Sally Cobau
Project Editor	Christal Niederer
Print Buyer	Barbara Britton
Permissions Editor	Joohee Lee

Cover Image: Andre Derain. "Effect of the Sun on the Water." © 2000 Artists Rights Society (ARS), New York/ADAGP, Paris.

ISBN: 0-15-506644-7
Library of Congress Cataloging-in-Publication Data
College reading with the active critical thinking method.
Book 1 / [compiled by] Janet Maker, Minnette Lenier.
-5th ed.
   Includes index.
   1. Reading (Secondary). 2. Reading (Higher education).
3. College readers. I.Maker, Janet. II. Lenier, Minnette.
III. College reading with active critical thinking. Book 1.
LB1632.C57   2000
428.6-dc21   99-42551

Address for Domestic Orders
Harcourt College Publishers, 6277 Sea Harbor Drive, Orlando, FL 32887-6777
800-782-4479

Address for International Orders
International Customer Service
Harcourt, Inc., 6277 Sea Harbor Drive, Orlando, FL 32887-6777
407-345-3800
(fax) 407-345-4060
(e-mail) hbintl@harcourt.com

Address for Editorial Correspondence
Harcourt College Publishers, 301 Commerce Street, Suite 3700, Fort Worth, TX 76102

Web Site Address
http://www.harcourtcollege.com

Printed in the United States of America

0 1 2 3 4 5 6 7 8 9   039   9 8 7 6 5 4 3 2 1

Harcourt College Publishers

Contents

UNIT I

Reading Fundamentals   1

Introduction   2

Word Comprehension   3

Context Clues   3
Word Parts   5
Dictionary   7

Word Memory   15
Word Comprehension Review   16

Paragraph Comprehension   38

Literal Comprehension   38

Inferential Comprehension   43

Critical Comprehension   46

Paragraph Comprehension Review   48

UNIT II

Introduction to the Active Critical Thinking (ACT) Method

Reading Selections

UNIT III

Using the ACT Method for Study   199

Textbook Reading Selections

Additional Resources

Tests: Comprehension and Vocabulary Checks   321

Contents by Skills

Word Comprehension

Comprehension

The Active Critical Thinking Method: Six Steps

Preface

The College Reading Series

College Reading with the Active Critical Thinking Method, Book 1, 5th Edition is the first book in a three-part reading series by Maker/Lenier for students reading at a developmental level. The books in this series include:

1. *College Reading with the Active Critical Thinking Method, Book 1.* Written at the sixth to ninth grade reading level, this book is intended for lower-level developmental reading courses. *Book 1* focuses on reading fundamentals such as vocabulary building, subject, main idea, theses, arguments, and supporting details through different types of readings (general interest and textbook). Students are introduced to the ACT Method.

2. *College Reading with the Active Critical Thinking Method, Book 2.* Written at the ninth to twelfth grade reading level, this book is intended for intermediate developmental reading courses. After a review of reading fundamentals, *Book 2* stresses general interest reading, study reading *and* critical reading. The study reading section contains challenging textbook selections from a variety of subjects. The critical reading section presents pairs of reading selections with opposing viewpoints on controversial subjects. Both sections utilize the six-step ACT Method.

3. *Academic Reading with Active Critical Thinking.* Written at the tenth to thirteenth (college) grade reading level, this book is intended for higher-level developmental reading courses. *Book 3* provides advanced practice with the ACT Method, helping students sharpen their critical reading and study skills together in real academic contexts.

The Maker/Lenier series teaches fundamental, study, and critical reading skills in the context of high-interest readings. As students become more confident in their newly acquired reading skills, they are expected to work more independently. The central component of their highly effective approach is the Active Critical Thinking Method.

The Active Critical Thinking Method

The Active Critical Thinking Method is an innovative six-step method that provides a unified approach to reading. Students can easily master this method and apply it to *any* reading, whether it's for pleasure, information, study, or analysis.

1. **Preread.** For general and study reading, the prereading step consists of skimming for subject and main idea, activating background knowledge, and generating questions. Readings are taken from actual college textbooks in a wide variety of content areas.

   For critical reading of persuasive material, students skim to ascertain the subject and the author's thesis. They then compare their own points of view with the author's, consider what they know and don't know about the subject, and generate questions. For most critical reading, we use pairs of articles taking opposing viewpoints on controversial subjects that are frequently debated by college students.

2. **Read.** As in SQ3R, students are asked to read without marking their texts; they concentrate on comprehension, and memory is a separate step. After reading, they mark any parts they didn't understand and make a plan to gain understanding (e.g., ask in class, read another source, and so on).

3. **Analyze What You Read.** Most of the teaching time is spent on this third step. Students use practice activities that are highly structured at first, moving toward increasing independence. For study reading, students prepare for both objective and subjective evaluation. They go back to the section they have read and predict what will be on the test. They underline only what they believe will be on the test and only what they don't think they will remember. They make marginal notes as in SQ3R to test themselves on what they have underlined. They practice marking the text differently for objective versus essay questions. They then create at least one graphic organizer for the article, such as an idea map, chart, time line, or outline.

   For critical reading, students identify the thesis (author's point of view), the arguments supporting the thesis, the support given for each argument, and finally they evaluate the support. They identify the type of support (facts, testimony, examples, reasons) and they evaluate the support by means of practice activities for whichever skills are relevant (e.g., fact versus opinion, provable versus unprovable data, valid versus invalid inferences, logical reasoning, credibility of sources, recognizing bias, and using criteria for evaluating research). They then create at least one graphic organizer for the article.

4. **Remember What's Important.** Students memorize by self-testing, using their underlining, marginal notes, and graphic organizers, all of which may be transferred to flash cards. Mnemonic devices are used as appropriate.

5. **Make Use of What You Read.** This step refers to output, such as class discussions, written assignments, oral reports, or tests. For each reading selection, we give our students a test which includes objective, short answer, and essay questions.

6. **Evaluate Your Active Critical Thinking Skills.** Students analyze feedback from the previous step using an evaluation checklist. For example, they decide whether wrong answers were caused by predicting the wrong questions; by not making sufficient use of the marginal notes, flash cards, and graphic organizers for memorization; and/or by poor test-taking skills, such as poor use of time or poor organization of the essay. They then make a plan for improvement, and evaluate their skills using a Progress Chart.

Key Features

Besides the innovative ACT Method, *College Reading, Book 1* offers the following benefits:

- All the skills instruction is based on 24 high-interest reading selections that appear after the expanded skills review in the introductory unit.

- A strong emphasis on vocabulary development, with vocabulary skills instruction in Unit I, review of the skills in Unit II, and vocabulary previews and checks for each reading, builds vocabulary skills in context, step-by-step.

- Two tables of contents: In addition to the regular table of contents, a skills-based table of contents allows instructors to assign activities that reinforce particular skills.

- The level of difficulty increases as students progress through the text.

New to the Fifth Edition

- New **high-interest reading selections.** One-third of the readings have been replaced or updated with particular regard to student interest. The 5th edition contains readings by Walter Cronkite, Rosie O'Donnell, Malcolm Forbes, Bill Cosby, and by financial wizards, The Motley Fools.

- **Expanded testing materials** to help instructors and students prepare for tests.
  - A new test section at the end of the book includes 24 Comprehension Checks and Vocabulary Checks.

- A Progress Chart has been added so students can measure their progress and use the results to analyze their strengths and weaknesses.

- The testing section of the Instructor's Manual has been expanded to include testing of cognitive understanding of the skills in each unit as well as testing for application of the skills.

■ **Improved clarity and design** of the ACT Method so that the steps are even easier for students to follow. The fifth edition has an easier-to-read font, and the pages are perforated so assignments can be torn out and submitted.

■ **Expanded coverage of key prerequisite and vocabulary skills.**

- Unit I now provides more vocabulary and critical reading skills practice.

- Expanded Vocabulary Skills Review activities now follow the reading selections in Unit II.

■ **Removable bookmark** attached to the cover helps students easily reference the ACT Method while reading this book or any others.

■ **Three alternate tables in the Instructor's Manual** correlate the text's activities to the skills required for the Texas, Florida, and Georgia state reading tests (TASP, CLAST, Regents).

Teaching and Learning Aids

Supplements for *College Reading with the Active Critical Thinking Method, Book 1*

■ **Instructor's Manual and Test Bank** (0-534-51855-9). Fully updated and revised to reflect key revisions in the main text, this 8½ x 11 resource now includes the following and more: tests, teaching philosophy, instructional suggestions, additional help for adjuncts, and reading efficiency perception exercises. Unit I tests cover vocabulary and comprehension. Units II and III feature cognitive, applications, and vocabulary tests.

■ **Web Site.** Visit Wadsworth's Developmental English Web site at **http://devenglish.wadsworth.com.** Here you will find many online teaching and learning aids.

Other Supplementary Materials Available from Wadsworth

Please contact your Wadsworth sales representative for additional information regarding policy, pricing, and availability for any of these products or services. You may locate your representative via the Internet at our Wadsworth home page: **http://www.wadsworth.com.**

- **Wadsworth Developmental English Internet-at-a-Glance Trifold** (0-534-54744-3). This handy guide shows your students where to find online reading and writing resources. Package this trifold card with any Wadsworth Developmental English text. (Please contact your Thomson Learning representative for pricing information.)

- **Newbury House Dictionary** (0-8384-5613-8). Make this developmental-level dictionary available to your students at a reduced cost by bundling it with this text. Contact your sales representative for information on this option.

- **InfoTrac® College Edition.** This fully searchable, online database with access to full-text articles from over 900 periodicals provides a great resource for additional readings and/or research. Now available **free** with this text, InfoTrac College Edition offers authoritative sources, updated daily and going back as far as four years. Both you and your students can receive unlimited online use for one academic term. (Please contact your Thomson Learning representative for policy, pricing, and availability; international and school distribution is restricted.)

- **Custom Publishing.** You can combine your choice of chapters from specific Wadsworth titles with your own materials in a custom-bound book. To place your order, call the Thomson Learning Custom Order Center at 1-800-355-9983.

- **Videos.** Wadsworth has many videos available to qualifying adopters on topics such as improving your grades, notetaking practice, diversity, and many more. Contact your local Wadsworth representative for more information.

Acknowledgments

Thanks to my children, Thomas and Jane Maker, for sharing the computer with their mom. Thanks to Kim Johnson, super editor, and to the entire Wadsworth Editorial and Production teams, especially Karen Allanson, Godwin Chu, and Christal Niederer for their hard work on this fifth edition. I am also grateful to the reviewers for all their helpful suggestions.

Reviewers of the Fifth Edition

L. David Allen, *University of Nebraska–Lincoln*
Linda Allen, *Hill College*
Jessica I. Carroll, *Miami-Dade Community College, Wilson Campus*

Joan Eberle, *Shasta College*
Lawrence Erickson, *Southern Illinois University–Carbondale*
Nadine Gandia, *Miami-Dade Community College, Inter-American Campus*
Alice K. Perry, *St. Charles County Community College*
Keflyn X. Reed, *Bishop State Community College*

Reviewers of the Previous Edition

L. David Allen, *University of Nebraska–Lincoln*
Naomi Barnett, *Lorain County Community College*
Ann M. Clark, *Hagerstown Business College*
William E. Loflin, *Catonsville Community College*
Keflyn X. Reed, *Bishop State Community College*
Richard Francis Tracz, *Oakton Community College*

To the Student

As a college student, you will probably spend about a fourth of your waking hours reading textbooks. The purpose of this book is to help you do that as efficiently as possible—to get the most out of your reading in the least amount of time and to succeed in your classes.

Using this book you will improve your reading and study skills by practicing them on reading selections. Because reading should be enjoyable, we have tried to make the reading selections as interesting as possible, choosing subjects such as *Obtaining Information About Employment Opportunities* and *The All-American Male.*

The book is divided into three units:

- **Unit I,** *Reading Fundamentals,* reviews the basic skills in vocabulary and comprehension that you will need for the other two units.

- **Unit II,** *Introduction to the Active Critical Thinking (ACT) Method*, begins with an introduction to the six-step ACT Method. You will then read ten selections of general interest and analyze them using the six steps. Two additional selections take opposing viewpoints on the use of lie-detector tests by employers. You again use the same six steps, adapted for critical reading.

- **Unit III**, *Using the ACT Method for Study,* begins by explaining how to use the six steps for study reading of college textbooks. You then will read twelve selections from college textbooks on a variety of subjects and prepare study guides using the six steps.

Each of the twenty-four reading selections in the book comes with two tests: one for comprehension and one for vocabulary. You will use the tests to evaluate your strengths and weaknesses and measure your progress.

Using this book will help you understand and remember what you read. You will learn what to study and how to study to get the grades you want.

UNIT I

Reading Fundamentals

Introduction

Before we get started, take this quiz to check your reading skills as they stand right now. Mark each question *yes* or *no*. You may answer *yes* to more than one in each group.

Vocabulary

1. When you see a word you don't know, do you regularly try to

    _____ a. figure out its meaning from the sentence it's in?

    _____ b. use its prefixes, suffixes, and roots as clues to the meaning?

    _____ c. sound it out?

2. After you look up a new word in the dictionary can you *usually*

    _____ a. pronounce it correctly using the pronunciation guide?

    _____ b. use it in the correct part of speech?

    _____ c. understand which definition to use if more than one is given?

    _____ d. use some kind of mental association to make sure you remember the word?

Comprehension

1. In reading a paragraph, can you *usually*

    _____ a. identify the subject, main idea, and supporting details?

    _____ b. identify the type of supporting details the author uses?

    _____ c. read between the lines to identify main ideas that are implied but not stated?

    _____ d. tell the difference between valid and invalid inferences?

2. When an author is trying to persuade you of something, can you *usually*

    _____ a. identify the author's point of view?

    _____ b. identify the arguments supporting the point of view?

    _____ c. identify the evidence supporting each argument?

All these questions should have been answered *yes*. Making sure you have all these basic vocabulary and comprehension skills is our goal in this first unit. In Unit II we focus on the more difficult skills needed for reading longer selections, and in Unit III we concentrate on textbook reading.

Word Comprehension

One of the biggest reasons for poor reading speed and comprehension is having a poor vocabulary. If you don't know the words, you will have trouble understanding the ideas.

Beginning in elementary school, many students are told, "If you don't know a word, look it up in the dictionary." We disagree. Going often to the dictionary interrupts your reading and can interfere with your comprehension. Instead, we recommend that every time you see an unfamiliar word, you do the following:

1. Try to figure the word out from the context of the sentence.

2. See if you can use the prefix and/or root as a clue to meaning.

3. Only if the first two steps fail, and if the word is important to understanding what you are reading, should you look it up in the dictionary.

Context Clues

The way babies learn to talk is by hearing words over and over until they figure out from the context what the words mean. When you learn to read, unfamiliar words are presented in the context of sentences. By thinking about the sentence you can usually figure out what the unfamiliar word means. People who read a lot have bigger vocabularies than people who don't because they have seen many more words in context.

In the following four sentences, you can figure out the meanings of the difficult words by using four types of context clues: definition clues, contrast clues, example clues, and experience clues. Circle the letter of the definition that comes closest to the meaning of the underlined word. **Do not use a dictionary.**

1. A theory is an accepted explanation of a set of observations.

   a. guess

   b. law

   c. fact

   d. explanation

   The answer is d. The context clue used in this sentence is a **definition** clue. The phrase "an accepted explanation of a set of observations" defines the word theory.

2. Teachers appreciate neatly written or typed assignments so they don't have to spend time trying to read <u>illegible</u> scrawls.

   a. easy to read

   b. misspelled

   c. hard to read

   d. foreign

   The answer is c. The context clue used in this sentence is a **contrast** clue. Illegible scrawls are contrasted with neatly written or typed assignments.

3. "Pretty as a picture," "poor as a churchmouse," and "sly as a fox" are examples of <u>clichés</u>.

   a. overused expressions

   b. new ideas

   c. insults

   d. flattery

   The answer is a. The context clue used is an **example** clue. The sentence gives examples of clichés.

4. Getting a chill, not eating right, and not getting enough sleep make us more <u>susceptible</u> to catching colds.

   a. open to

   b. resistant to

   c. happy about

   d. angry about

   The answer is a. The context clue used is an **experience** clue. Anyone who has ever had the experience of catching a cold knows that unhealthy behaviors lower our resistance.

   In the following exercise, circle the correct answer and then write the type of clue (definition, contrast, example, experience) in the blank. (The answers appear upside down at the bottom of the next page.)

1. ZIP code is <u>an acronym</u> for Zone Improvement Plan.

   a. a word with more than one meaning

   b. a word that sounds like another word

   c. a rhyming word

   d. a word made up from other words

   Type of clue _____

2. A <u>hypothesis</u> is a type of guess, a theory that remains to be proved.

   a. fact

   b. theory

   c. lie

   d. promise

   Type of clue _____

3. Physics is considered a more intellectually <u>demanding</u> major than is education or P.E.

   a. well paid

   b. enjoyable

   c. difficult

   d. unusual

   Type of clue _____

4. If someone who is widely respected <u>endorses</u> a candidate or program, you are more likely to vote for the candidate or program.

   a. loudly opposes

   b. carefully ignores

   c. decides to become

   d. publicly favors

   Type of clue _____

5. A <u>conscientious</u> police officer never takes bribes or uses unnecessary force.

   a. A crooked

   b. An honest

   c. A well educated

   d. An overpaid

   Type of clue _____

Word Parts

A second important skill in figuring out unfamiliar words is using word parts. Most of the difficult words in English come from Latin or Greco-Latin. Latin is very closely related to Spanish, French, Italian, Portuguese, and

Romanian. If you know any of these languages you have a huge advantage in figuring out difficult words in English. However, even if the only language you know is English, you still know many of the important Latin word parts. For example, guess the meanings of the following word parts (the first item is done for you; the answers appear upside down at the bottom of the page).

Word part	Example	Meaning of word part
1. tri	triangle	three
2. non	nonprofit	_____
3. max	maximum	_____
4. vid	video	_____
5. pre	preview	_____

There are three types of word parts: prefixes, roots, and suffixes. A **prefix** is a syllable added to the beginning of a word to change its meaning. For example, the word *insincere* means "not sincere," because one meaning of *in* is "not." A **root** forms the base of a word. *Cur,* meaning "to run," is a root that is used with different prefixes to form many words. A **suffix** is a syllable that is added to the end of a word to change its meaning or part of speech. An example of a suffix that changes a word's meaning is the suffix *ist,* which means "one who." A *pianist* is "one who" plays the piano. An example of a suffix that changes a word's part of speech is the suffix *ness.* Adding the suffix *ness* to the adjective *great* changes it to the noun *greatness.*

For practice, write the correct word part from the following list in the blanks provided. Make sure that the words match their definitions. Use the underlined words as clues. (The answers appear upside down at the bottom of the next page.)

Prefixes	Roots	Suffixes
com = together	pose = put	er = someone who
pro = forth, forward	gress = go	or something that
re = back	pel = push, drive	
de = away	port = carry	
ex = out		

Word	**Definition**
1. _ _ _ _ able	able to be <u>carried</u>
2. pro _ _ _ _ _	to <u>go</u> forward
3. re _ _ _	to <u>push</u> back
4. _ _ _ poser	someone who writes music (puts notes <u>together</u>)
5. report _ _	<u>someone who</u> reports information (carries back information)
6. _ _ _ peller	a machine with blades for driving a ship or an airplane (something that drives <u>forward</u>)
7. _ _ gress	to go <u>back</u>
8. pro _ _ _ _	to <u>put</u> forward an idea or a plan
9. _ _ port	to send someone out of the country (carry <u>away</u>)
10. _ _ pel	to push <u>out</u>

In the back of this book (see p. 423) there is a section with 60 common prefixes and 150 common roots. Most of them you probably know already. Learning them all will make a huge difference in your vocabulary. This section contains suggestions about the best ways to learn these word parts. Whenever you have time, we recommend that you work with them.

Dictionary

Sometimes the context does not provide a clue to meaning, or sometimes you cannot understand the ideas being presented without finding out what a word means. In such cases, you will have to use a dictionary. Most people know how to look words up, but very few know how to make the most out of the information that a good dictionary provides.

A dictionary entry has five major parts:

1. the main entry

2. the pronunciation

3. the part or parts of speech

4. the etymology (word history)

5. the definitions

ANSWERS
1. port 2. gress 3. pel 4. com 5. er 6. pro 7. re 8. pose 9. de 10. ex

con•cur (kən kur′) *vi.* **-curred′, -cur′ring** [ME. *concurren* < L. *concurrere*, to run
together < *com-*, together + *currere*, to run] **1.** to occur at the same time; happen
together; coincide **2.** to combine in having an effect; act together [several events
concurred to bring about this result] **3.** to agree (*with*); be in accord (*in* an
opinion, etc.) −*SYN.* see CONSENT

Main Entry

When you look up a word in the dictionary, the first thing you see is the
main entry. The main entry word is divided into syllables, and the syllables
are separated by dots.

Pronunciation

The **pronunciation** appears in parentheses after the main entry. You can
figure out how to pronounce words by using the brief pronunciation guide,
which is usually located at the bottom of every other page. A full explanation
of pronunciation is usually found at the beginning of a dictionary. Here is an
example of a brief pronunciation guide:

**cat, āte, fäther; pen, ēvil; if, kīte; nō, ôr, fo͞od, book; boil, house; up,
tʉrn; chief, shell; thick, *the*; zh, treasure; ŋ, sing; ə for *a* in *about*; ′ as
in *able* (ā′b'l)**

It is sometimes necessary to use the pronunciation guide because you
can't always tell how to pronounce a word from its spelling. There are
twenty-six letters in English representing about forty-four sounds, depending
on one's dialect. For example, the letter *a* is pronounced differently in the
words *cat* (kat), *father* (fä′ther), *ago* (ə gō′), *all* (ôl), and *late* (lāt).

One sound that is common in English is the **schwa sound.** It is written ə
and is pronounced "uh." It occurs in unstressed syllables. A stressed syllable
is pronounced in a louder voice than an unstressed syllable. For example, in

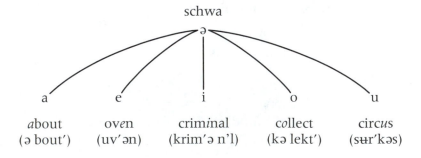

schwa

ə

| a | e | i | o | u |

about | oven | crim*i*nal | collect | circ*u*s
(ə bout′) | (uv′ən) | (krim′ə n'l) | (kə lekt′) | (sʉr′kəs)

the word *ago* (ə gō′), the stress is on the second syllable. The schwa sound can be spelled with any vowel letter, but it is always pronounced the same way.

When you look up a word in the dictionary, you should always take the time to figure out its pronunciation. If you can pronounce a word to yourself, you are more likely to remember it.

For example, let's go back to the word *concur.* The pronunciation is presented in the dictionary as kən kʉr′.

First syllable (kən):	k	does not appear in the pronunciation guide, because it can be pronounced only one way, unlike *c,* which can be pronounced either as *k* or as *s* (city).
	ə	is pronounced "uh" (schwa). The example in the pronunciation guide is the word *about.*
	n	does not appear in the guide, because it has only one pronunciation.
		The syllable *kən* rhymes with *fun.*
Second syllable (kʉr):	k	has only one pronunciation.
	ʉ⎫ r⎭	sounds like the ur in *turn*

The accent mark on the second syllable (kʉr′) means that the second syllable is stressed.

Using the pronunciation guide is very important. If you learn the meaning of an unfamiliar word but can't pronounce it, then you can't use the word in conversation.

Some people have problems hearing some of the sounds, either because the sound does not exist in their native language or dialect, because they have a hearing or learning disability, or because they weren't taught any phonics in elementary school. However, nobody has problems hearing *all* the sounds. In addition, there are many different dialects spoken in English-speaking countries. For the sake of simplicity, American English dictionaries have chosen Standard Midwestern English. If your pronunciation of a word does not match the pronunciation in your dictionary, you are not incorrect. If you have problems, here is what to do:

1. Make sure you are comparing each word with the key words. For example, if the key word for short a is *cat* and the key word for long a is *ate,* you listen for the vowel sound in each word and decide whether you hear the sound in *cat* or the sound in *ate.* In the table on the next page, mark an **X** under the correct key word.

	cat	ate
1. change		
2. dance		
3. gate		
4. ran		
5. stay		

The vowel sounds in *change, gate,* and *stay* match the vowel sound in *ate.* The vowel sounds in *dance* and *ran* match the vowel sound in *cat.*

2. Make sure you listen to the *sound* rather than look at the spelling. For example, the word *eight* has the vowel sound in *ate* even though there is no letter *a* in the word.

3. If you have used the key words correctly and listened for the sound and still can't hear the difference, mark that sound and go on to the next one. Your instructor may be able to assign tapes to help you with sounds, but you should review only those few sounds that really give you trouble. Otherwise, you'll spend too much time on phonics.

A detailed "Practice for Pronunciation" can be found on p. 430.

Part of Speech

In order to use a word you look up in the dictionary, you not only have to be able to pronounce it, but you also have to be able to use it correctly in a sentence. That means knowing what part of speech it is and what that part of speech means.

The **part of speech** appears after the pronunciation in a dictionary entry. Here are a few of the abbreviations you will see in dictionary entries:

n. = noun:	a word that names a person, a place, or a thing
v. = verb:	a word that shows an action or a state of being
vt. = transitive verb:	an action word that affects a person or thing: "Jim dropped the pencil." A transitive verb requires a direct object to complete its meaning.
vi. = intransitive verb:	an action word that does not affect a person or thing: "The apple fell to the ground."

| *adj.* = adjective: | a word that modifies a noun |
| *adv.* = adverb: | a word that modifies a verb, an adjective, or another adverb |

If you know parts of speech, you can use words correctly in a sentence.

Practice A: Circle the letter before the correct part of speech of the under-lined words in the following sentences. Use the dictionary if you need help. (The answers appear upside down at the bottom of the page.)

1. Farmer's markets usually have better <u>produce</u> than supermarkets.

   a. *n.* (präd′o͞os)

   b. *v.* (prə do͞os′)

2. UFO stands for unidentified flying <u>object</u>.

   a. *n.* (äb′jikt)

   b. *v.* (əb jekt′)

3. Extreme cold causes metals to <u>contract</u>.

   a. *n.* (kän′trakt)

   b. *v.* (kən trakt′)

Practice B: Complete the table on the next page. The first item is done for you as an example. If you don't know the part of speech, you will have to use the dictionary. Begin with the word on the left. If you find it, look up its part of speech. Then look around for a similar word in the new part of speech, and check its meaning. Be aware that not all words have their parts of speech listed in the dictionary. They are sometimes listed at the bottom of another entry. For example, in some dictionaries the word *bashful* (adjective) has its own entry, but *bashfully* (adverb) and *bashfulness* (noun) do not. Instead, they are listed at the bottom of the entry for *bashful*. Another possibility is that the word may change its spelling in another part of speech. For example, *receive* is a verb, but the noun form is *reception*. You may need to look around in the dictionary to find the word you want. (The answers appear upside down at the bottom of the next page.)

Word	Part of speech	New part of speech	New word
1. sad	adjective	noun	sadness
2. joy		adjective	
3. sales		verb	
4. quick		adverb	
5. lose		noun	

Etymology

The **etymology,** or origin of the word, appears in brackets after the part of speech.

> **con•cur** (kən kʉr´) *vi.* **-curred´, -cur´ring** [ME. *concurren* < L. *concurrere,* to run together < *com-,* together + *currere,* to run] **1.** to occur at the same time; happen together; coincide **2.** to combine in having an effect; act together [several events **concurred** to bring about this result] **3.** to agree (*with*); be in accord (*in* an opinion, etc.) –*SYN.* see CONSENT

The etymology for *concur* says that in Middle English (ME.) the word was *concurren,* which originally came from the Latin word *concurrere,* to run together. The symbol < (meaning "comes from") and the abbreviation L. (for Latin) are defined in the front of the dictionary along with other symbols and abbreviations. *Concurrere* is further broken down into the word parts it comes from: *com* = together + *currere* = to run.

Taking the time to read the etymology is important in vocabulary building. For example, if you know that *cur* means to run, you will have an important clue to an entire word family, including the following:

Word	Meaning
cursive	handwriting (letters running)
courier	messenger (runner)
concurrent	at the same time (running together)
recur	to happen again (rerun)
cursory	quick or brief (on the run)
occur	to come to mind (run up to)

precursor	forerunner
current	flowing (running)
currency	something that passes from hand to hand, as money (running around)
discursive	wandering from one topic to another (running away)
incur	to bring upon oneself (run into)

You have seen how the dictionary etymology of the word *concur* helped you with the meaning. It also helped you discover the meaning of a whole group of words based on *cur*. You can understand thousands of new words by gaining a knowledge of basic word parts.

Definition

The next part of the dictionary entry is the **definition.** Many words have more than one definition. The dictionary entry that follows shows that the word *concur* has three definitions. You must choose the one that best fits the context in which the word is used. For example, in the sentence "Thunder and lightning do not *concur* in time, because light travels faster than sound," definition 1 is the one that is meant.

> **con•cur** (kən kʉr´) *vi.* **-curred´, -cur´ring** [ME. *concurren* < L. *concurrere*, to run together < *com-*, together + *currere*, to run] **1.** to occur at the same time; happen together; coincide **2.** to combine in having an effect; act together [several events **concurred** to bring about this result] **3.** to agree (*with*); be in accord (*in* an opinion, etc.) –*SYN.* see CONSENT

The following words have more than one meaning. There are two sentences for each word. Read each sentence and identify the dictionary meaning that best describes how the underlined word is used. Write the number of the definition in the space provided. Be sure to choose the definition that matches the part of speech written under the blank. (The answers appear upside down at the bottom of the next page.)

> **A. fast** (fast) *adj.* [OE. *fæst*] **1.** firm; firmly fastened **2.** loyal; devoted **3.** nonfading [*fast* colors] **4.** swift; quick **5.** ahead of time [a *fast* watch] **6.** wild, promiscuous, or dissipated **7.** [Colloq.] glib –*adv.* **1.** firmly; fixedly **2.** thoroughly [*fast* asleep] **3.** rapidly **–fast´ness** *n.*

_____ 1. Mary's older brother ran with the fast crowd in school.
adj.

_____ 2. Sam and Joe have been fast friends since childhood.
adj.

B. muz•zle (muz′′l) *n.* [< M. L. *musum*] **1.** the nose and jaws of a dog, horse, etc. **2.** a device put over the mouth of an animal to prevent its biting or eating **3.** the front end of the barrel of a firearm —*vt.* **-zled, -zling 1.** to put a muzzle on (an animal) **2.** to prevent from talking

——————— **1.** Dictators try to <u>muzzle</u> the opposition.
vt.

——————— **2.** My dog likes to have his <u>muzzle</u> rubbed.
n.

C. ground (ground) *n.* [OE. *grund*, bottom] **1.** the solid surface of the earth **2.** soil; earth **3.** [*often pl.*] a tract of land [*grounds* of an estate] **4.** area, as of discussion **5.** [*often pl.*] *a)* basis; foundation *b)* valid reason or motive **6.** the background, as in a design **7.** [*pl*] sediment [coffee *grounds*] **8.** the connection of an electrical conductor with the ground —*adj.* of, on or near the ground —*vt.* **1.** to set on the ground **2.** to cause to run aground **3.** to base; found; establish **4.** to instruct in the first principles of **5.** to keep (an aircraft or pilot) from flying **6.** *Elec.* to connect (a conductor) with the ground —*vi.* **1.** to run ashore **2.** *Baseball* to be put out on a grounder (usually with *out*) **–gain** (or **lose**) **ground** to gain (or lose) in achievement, popularity, etc. **–give ground** to retreat; yield **–hold** (or **stand**) **one's ground** to remain firm, not yielding **–run into the ground** [Colloq.] to overdo

——————— **1.** Some people are nervous on an airplane until it touches <u>ground</u>.
n.

——————— **2.** The hurricane will <u>ground</u> all air traffic.
vt.

Whenever you read a definition in the dictionary, you should do two things to make sure you really understand it. First, put the definition into your own words. Second, make up a sentence using the word. Define the word *concur* and use it in a sentence. (The sample answers appear upside down at the bottom of the page.)

Definition _____

_____

Sentence _____

_____

Word Memory

You will learn hundreds of new words in your college classes, but you may have a problem remembering them all. Pronouncing the word, checking the etymology, putting the definition in your own words, and using the word in a sentence are all aids to memory. In addition, there are two more ways to remember words: using word association and using flashcards.

Word association means linking the new word with one you already know. For example, to remember that *erroneous* means "mistaken," you could associate it with the word *error*. Or to remember that *nonpartisan* means "unconnected with a political party," you could associate it with the phrase *no party*.

For practice in word association, make up a word or a phrase that you could use to remember each of the following words. (Some possible word associations appear upside down at the bottom of the page.)

1. brevity (brev′ə tē): shortness

   _____

2. fluent (floo′ənt): able to write or speak easily

   _____

3. conviction (kən vik′*sh*ən): strong belief

   _____

4. summation (sə mā′*sh*ən): a final review or summary

   _____

5. sector (sek′tər): part of an area or district

   _____

Another way to memorize a word is to put it on a **flash card.** Write the word and its pronunciation on one side of the card, and write the definition and a sentence using the word on the other side. Your cards should look like the sample card on the next page.

Test yourself by looking at the front of the card and trying to give the definition. When you are sure you can remember a word, you can retire the card. Carry ten to twenty cards with you so you can use spare moments (such as when you are standing in line or eating lunch by yourself) to memorize vocabulary. That way you won't have so much work to do the night before an exam.

ANSWERS
1. brief 2. flow 3. convince 4. sum 5. section

Front

avid
(av′id)

Back

eager and enthusiastic
He was an avid reader.

Word Comprehension Review

The following twenty-five vocabulary exercises provide practice in building word-comprehension skills.

For explanation see pp. 13–14

Exercise 1

Most words have more than one meaning. Here is the dictionary entry for the word *run*, followed by ten sentences using *run* in different ways. In the space before each sentence, write the number of the definition that fits the way the word *run* is used. To make it easier for you to find the answer, the part of speech of the correct definition is written under the blank.

> **run** (run) *–vi.* **ran, run, run′ning** [< ON. & OE.] **1.** to go by moving the legs faster than in walking **2.** to go, move **3.** to flee **4.** to make a quick trip (*up to, down to,* etc.) **5.** to compete in a race, election, etc. *–vt.* **1.** to manage (a business, etc.) **2.** to undergo (a fever, etc.) **3.** to publish (a story, etc.) in a newspaper *–n.* **1.** an enclosed area for domestic animals **2.** freedom to move about at will [the *run* of the house] **3.** a large number of fish migrating together **4.** a ravel, as in a stocking **5.** *Baseball* a scoring point, made by a successful circuit of the bases **6.** a continuous course of performances, etc., as of a play **7.** a continued series of demands, as on a bank

_____   1. Some clocks <u>run</u> on batteries.
vi.

_____   2. She had a <u>run</u> in her stockings.
n.

_____   3. If you see that the bus is about to leave, <u>run</u> to catch it.
vi.

_____   4. *My Fair Lady* had the longest <u>run</u> of any musical on Broadway.
n.

_____ 5. The young boy wants to <u>run</u> away from home.
vi.

_____ 6. Most newspapers <u>run</u> the Sunday comics in color.
vt.

_____ 7. Hank Aaron hit 755 home <u>runs</u> during his career.
n.

_____ 8. In a kennel, dogs are let out in <u>runs</u> instead of in open areas so
n.   that they won't get into fights.

Exercise 2

Here are dictionary entries for five words that appear in articles in this book.
Write a sentence that shows the meaning of each word.

> **so•phisti•cated** (sə fis′tə kāt′id) *adj.* **1.** not simple, naive, etc.; worldly-
> wise or knowledgeable, subtle, etc. **2.** for sophisticates **3.** highly
> complex or developed in form, technique, etc., as equipment
> **–so•phis′ti•ca′tion** *n.*

1. Sentence _____

_____

> **an•ni•hi•late** (ə nī′ə lāt′) *v.* **-lat′ed, -lat′ing** [< L. *ad.* to + *nihil,*
> nothing] to destroy entirely; kill off; crush **–an•ni′hi•la′tion** *n.*
> **–an•ni′hi•la′tor** *n.*

2. Sentence _____

_____

> **col•league** (käl′ēg) *n.* [< Fr. < L. *com-,* with + *legare,* appoint as deputy]
> a fellow worker; associate in office

3. Sentence _____

_____

> **i•tal•ic** (i tal′ik; also ī-) *adj.* [see fol.: so called because first used in an
> Italian edition of Virgil (1501)] designating or of a type in which
> the characters slant upward to the right, used variously, as to
> emphasize words, indicate foreign words, set of book titles, etc.
> (Ex.: *this is italic type*)

4. Sentence _____

_____

corre•spondence (kôr′ə spänd′əns) *n.* **1.** agreement **2.** similarity **3.** *a)* communication by letters *b)* the letters

5. Sentence _____

_____

For explanation see pp. 3–5

Exercise 3

Circle the letter before the best definition of each underlined word and write in the type of context clue (definition, contrast, example, experience). The words shown here are in the context of reading selections from Units II and III.

1. You can prove <u>an observation</u>, such as "some stars are brighter than others," by pointing it out yourself or by testing it scientifically.

   a. a comment on something you noticed

   b. a disagreement with another person

   c. a well-known fact

   d. an opinion

   Type of clue _____

2. Some opinions are <u>sounder</u> than others. While they cannot be proved, they can be backed up with facts.

   a. more common

   b. stranger

   c. weaker

   d. stronger

   Type of clue _____

3. Business <u>jargon</u> too often is cold, stiff, unnatural. Suppose I came up to you and said, "I acknowledge receipt of your letter and I beg to thank you."

   a. competition

   b. humor

   c. bookkeeping

   d. vocabulary

   Type of clue _____

4. Your opinions may be the best in the world, but they're not <u>gospel</u>.

   a. completely false

   b. absolute truth

c. more or less factual

d. religious

Type of clue _____

5. Review material that is <u>enumerated</u>. Pay attention to any numbered lists.

a. long

b. stressed

c. numbered

d. difficult

Type of clue _____

For explanation see pp. 8–10

Exercise 4

Circle the word in each pair on the right that matches the pronunciation on the left. Use the dictionary pronunciation guide.

cat, āte, fäther; pen, ēvil; if, kīte; nō, ôr, fōōd, book; boil, house; up, tᵤrn; chief, shell; thick, *the*; zh, treasure; ŋ, sing; ə for *a* in *about*; ' as in *able* (ā′b'l)

Pronunciation	Words	
1. hīt	height	hit
2. räb	robe	rob
3. blō	blue	blow
4. kär tōōn′	carton	cartoon
5. bāt	bait	bat

For explanation see pp. 15–16

Exercise 5

Make up a word or phrase that you could use to remember each of the following words.

> **de•plete** (di plēt′) *vt.* **-plet′ed, -plet′ing** [< L. *de-*, from + *plere*, fill] **1.** to use up (funds, etc.) **2.** to use up the resources, etc. of **–de•ple′tion** *n.*

1. Word association _____

> **me•thod•i•cal** (mə thäd′i k'l) *adj.* [<fr. < Gr. *meia*, after + *hodos*, away] characterized by method; orderly; systematic **–me•thod′i•cal•ly,** *adv.*

2. Word association _____

as•i•nine (as′ə nīn′) *adj.* [< L. *asinus,* ass] stupid; silly

3. Word association _____

For explanation see pp. 10–12

Exercise 6

Identify the part of speech of the word on the left. Then change it into the new part of speech listed. Use each *new* word in a sentence.

Word	Part of speech	New part of speech	New word
1. pretense		verb	
Sentence:			
2. hazardous		noun	
Sentence:			
3. phenomenon		adjective	
Sentence:			
4. premature		adverb	
Sentence:			
5. penalize		noun	
Sentence:			
6. priority		adjective	
Sentence:			
7. inference		verb	
Sentence:			
8. origin		verb	
Sentence:			

Word	Part of speech	New part of speech	New word
9. intimidate		noun	
Sentence:			
10. invariably		adjective	
Sentence:			

Exercise 7

Some pairs of words are confused in writing because they look very similar or because they sound alike. Use the dictionary entries below to help you choose the correct words to fill in the blanks.

1. Little League used _____ be only for boys, but now girls can join, _____ .

2. It's twenty minutes _____ _____ o'clock.

3. It's _____ late _____ go _____ the party.

> **to** (tōō; unstressed, too, tə) *prep.* [ME. < OE., akin to Ger. *zu* < IE. *-*dō*-, up toward > L. *(quan)do,* when, then, *do(nec),* until] **1.** *a)* in the direction of; toward [turn *to* the left; traveling *to* Pittsburgh] *b)* in the direction of and reaching [he went *to* Boston; it dropped *to* the ground] **2.** as far as [wet *to* the skin; a fight *to* the death] **3.** *a)* toward or into a condition of [to grow *to* manhood; a rise *to* fame] *b)* so as to result in [sentenced *to* ten years in prison] **4.** on, onto, against, at, next, etc.: used to indicate nearness or contact [to apply lotion *to* the skin; a house *to* the right] **5.** *a)* until [no parking from four *to* six] *b)* before [the time is ten *to* six] **6.** for the purpose of; for [come *to* dinner] **7.** *a)* as concerns; in respect of; involving [that's all there is *to* it; open *to* attack] *b)* in the opinion of [it seems good *to* me] **8.** producing, causing, or resulting in [*to* his amazement; torn *to* pieces] **9.** along with; accompanied by; as an accompaniment for [add this *to* the others; dance *to* the music] **10.** being the proper appurtenance, possession, or attribute of; of [the key *to* the house] **11.** as compared with; as against [a score of 7 *to* 10; superior *to* the others] **12.** *a)* in agreement, correspondence, or conformity with [not *to* one's taste] *b)* as a reaction or in response toward [the dog came *to* his whistle] **13.** constituting; in or for each [four quarts *to* a gallon] **14.** as far as the limit of [moderate *to* high in price] **15.** with (a specified person or thing) as the recipient, or indirect object, of the action [listen *to* him; give the book *to* her] **16.** in honor of [a toast *to* your success] **17.** [Colloq. or Dial.] with [a field planted *to* corn]

18. [Dial.] at or in (a specified place) [he's *to* home] To is also used before a verb as a sign of the infinitive (Ex.: it was easy *to* read; *to* live is sweet) or, elliptically, to denote the infinitive (Ex.: tell him if you want *to*) –*adv.* **1.** forward [his hat is on wrong side *to*] **2.** in the normal or desired direction, position, or condition; esp., shut or closed [the door was blown *to*] **3.** into a state of consciousness [the boxer came *to*] **4.** at hand [we were close *to* when it happened] To is used in many idiomatic phrases entered in this dictionary under their key words (e.g., bring *to*, come *to*, go *to*) **–to and fro** first in one direction and then in the opposite; back and forth

too (to͞o) *adv.* [stressed form of TO, with differentiated sp.] **1.** in addition; as well; besides; also **2.** more than enough; superfluously; overly [the hat is *too* big] **3.** to a regrettable extent [that's *too* bad!] **4.** extremely; very [it was just *too* delicious!] Too is often used as a mere emphatic [I will *too* go!] and is sometimes construed as an adjective in modifying much, little, etc. [there was not *too* much to see]

two (to͞o) *adj.* [ME. *two, tu* < OE. *twa,* fem. & neut., *tu,* neut., akin to Ger. *zwei* < IE. base **dwōu-,* two > L. *duo,* two, Gr. *duo,* Sans. *dvau*] totaling one more than one –*n.* **1.** the cardinal number between one and three; 2; II **2.** any two people or things; pair; couple **3.** something numbered two or having two units, as a playing card, domino, face of a die, etc. **–in two** in two parts; asunder **–put two and two together** to reach an obvious conclusion by considering several facts together

For explanation see pp. 12–13

Exercise 8

English words come from many different languages. Following is a list of ten English words, each from a different language. The languages that the words come from are written under the list. Use a dictionary that includes etymology and fill in each blank with the correct language.

_____ 1. canyon   _____ 6. noodle

_____ 2. health   _____ 7. tea

_____ 3. autograph   _____ 8. coffee

_____ 4. ketchup   _____ 9. husband

_____ 5. coleslaw   _____ 10. magazine

French   English   Norwegian   Arabic   Chinese

Greek   Dutch   Spanish   Malaysian   German

For explanation see pp. 13–14

Exercise 9

Here is the dictionary entry for the word *hard*. In the space before each sentence, put the number of the definition that fits the way the word *hard* is used. To make it easier for you to find the answer, the part of speech of the correct definition is written under the blank.

> **hard** (härd) *adj.* [OE. *heard*] **1.** firm and unyielding to the touch; solid and compact **2.** powerful [a *hard* blow] **3.** difficult to do, under-stand, or deal with **4.** *a)* unfeeling [a *hard* heart] *b)* unfriendly [*hard* feelings] **5.** harsh; severe **6.** having mineral salts that interfere with lathering **7.** energetic [a *hard* worker] **8.** containing much alcohol [*hard* liquor] **9.** addictive and harmful [heroin is a *hard* drug] —*adv.* **1.** energetically [work *hard*] **2.** with strength [hit *hard*] **3.** with difficulty [*hard*-earned] **4.** close; near [we live *hard* by] **5.** so as to be solid [frozen *hard*] **6.** sharply [turn *hard* right]

_____   1. Diamonds are so <u>hard</u> that they can be scratched only by other
adj.   diamonds.

_____   2. The math problem was <u>hard</u> to do.
adj.

_____   3. The landlord was so <u>hard</u> that he evicted the elderly couple in
adj.   freezing weather when he knew that they had no place to go.

_____   4. Some states will not let stores sell <u>hard</u> liquor on Sundays.
adj.

_____   5. The player hit the baseball so <u>hard</u> that it went out of the
adv.   stadium and into the parking lot.

_____   6. During a <u>hard</u> winter there can be several feet of snow on the
adj.   ground for months.

_____   7. <u>Hard</u> water does not wash clothes very well.
adj.

For explanation see pp. 15–16

Exercise 10

See the two sample flash cards on the next page. On the front, write the word and its pronunciation. On the back, write a brief definition of the word and a sentence to help you remember it.

> **doctor•ate** (däk′tər it) *n.* the degree of doctor conferred by a university
>
> **extra•cur•ricu•lar** (eks′trə kə rik′yə lər) *adj.* not part of the required curriculum

Front

Front

Back

Back

Exercise 11

Here are the dictionary entries for five words that appear in articles in this book. Write a sentence that shows the meaning of each word.

> **cap•tion** (kap′shən) *n.* [< L. *capere,* take] **1.** a heading or title, as of a newspaper article or an illustration **2.** *Motion Pictures* a subtitle —*vt.* to supply a caption for

1. Sentence _____

_____

> **a•naly•sis** (ə nal′ə sis) *n., pl.* -ses (-sēz) [< Gr. < *ana-,* up + *ly*sis, a loosing] **1.** a breaking up of a whole into its parts to find out their nature, etc. **2.** a statement of these findings **3.** psychoanalysis **4.** *Chem.* separation of compounds and mixtures into their constituents to determine their nature or proportion —**an•a•lyt•i•cal** (an′ə lit′i k'l), —**an′a•lyt′ic** *adj.* —**an′a•lyt′i•cal•ly** *adv.*

2. Sentence _____

_____

flippant (flip′ənt) *adj.* [prob. FLIP¹] frivolous and disrespectful; saucy
—**flip′pan•cy** *n., pl.* **-cies** —**flip′pant•ly** *adv.*

3. Sentence _____

_____

heft (heft) *n.* [base of HEAVE] [Colloq.] **1.** weight; heaviness **2.** importance;
influence —*vt.* [Colloq.] to try to judge the weight of by lifting

4. Sentence _____

_____

e•go (ē′gō) *n., pl.* **-gos** [L., I] **1.** the individual as aware of himself; the
self **2.** conceit **3.** *Psychoanalysis* the part of the psyche which governs
action rationally

5. Sentence _____

_____

For explanation see pp. 5–7

Exercise 12

Here is a list of ten common prefixes and their meanings. Fill in the blank
with a word that has the same prefix. If you need help, use your dictionary.
The first item is done for you as an example.

Prefix	Meaning	Example	Another word
1. re	again, back	replay	return
2. de	from, away	defrost	
3. e, ex	out	exterior	
4. inter	between	interrupt	
5. sub, sup	under	submerge	
6. super	over	superior	
7. trans	across	transfer	
8. bi	two	binoculars	
9. pre	before	preheat	
10. in, im	into	inside	

Check the etymology in your dictionary for the answers.

For explanation see pp. 8–10

Exercise 13

Circle the word in each pair on the right that matches the pronunciation on the left. Use the dictionary pronunciation guide.

cat, āte, fäther; pen, ēvil; if, kīte; nō, ôr, fōōd, book; boil, house; up, tʉrn; chief, shell; thick, *the*; zh, treasure; ŋ, sing; ə for *a* in *about*; ' as in *able* (ā'b'l)

Pronunciation	Words	
1. (mān)	man	main
2. (bēt)	bet	beat
3. (sō)	sew	sue
4. (sīt)	sit	sight
5. (gät)	got	goat

For explanation see pp. 3–5

Exercise 14

Circle the best definition for each underlined word and write in the type of context clue (example, definition, contrast, experience). The words are shown here in the sentences in which they appear in later reading selections.

1. Many words that mean the same thing can have opposite <u>connotations</u>. For example, *slender* and *thrifty* are positive words, but *skinny* and *cheap* are negative.

   a. definitions

   b. suggestions

   c. questions

   d. opposites

   Type of clue _____

2. By using card stacking, a <u>mediocre</u> politician can appear to be a great statesman.

   a. very good

   b. terrible

   c. average

   d. new

   Type of clue _____

3. It uses <u>deception</u> and "stacks the cards" against the truth.

    a. lies

    b. honesty

    c. payoffs

    d. force

Type of clue _____

4. <u>Mediation</u> means attaching the items in a list to some easily remembered "mediating" device, such as the jingle most adults use to recall the lengths of the months: "Thirty days hath September, . . ."

    a. making a decision

    b. connecting two things together

    c. making a division

    d. separation

Type of clue _____

5. Stress is commonly defined as intense <u>exertion</u>—strain and effort—the wear and tear of life.

    a. relaxation

    b. recreation

    c. effort

    d. fatigue

Type of clue _____

Exercise 15

Some pairs of words are confused in writing because they look very similar or because they sound alike. Use the dictionary entries on the next page to help you choose the correct words to fill in the blanks

1. At first they didn't want to go _____, but now _____ glad they went.

2. _____ glad that _____ television was not stolen when _____ house was robbed.

3. _____ were three reasons why they decided to go _____ for _____ vacation.

their (ther; unstressed, thər) *possessive pronominal adj.* [ME. *theyr* < ON. *theirra,* gen. pl. of the demonstrative pron. replacing ME. *here,* OE. *hira:* see THEY] of, belonging to, made, or done by them: often used with a singular antecedent (as *everybody, somebody, everyone*) [did everybody finish *their* lunch?]

there (ther) *adv.* [ME. *ther,* there, where < OE. *ther, thær,* there, where < IE *tor-, *ter-,* there <*to-, *tā-,* demonstrative base > THAT, THEN] **1.** at or in that place: often used as an intensive [Mary *there* is a good player]: in dialectal or nonstandard use, often placed between a demonstrative pronoun and the noun it modifies [that *there* hog] **2.** toward, to, or into that place; thither [go *there*] **3.** at that point in action, speech, discussion, etc.; then [*there* I paused] **4.** in that matter, respect, etc.; as to that [*there* you are wrong] **5.** at the moment; right now [*there* goes the whistle] *There* is also used *a)* in interjectional phrases of approval, encouragement, etc. [*there*'s a fine fellow!] *b)* with pronominal force in impersonal constructions in which the real subject follows the verb [*there* is very little time, *there* are three people here] *–n.* that place or point [we left *there* at six] *–interj.* an exclamation expressing: **1.** defiance, dismay, satisfaction, etc. [*there,* that's done!] **2.** sympathy, concern, etc. [*there, there!* don't worry]
—**(not) all there** [Colloq.] (not) in full possession of one's wits; (not) mentally sound

they're (ther, thā'ər) they are

For explanation see pp. 5–7

Exercise 16

Negative Prefixes. The prefixes in the following group change the base words that come after them into negatives. A negative is a word that expresses the idea of *no* or *not.* Place the correct negative prefix in front of each base. The first item is done for you as an example.

anti = against   **dis = not**   **in = not**

mis = not or wrong   **n, non = not or no**   **un = not**

1. anti _____   war   against war

2. _____   necessary   not necessary

3. _____   pronounce   to pronounce wrong

4. _____   correct   not correct

5. _____   sense   something that does not make sense

6. _____   expensive   not expensive

7. _____   attached   not attached

8. _____	dote	against poison	
9. _____	fat	no fat	
10. _____	continue	to stop (not continue)	
11. _____	count	to count wrong	
12. _____	honest	not honest	

<table>
<tr><td>For explanation
see pp. 10–12</td></tr>
</table>

Exercise 17

Identify the part of speech of the word printed on the left. First remove the suffix, write the word that remains, and identify the new part of speech. Then make a sentence using the new word. Use your dictionary if you need help. The first item is done for you as an example.

Word	Part of speech	New word	New part of speech
1. gladly	adverb	glad	adjective
Sentence: I'm *glad* to see you.			
2. protective			
Sentence:			
3. assistance			
Sentence:			
4. depression			
Sentence:			
5. suggestible			
Sentence:			
6. criticize			
Sentence:			

continued

Word	Part of speech	New word	New part of speech
7. weaken			
Sentence:			
8. cleverness			
Sentence:			
9. acceptable			
Sentence:			
10. friendly			
Sentence:			

For explanation see pp. 13–14

Exercise 18

Here are eight verb definitions for the word *call*. Write the number of the correct definition of *call* in the space provided.

> **call** (kôl) *vt.* [< ON. *kalla*] **1.** to say in a loud tone; shout **2.** to summon **3.** to give or apply a name to **4.** to telephone **5.** to stop (a game, etc.) **6.** to demand payment of (a loan, etc.) **7.** *vi. Poker* to require (a player) to show his hand by equaling his bet **8.** to visit for a while (often with *on*)

_____ 1. <u>Call</u> me tomorrow evening about 9:00 P.M.
vt.

_____ 2. The banker <u>called</u> in the loan.
vt.

_____ 3. Some people in the Alps use yodeling to <u>call</u> to each other across
vt.   long distances.

_____ 4. They <u>called</u> the game because of rain.
vt.

_____ 5. If we did not agree on what to <u>call</u> things, we would have to use
vt.   many words to describe each item.

Exercise 19

Here are the dictionary entries for five words that appear in articles in this book. Write a sentence that shows the meaning of each word.

> **eth•nic** (eth′nik) *adj.* [< Gr. *ethnos,* nation] of any of the basic divisions of mankind, as distinguished by customs, language, etc. *–n.* a member of a minority or nationality group that is part of a larger community **–eth′ni•cal•ly** *adv.*

1. Sentence _____

   _____

> **mun•dane** (mun dān′) *adj.* [< L. *mundus,* world] **1.** of the world; worldly **2.** commonplace; ordinary

2. Sentence _____

   _____

> **psy•cho•so•mat•ic** (sī kō sō mat′ik) *adj.* [< Gr., *Psycho,* soul + *soma,* body] designating or of a physical disorder originating in or aggravated by emotional processes

3. Sentence _____

   _____

> **nov•el** (näv′əl) *adj.* [< L. dim. of *novus,* new] new and unusual *–n.* a relatively long fictional prose narrative

4. Sentence _____

   _____

> **ex•cess** (ik ses′; *also & for adj. usually* ek′ses′) *n.* [see EXCEED] **1.** action that goes beyond a reasonable limit. **2.** an amount greater than is necessary **3.** the amount by which one thing exceeds another; surplus *–adj.* extra; surplus

5. Sentence _____

   _____

For explanation see pp. 5–7

Exercise 20

Here are five roots and their meanings. Fill in the missing root for the difficult words on the left to make them match the definition provided. The meaning of the root is underlined.

dic or dict = say   graph = write   syn = together or same

bene = good   chron = time

1. __ __ __ __ um   a <u>saying</u>; rule

2. __ __ __ __ __ ite   the mineral in pencil "lead" that <u>writes</u>

3. __ __ __ onymous   means the <u>same</u> thing

4. __ __ __ __ ficial   <u>good</u>, helpful, favorable

5. __ __ __ __ __ ic   lasting over a long <u>time</u>

6. __ __ __ thesis   putting <u>together</u> parts to form a whole

7. ab __ __ __ ate   to give up formally; to <u>say</u> you won't do it

8. __ __ __ __ __ ologist   a person who studies hand<u>writing</u>

9. __ __ __ __ __ icle   a historical record in order of <u>time</u>

10. __ __ __ __ factor   one who does <u>good</u>, especially one who offers financial support

For the following words, combine *two* of the roots to fill in the blanks.

11. __ __ __ __ __ __ __ __ ize   to move or occur at the <u>same</u> <u>time</u>

12. __ __ __ __ __ __ __ __ ion   a <u>good</u> <u>saying</u>; a blessing

For explanation see pp. 5–7, 10–12

Exercise 21

In the table on the next page, identify the part of speech of the word printed on the left. First remove the suffix, write the word that remains, and identify the new part of speech. Then use the new word in a sentence. Use your dictionary if you need help.

Word	Part of speech	New word	New part of speech
1. superiority			
Sentence:			
2. freely			
Sentence:			
3. brewery			
Sentence:			
4. thankful			
Sentence:			
5. silky			
Sentence:			
6. grandeur			
Sentence:			
7. advertisement			
Sentence:			
8. greenness			
Sentence:			
9. happily			
Sentence:			
10. successful			
Sentence:			

For explanation see pp. 13–14

Exercise 22

Here is the dictionary entry for the word *cast*. In the space before each sentence, write the number of the definition that fits the way *cast* is used. To make it easier for you to find the answer, the part of speech of the correct definition is written under the blank.

> **cast** (kast) *vt.* **cast, cast'ing** [< ON. *kasta*] **1.** to throw with force; fling; hurl **2.** to deposit (a ballot or vote) **3.** to direct [to *cast* one's eyes] **4.** to project [to *cast* light] **5.** to throw off or shed (a skin) **6.** to shape (molten metal, etc.) by pouring into a mold **7.** to select (an actor) for (a role or play) –*vi.* to throw; hurl –*n.* **1.** a casting; throw **2.** something formed in a mold **3.** a plaster form for immobilizing a limb **4.** the set of actors in a play or movie **5.** an appearance, as of features **6.** kind; quality **7.** a tinge; shade

_____   1. To vote you must <u>cast</u> your ballot.
vt.

_____   2. When you break your leg, the doctor sets it in a plaster <u>cast</u>.
n.

_____   3. Overhead lights <u>cast</u> dark shadows that look bad in photographs.
vt.

_____   4. The <u>cast</u> had a huge party on the opening night of the play.
n.

For explanation see pp. 5–7

Exercise 23

Here are five roots and their meanings. Fill in the missing root of the difficult words on the left to make them match the definition provided. The meaning of the root is underlined.

path = feeling   **capit or cap = head**   **voc or voke = call**

viv = live   **scribe = write**

1. re __ __ __ e   to bring back to <u>life</u>

2. a __ __ __ __ y   without <u>feeling</u>; without emotion

3. __ __ __ ation   a <u>calling</u> or an occupation

4. sub __ __ __ __ __ __   to <u>write</u> in or apply for

5. __ __ __ tion   a <u>heading</u> under a picture

6. de __ __ __ __ __ ate   to be<u>head</u>

7. re __ __ __ __   to <u>call</u> back; cancel

8. __ __ __ acious   <u>lively</u>

9. __ __ __ __ etic   expressing or arousing <u>feelings</u> of pity,
                                     sorrow, or sympathy

10. in __ __ __ __ __ __   to <u>write</u>, mark, or engrave words or
                                     symbols on a surface

Exercise 24

Use the annotated dictionary sample on the next page to answer the following questions.

   A list of all the symbols and abbreviations used in a dictionary can be found either in the front or in the back. If you do not have a copy of *Webster's New World Dictionary*, you may have to guess at the etymologies below.

1. Find a word on the annotated dictionary page (p. 36) for each of the following etymologies. Then state what you think each abbreviation means. The first item is done for you as an example.

	Sample word	**Meaning of abbreviation**
a. <	ratify	comes from
b. [OE]		
c. [OFr]		
d. [?]		
e. [prob. echoic]		
f. [L]		
g. [It]		
h. [Ger]		
i. [see prec.]		
j. [MDu]		

guide words —

raspberry
ravine   488

irregular plural —

rasp·ber·ry (raz′ber′ē, -bar-) *n., pl.* **-ries** [< earlier *raspis*] 1 a small, juicy, edible, reddish fruit related to the rose 2 a plant bearing this fruit 3 [Slang] a sound of derision

rat (rat) *n.* [OE *ræt*] 1 a long-tailed rodent, resembling, but larger than, the mouse 2 [Slang] a sneaky, contemptible person; esp., an informer —*vi.* **rat′ted, rat′ting** [Slang] to inform (on) —**smell a rat** to suspect a trick, plot, etc.

idiomatic expression —

ratch·et (rach′it) *n.* [< It *rocca*, distaff] 1 a toothed wheel (in full **ratchet wheel**) or bar whose sloping teeth catch a pawl, preventing backward motion 2 such a pawl

rate¹ (rāt) *n.* [< L *reri*, reckon] 1 the amount, degree, etc. of anything in relation to units of something else /*rate* of pay/ 2 price, esp. per unit 3 [Now Rare] a class or rank /of the first *rate*/ —*vt.* **rat′ed, rat′ing** 1 to appraise 2 to consider; esteem 3 [Colloq.] to deserve —*vi.* to have value, status, etc. —**at any rate** 1 in any event 2 anyway

multiple entries —

rate² (rāt) *vt., vi.* **rat′ed, rat′ing** [< L *reputare*, to count] to scold; chide

rath·er (rath′ər) *adv.* [OE *hræthe*, quickly] 1 more willingly; preferably 2 with more justice, reason, etc. /I, *rather* than you, should pay/ 3 more accurately /my son, or *rather*, stepson/ 4 on the contrary 5 somewhat /*rather* hungry/ —**rather than** instead of

main entries —

raths·kel·ler (rät′skel′ər, rath′-) *n.* [Ger < *rat*, council + *keller*, cellar] a restaurant, usually below the street level, where beer is served

rat·i·fy (rat′ə fī′) *vt.* **-fied′, -fy′ing** [< L *ratus*, reckoned + *facere*, make] to approve; esp., to give official sanction to —**rat′i·fi·ca′tion** *n.*

rat·ing (rāt′in) *n.* 1 a rank or grade, as of military personnel 2 a placement in a certain rank or class 3 an evaluation; appraisal 4 [Film] a classification, based on content, restricting the age of those who may attend 5 [Radio, TV] the relative popularity of a program according to sample polls

specialized definitions —

ra·tio (rā′shō, -shē ō′) *n., pl.* **-tios** [L, a reckoning] a fixed relation in degree, number, etc. between two similar things; proportion

ra·ti·oc·i·nate (rash′ē äs′ə nāt′) *vi.* **-nat′ed, -nat′ing** [see prec.] to think or argue logically; reason —**ra′ti·oc′i·na′tion** *n.*

ra·tion (rash′ən, rā′shən) *n.* [see RATIO] 1 a fixed portion; share 2 a fixed allowance of food, as a daily allowance for a soldier 3 [pl.] food supply —*vt.* 1 to supply with rations 2 to distribute (food, clothing, etc.) in rations, as in times of scarcity

parts of speech —

ra·tion·al (rash′ən əl) *adj.* [see RATIO] 1 of or based on reasoning 2 able to reason; reasoning 3 sensible or sane —**ra′tion·al′i·ty** (-a nal′ə tē) *n.* —**ra′tion·al·ly** *adv.*

main entries —

ra·tion·ale (rash′ə nal′) *n.* [< L *rationalis*, rational] 1 the reasons or rational basis for something 2 an explanation of principles

ra′tion·al·ism *n.* the practice of accepting reason as the only authority in determining one's opinions or course of action —**ra′tion·al·ist** *n., adj.* —**ra′tion·al·is′tic** *adj.*

— different form for different part of speech

ra′tion·al·ize′ *vt., vi.* **-ized′, -iz′ing** 1 to make or be rational or reasonable 2 to devise plausible explanations for (one's acts, beliefs, etc.), usually in self-deception —**ra′tion·al·i·za′tion** *n.*

rat·line (rat′lin) *n.* [< ?] any of the horizontal ropes which join the shrouds of a ship and serve as a ladder Also **rat′lin**

rat race [Slang] a mad scramble or intense struggle, as in the business world

rat·tan (ra tan′) *n.* [Malay *rotan*] 1 a tall palm tree with long, slender, tough stems 2 its stem, used in making furniture, etc.

rat·tle (rat′l) *vi.* **-tled, -tling** [prob. echoic] 1 to make a series of sharp, short sounds 2 to chatter: often with *on* —*vt.* 1 to cause to rattle 2 to confuse or upset —*n.* 1 a series of sharp, short sounds 2 a series of horny rings at the end of a rattlesnake's tail 3 a baby's toy, a percussion instrument, etc. made to rattle when shaken

— definitions

rat′tle·brain′ *n.* a frivolous, talkative person —**rat′tle·brained′** *adj.*

rat′tler *n.* a rattlesnake

DIAMONDBACK
RATTLESNAKE

— illustration

— words used in context

rat′tle·snake′ *n.* a poisonous American snake with horny rings at the end of the tail that rattle when shaken

rat′tle·trap′ *n.* a rickety old car

rat′tling *adj.* 1 that rattles 2 [Colloq.] very fast, good, etc. —*adv.* [Colloq.] very /a *rattling* good time/

— usage

rat′trap′ *n.* 1 a trap for rats 2 [Colloq.] a dirty, run-down building

rat·ty (rat′ē) *adj.* **-ti·er, -ti·est** [Slang] shabby or run-down

rau·cous (rô′kəs) *adj.* [L *raucus*] 1 hoarse 2 loud and rowdy —**rau′cous·ly** *adv.* —**rau′cous·ness** *n.*

raun·chy (rôn′chē, rän′-) *adj.* **-chi·er, -chi·est** [< ?] [Slang] 1 dirty, sloppy, etc. 2 risqué, lustful, etc.

rav·age (rav′ij) *n.* [see RAVISH] destruction; ruin —*vt.* **-aged, -ag·ing** to destroy violently; devastate; ruin —*vi.* to commit ravages

— cross reference

rave (rāv) *vi.* **raved, rav′ing** [< OFr *raver*, roam] 1 to talk incoherently or wildly 2 to talk with great enthusiasm (*about*) —*n.* [Colloq.] a very enthusiastic commendation

rav·el (rav′əl) *vt., vi.* **-eled or -elled, -el·ing or -el·ling** [MDu *ravelen*] to separate into its parts, esp. threads; untwist; fray —*n.* a raveled part in a fabric

— alt. spellings

ra·ven (rā′vən) *n.* [OE *hræfn*] the largest crow, with a straight, sharp beak —*adj.* black and lustrous

— pronunciations

rav·en·ing (rav′ən in) *adj.* [ult. < L *rapere*, seize] greedily searching for prey /*ravening* wolves/

rav·e·nous (rav′ə nəs) *adj.* [< L *rapere*, seize] 1 greedily hungry 2 rapacious —**rav′e·nous·ly** *adv.*

— etymologies

ra·vine (rə vēn′) *n.* [Fr, flood] a long, deep hollow in the earth, esp. one worn by a stream; gorge

Exercise 25

1. Using the same annotated dictionary page, find examples of the following usages and explain what the usage means.

	Sample word	**Meaning of usage**
a. Slang	_____	_____
b. Colloq.	_____	_____

2. Why does *rate* have two entries? _____

_____

3. As which parts of speech can *rave* be used?

a. _____   b. _____

4. How many noun definitions does *rattle* have? _____

5. What does *n., pl.* in the entry for *ratio* mean? _____

6. What is the noun form of *ratify*? _____

7. Which words come from a Latin word that means "a reckoning"?

a. _____

b. _____

c. _____

d. _____

Paragraph Comprehension

Literal Comprehension

The most important skills in literal comprehension of paragraphs are under-standing the subject, main idea, and supporting details.

Subject

A good paragraph is a group of sentences that explain one central idea, called the **subject,** or topic, of the paragraph. You can find the subject of a para-graph by asking yourself who or what the whole paragraph is about. Circle the letter that precedes the subject of Paragraph A.

A. Twenty-four karat gold is not pure gold as most people believe. This is because pure gold is too soft to be used. It is so soft that it can be molded in the hand and, therefore, cannot hold a shape. Twenty-four karat gold has a small amount of copper in it to make it stronger.

    a. the purity of gold

    b. gold

    c. gold jewelry

    d. how to get gold from ore

The answer is a. Choice b is too broad. If b were the subject, the para-graph would have to discuss general aspects of gold, such as the use of gold as money, the mining of gold, the value of gold, and so forth. Choices c and d are off the subject; the paragraph doesn't discuss gold jewelry or how to get gold from ore.

Circle the letter that precedes the subject of Paragraph B.

B. Houdini, the master magician, was a pioneer in many fields. Of course, he is probably the most famous escape artist that ever lived. But he was a silent-picture actor as well, although few people know it. He was also the first man to fly an airplane solo into Australia.

    a. master magicians

    b. Houdini as an escape artist

    c. Houdini's acting career

    d. Houdini's career

The answer is d. Choice a is too broad. Only one master magician is discussed in the paragraph. Choices b and c are too narrow; the paragraph mentions Houdini's work as an escape artist, an actor, and a pilot.

Main Idea

Every paragraph should have a **main idea,** or a central point. The main idea of a paragraph is usually a complete sentence. To find the main idea, ask yourself what the subject is and what the author is saying about the subject.

Look again at Paragraph A. Circle the letter that precedes the main idea.

a. The more impure the gold, the harder it is.

b. The purer the gold is, the more expensive it is.

c. It is difficult to mold soft metal.

d. Twenty-four karat gold is not pure.

The answer is d. Choices a and b are true, but they are not stated in the paragraph. Choice c is not true.

Look again at Paragraph B. Circle the letter that precedes the main idea.

a. Houdini was rich and famous.

b. Houdini was brilliant.

c. Houdini could do many things.

d. Houdini died young.

The answer is c. Choices a, b, and d may or may not be true, but they are not discussed in the paragraph.

Supporting Details

A good paragraph should have details that support the main idea. The **supporting details** explain, clarify, or justify the main idea. Supporting details can be reasons, facts, examples, or testimony.

Reasons: In Paragraph A, the main idea is supported by **reasons.** The author explains the reasons why twenty-four karat gold is not pure by saying that if it were pure, it would be too soft to use. One way you can identify what type of supporting details an author is using is to look for **signal words.** In this paragraph, the word *because* signals you that reasons will be given.

Go back and reread Paragraph A and then fill in the blanks below.

Subject_____

Main idea _____

Reason_____

Signal word _____

The subject is the purity of gold. The main idea is that twenty-four karat gold is not pure. The reason is that pure gold is too soft to use. The signal word is *because.*

Facts: In Paragraph B, the main idea is supported by **facts**—things that have actually happened or that are true. Facts can include numbers, scientific laws, historical information, and so forth. The author of Paragraph B gives historical facts about Houdini's life to show that Houdini did many things. The words *of course* signal you that facts will be given as support for the main idea.

Go back and reread Paragraph B and then fill in the blanks below.

Subject _____

Main idea _____

Fact 1 _____

Fact 2 _____

Fact 3 _____

Signal words_____

The subject is Houdini's career. The main idea is that Houdini could do many things. The first fact is that he was the most famous escape artist that ever lived. The second fact is that he was a silent-picture actor. The third fact is that he was the first man to fly an airplane solo into Australia. The signal words are *of course.*

Examples: Sometimes an author uses one or more **examples** to support the main idea. Phrases such as *for example, such as,* or *for instance* may be used to signal that examples will be given. Read Paragraph C and fill in the blanks.

C. Sticking to a study schedule is not easy, but you can be more successful if you offer yourself some rewards. For example, save the most interesting work until last so that you can look forward to the end of the day. Then, when you have successfully completed your work, give yourself time off as a reward. Also, at the end of each day, go over your completed assignments so you can really see how much you have accomplished.

Subject _____

Main idea _____

Example 1 _____

Example 2 _____

Example 3 _____

Signal words _____

The subject is sticking to a study schedule. The main idea is that sticking to the schedule is easier if you offer yourself some rewards. The first example is saving the most interesting work until last. The second example is giving yourself time off as a reward. The third example is going over completed assignments to see how much you have accomplished. The signal words are *for example.*

Testimony: To give **testimony** means to give opinions or findings of people other than the author as support for the main idea. Sometimes signal words such as *according to* are used. Read paragraph D and fill in the blanks.

D. People who exercise regularly tend to look and feel better than their inactive friends. According to Gail Butterfield, a professor of nutritional sciences, the reason may be that active people are better able to use certain vitamins and proteins.

Subject _____

Main idea _____

Testimony _____

Signal words _____

The subject is people who exercise. The main idea is that people who exercise regularly tend to look and feel better than their inactive friends. The testimony is from Gail Butterfield. The signal words are *according to.*

Mixed Category: Sometimes, more than one type of support may be used. For example, the author may rely on reasons for the main type of support but may reinforce those reasons with facts.

In Paragraph E the main type of supporting detail is testimony, but factual information is also given.

E. People have subconscious reasons for liking to wear certain shades of colors rather than others. Some shades look better on certain people because of their skin tone, eye color, and hair color. According to Professor Robert L. Beadmore, people choose the colors that look best on them. In experiments he did, every person was able to choose the colors that were most flattering to his or her natural tones. Dr. Beadmore says that we must assume that a sixth sense leads a person to select the right shades.

Subject _____

Main idea _____

Testimony _____

Fact _____

The subject is the reasons people wear certain colors. The main idea is that people subconsciously wear colors that are flattering. The testimony is from Professor Beadmore. The facts are from Dr. Beadmore's experiments.

Finding the Main Idea

In the paragraphs you have read so far, the main idea has been in the first sentence. A main idea can usually be found in the first sentence of a paragraph, but it can sometimes be found in the middle or at the end.

In Paragraphs F and G the main ideas are not in the first sentence. Fill in the blanks and identify the type of supporting details used.

F. The skin is the largest organ of the human body. An adult has about twenty square feet of skin weighing about six or seven pounds. Skin varies in thickness; it is thinner than a sheet of paper on the eyelids, but it is about one-quarter of an inch thick on the soles of the feet. Skin is certainly different from any other organ in the human body.

Subject _____

Main idea _____

Supporting detail 1_____

   Minor detail _____

   Minor detail _____

Supporting detail 2_____

   Minor detail _____

   Minor detail _____

Type of supporting details _____

The subject is the skin. The main idea is that skin is different from any other organ in the human body. The first major detail is that the skin is the largest organ of the human body. Minor details are (1) the skin of an adult measures about 20 square feet and (2) it weighs about six or seven pounds. The second major detail is that it varies in thickness. Minor details are that (1) it is thinner than a sheet of paper on the eyelids and (2) it is about one-fourth-inch thick on the soles of the feet. The supporting details are facts.

G. Most of us identify precious stones such as rubies and sapphires by their colors. A ruby is red. A sapphire is blue. But most precious gems are formed from colorless minerals and get their color from impurities in the stones. For example, rubies and sapphires are both varieties of corundum, a mineral that contains other trace minerals that give corundum its color.

Subject _____

Main idea _____

Supporting detail _____

Type of support_____

The subject is the colors of precious stones. The main idea is that most precious gems are formed from colorless minerals and get their color from impurities in the stones. The supporting detail is that both rubies and sapphires come from corundum. The type of support is examples.

Inferential Comprehension

Implied Main Idea

In the two preceding paragraphs the main idea was stated somewhere in the paragraph. In some paragraphs, however, the main idea is implied rather than stated. You will have to "read between the lines" to infer (reason out) the main idea. To do this, first ask yourself who or what the paragraph is about (the subject). Then ask yourself the main thing the writer is telling you about the subject (the main idea). Fill in the blanks for Paragraphs H and I.

H. A baby penguin is called a chick. A baby kangaroo is called a joey. A baby elephant is a calf. A baby turkey is a poult. A baby fish is a fry. But a baby monkey is just a baby.

Subject _____

Supporting detail 1_____

Supporting detail 2_____

Supporting detail 3_____

Supporting detail 4_____

Supporting detail 5_____

Supporting detail 6_____

Type of supporting details _____

Implied main idea _____

The subject is the names of baby animals. The supporting details are (1) chick, (2) joey, (3) calf, (4) poult, (5) fry, (6) baby. The type of support is examples. The implied main idea is that many baby animals have names different from those of the adults.

I.   The hippopotamus is born underwater, but it cannot breathe underwater. It is the second heaviest land mammal. Only an elephant weighs more. It is a close relative of the pig. It can open its mouth more than four feet. Its skin is more than an inch thick and so tough that bullets cannot penetrate it. Finally, it has a stomach ten feet long.

Subject _____

Supporting detail 1_____

Supporting detail 2_____

Supporting detail 3_____

Supporting detail 4_____

Supporting detail 5_____

Supporting detail 6_____

Type of supporting details _____

Implied main idea _____

The subject is the hippopotamus. Supporting details are (1) it is born underwater but cannot breathe underwater, (2) it is the second heaviest land animal, (3) it is a close relative of the pig, (4) it can open its mouth more than four feet, (5) its skin is very thick and tough, and (6) its stomach is more than ten feet long. The supporting details are facts. The implied main idea is that it is an unusual animal.

Valid and Invalid Inferences

When you found the implied main ideas in the preceding paragraphs, you were using inference. Making inferences is important in daily life. For example, if you see storm clouds, you might infer that it will rain. Inference in reading is a type of informed guesswork in which the reader makes judgments about the author's meaning. You must read "between the lines." Some inferences are valid because they are supported by what the author has implied. All others are invalid.

Fill in the blanks for Paragraph J. Then mark each inference V if it is valid or I if it is invalid.

J.   During his lifetime, Samuel Morse (1791–1872) was more famous for his painting than for his invention of the telegraph and Morse code. He was known first for his ivory carving, which he studied at Yale University. He was later known for his portrait painting. By 1822, at the age of 31, he was internationally recognized. It was another ten years before he became interested in telegraphic communication.

Subject _____

Main idea _____

Supporting detail 1_____

   Minor detail _____

Supporting detail 2_____

   Minor detail _____

Type of supporting details _____

The subject is Samuel Morse. The main idea is that during his lifetime he was more famous for his painting than for his inventions. The first supporting detail is that he was first known for his ivory carving. The minor detail is that he studied ivory carving at Yale University. The second major detail is that he was later known for his portrait painting. The minor detail is that he was internationally recognized by 1822 when he was 31. The supporting details are facts.

Inferences: Mark each sentence V or I.

_____ 1. Today, Morse is better known for his invention of the telegraph.

_____ 2. Morse died young.

_____ 3. Morse was not famous as a scientist during his lifetime.

_____ 4. Morse's art was seen in different countries.

_____ 5. Morse studied to be an artist.

_____ 6. Morse was an unusually talented man.

Statements 1, 4, 5, and 6 can be inferred from the paragraph. It can be inferred that statement 1 is true from the first sentence in the paragraph. Statement 4 can be inferred from the phrase "internationally recognized." Statement 5 can be inferred from the reference to Yale University. Statement 6 can be inferred from all the things Morse was able to do. Statement 2 is not a valid inference, because Morse lived from 1791 to 1872. Statement 3 cannot be inferred; Morse started working on the telegraph in 1832, but he didn't die until 1872.

Fill in the blanks for Paragraph K; then write V or I next to each sentence.

K. Pet overpopulation has become a major problem in the United States. No one wants to kill dogs and cats, and people don't want to keep their pets from breeding, so there is an epidemic of unwanted pets. Every hour 12,500 puppies are born in the United States. Most will never have a permanent home. In New York City, there are at least one million stray dogs and five hundred thousand stray cats.

Subject _____

Main idea _____

Supporting detail _____

    Minor detail _____

    Minor detail _____

Type of supporting details _____

The subject is pet overpopulation. The main idea is that pet overpopulation is a major problem in the United States. The supporting detail is a reason: Nobody wants to kill dogs and cats, yet people don't keep pets from breeding. The minor details are (1) that every hour 12,500 puppies are born and most will never have a permanent home, and (2) that in New York City there are at least one million stray dogs and five hundred thousand stray cats.

Inferences: Mark each sentence V or I.

_____ 1. There are more cats born than dogs.

_____ 2. People don't want to take responsibility for their pets.

_____ 3. People will begin killing more animals in the next century.

_____ 4. Many dogs and cats are abandoned by their owners.

_____ 5. New York City has a worse problem than any other city.

_____ 6. Cats and dogs are the only pets that have a problem with overpopulation.

Statements 2 and 4 can be inferred from the paragraph. Statement 2 can be inferred from the assertion that people don't want to keep their pets from breeding and statement 4 can be inferred from the number of stray cats and dogs that exist. Sentences 1, 3, 5, and 6 cannot be inferred, because (in 1) a comparison of the numbers of cats and dogs is mentioned only in the last sentence, which states that there are more dogs in New York City; (in 3) the future is not mentioned; (in 5) New York's problem is not compared with that of other cities; and (in 6) other pets, such as rabbits and hamsters, are not mentioned.

Critical Comprehension

Thesis, Argument, and Support

When an author or speaker is trying to persuade us of something, we have to read or listen critically. Instead of a main idea, we have the author's thesis, or point of view. It is the major point the author is making about the subject.

The thesis can be either stated or implied. The arguments are the main points the author makes in support of the thesis; they are like the major supporting details. Minor details consist of support for the arguments.

Fill in the blanks for Paragraphs L and M.

L. We have no more right to use other species for medical experiments than the Nazis had the right to use humans for experimentation in the concentration camps. Recent research proves that animals are more intelligent than previously thought and that they have feelings not very different from ours.

Subject _____

Thesis _____

Argument _____

Type of supporting details _____

The subject is using animals for medical experiments. The thesis is that we have no right to use them. The argument is that research has found that animals are more intelligent than previously thought and that they have feelings similar to ours. The type of support is facts (research).

M. The animal-rights movement is strangling medical research. Among the medical advances that would have been impossible without animal research are kidney dialysis, the artificial heart, the polio vaccine, and a leukemia vaccine for *cats.* Because of the animal-rights protests, other important research projects have been dropped. We cannot reasonably expect to find a cure for cancer by experimenting on vegetables.

Subject _____

Thesis _____

Argument 1 _____

   Minor detail 1 _____

   Minor detail 2 _____

   Minor detail 3 _____

   Minor detail 4 _____

Argument 2 _____

Type of supporting details _____

The subject is the animal-rights movement. The thesis is that we need to experiment on animals. The first argument is that many medical advances

would have been impossible without research. The minor details are examples: (1) kidney dialysis, (2) the artificial heart, (3) the polio vaccine, and (4) a
leukemia vaccine for cats. The second argument is that important research
projects have been dropped because of the animal-rights protests. The main
type of support (Arguments 1 and 2) is reasons.

Paragraph Comprehension Review

The following twenty-five exercises will help you practice paragraph comprehension. Read each exercise and fill in the blanks.

Exercise 1

The death penalty should be used. The main reason is the evidence that it
deters others from committing capital crimes. Common sense tells us that
the greater the punishment, the less likely it is that people will commit the
crime. So killing a few criminals will save many innocent people from being
victimized.

Subject _____

Thesis _____

Argument _____

_____

Type of supporting details _____

Exercise 2

The death penalty is immoral for several reasons. First, it has never been
proved that the death penalty deters crime, since most criminals hope they
will not be caught. Second, a less severe penalty, such as life imprisonment,
would deter crime just as effectively. Finally, the criminal justice system frequently convicts innocent people while letting the guilty go free, particularly
when the innocent are poor and the guilty are rich.

Subject _____

Thesis _____

Argument 1 _____

_____

Argument 2 _____

_____

Argument 3 _____

_____

Type of supporting details _____

Exercise 3

Saudi Arabia must import sand. This may seem strange, because most of the country is desert. But desert sand is too coarse to use in building. Building materials must be mixed with fine sand to make strong cement blocks. It would be too expensive and too difficult to grind up the desert sand so that it could be used. Therefore, the Saudis must import river sand from Scotland.

Subject _____

Main idea _____

Supporting detail _____

Type of supporting details _____

If the statement is a valid inference, write V. If it is not a valid inference, write I.

_____   1. Scottish river sand is finer than Saudi Arabian sand.

_____   2. Scottish sand is more useful for building than Saudi Arabian sand.

_____   3. Sand is necessary in making cement.

_____   4. The Saudis export their own sand to other countries.

_____   5. Saudi Arabia has little or no river sand.

_____   6. Saudi Arabia has no water.

Exercise 4

Although it has never been possible to produce a violin like the Stradivarius, it may be possible to produce its sound in the future. According to Janos Negyesy at the University of California, San Diego, some day there may be a way to produce the same quality of sound by computer.

Subject _____

Main idea _____

_____

Supporting details _____

Type of supporting details _____

If the statement is a valid inference, write V. If it is invalid, write I.

_____ 1. A Stradivarius is a very good violin.

_____ 2. A Stradivarius was made by using a computer.

_____ 3. Negyesy made Stradivarius violins.

_____ 4. Many violinists would like to own a Stradivarius violin.

_____ 5. The new computer reproduction will look like the original.

_____ 6. The same note played on different violins can sound different.

Exercise 5

Let's say you want to memorize the names of all fifty states in the United States. You could organize them alphabetically, beginning with Alabama and ending with Wyoming. Another way to organize them might be geographically, by sections of the country. You could try to picture a map of the states in the Northeast, in the South, and so on. A third way might be to remember them in the order in which they were admitted to the Union, beginning with the thirteen original colonies and ending with Alaska and Hawaii.

Subject _____

Supporting detail 1 _____

Supporting detail 2 _____

Supporting detail 3 _____

Type of supporting details _____

Implied main idea _____

_____

Mark each sentence V or I.

_____ 1. Alphabetizing a list is the most efficient method of memorization.

_____ 2. It is difficult to remember the names of the states without putting them in some type of order.

_____ 3. There are only three ways to organize the fifty states.

_____ 4. The Union is another name for the United States.

_____ 5. Alaska was admitted to the Union before Wyoming.

_____ 6. The thirteen colonies became states.

Exercise 6

According to the National Safety Council, drinking chemicals such as detergents, furniture polish, or paint is not the major cause of poisoning among children. The Council says that the most frequent cause of poisoning among children is eating deadly plants. Children find these deadly plants in and around their own homes. Common household plants such as oleanders and daffodils are poisonous if eaten.

Subject _____

Main idea _____

_____

Supporting detail _____

Type of supporting details _____

Mark each sentence V or I.

_____ 1. Common plants can be dangerous.

_____ 2. Children will eat things that adults won't.

_____ 3. Children can tell whether a plant is poisonous.

_____ 4. All household plants are poisonous plants.

_____ 5. If a child eats an unknown plant, you should call a doctor or a poison control center to be sure the child hasn't been poisoned.

_____ 6. Parents should learn which plants are poisonous.

Exercise 7

In 1980, the National Turkey Federation studied the sales of turkey and turkey parts. The results were surprising. According to the study, supermarket chains showed that more than 60 percent of all turkey products are bought in the first nine months of the year. A similar study thirty years earlier showed that 99 percent of all turkey was sold during November and December. The 1980 study also showed that people are eating more turkey than ever before. Now the average person eats 10.7 pounds of turkey per year. Twenty years ago, the average person ate only 6.15 pounds per year. Turkey, known as America's favorite Thanksgiving meal, now appears on American tables year-round.

Subject _____

Main idea _____

Supporting detail _____

Type of supporting details _____

Mark each sentence V or I.

_____ 1. People eat more turkey because it is good for them.

_____ 2. In 1950, people ate most of their yearly consumption of turkey in November and December.

_____ 3. People now eat more turkey in February than in December.

_____ 4. People ate less turkey in the 1950s because it was very expensive.

_____ 5. Today, 40 percent of all turkey is bought between October and December.

_____ 6. People eat turkey more times throughout the year than they did twenty years ago.

Exercise 8

We should legalize cocaine and marijuana. First, research indicates that trying to reduce the flow of drugs into the country drives prices up. This causes more people to produce and sell drugs domestically. Second, legalizing drugs would allow the government to set standards for purity and strength and to eliminate the black market, as it has for alcohol. Finally, drugs aren't the real problem. The war on drugs serves as a smoke screen for the issues we don't want to deal with, such as poverty and racism.

Subject _____

Thesis _____

Argument 1 _____

_____

Argument 2 _____

_____

Argument 3 _____

_____

Type of supporting details _____

Exercise 9

We can win the war against drugs if we focus on discouraging the user. One way is to devote more time and money to detecting and punishing users. Prison sentences are one possibility. Alternative punishments include seizing the property of users; making them ineligible for government programs such as unemployment insurance, Social Security, disability insurance, Medicaid, and public assistance; and revoking their driver's licenses. Another effective tool is drug testing. The Department of the Navy reports that its testing program reduced use from 33 percent in 1980 to 10 percent in 1985. Drug-testing programs in the workplace have produced similar results.

Subject _____

Thesis _____

Argument 1 _____

_____

   Minor detail 1 _____

   Minor detail 2 _____

   Minor detail 3 _____

   Minor detail 4 _____

Argument 2 _____

   Minor detail _____

_____

Type of supporting details _____

Exercise 10

One of the most helpful spelling rules is "*i* before *e* except after *c* or when sounded like *a* as in *neighbor* and *weigh.*" Based on this rule, you know that words such as *piece, believe,* and *brief* are spelled with *ie* rather than *ei*. You also know that words such as *receive, receipt,* and *ceiling* are spelled with *ei* rather than *ie,* since the letters follow a *c*. Finally, you know that when the two letters sound like *a* in words such as *veil, weight,* and *sleigh,* the order is *ei* rather than *ie.*

Subject _____

Main idea _____

_____

Supporting detail 1 _____

_____

Supporting detail 2 _____

_____

Supporting detail 3 _____

_____

Type of supporting details _____

If you can infer that the spelling is correct from the rule in the paragraph, write V. If the spelling is incorrect, write I.

_____ 1. decieve

_____ 2. freight

_____ 3. obedeint

_____ 4. sieve

_____ 5. weiner

_____ 6. priest

Exercise 11

In order from three sides to ten, the names of the shapes are triangle, quadrilateral, pentagon, hexagon, heptagon, octagon, nonagon, and decagon. The first two come from Latin: *triangle* means "three angles," and *quadrilateral* means "four sides." *Gon* is a Greek root meaning "angles."

Subject _____

Supporting details _____

_____

Type of supporting details _____

Implied main idea _____

_____

Mark each sentence V or I.

_____ 1. We use some Latin and Greek words in English.

_____ 2. The best way to learn English is to study Latin and Greek.

_____ 3. We can infer that *trilateral* means "three sides."

_____ 4. We can infer that October was the eighth month in the ancient Roman calendar.

_____ 5. We can infer that the Pentagon building in Washington, D.C. has ten sides.

Exercise 12

The moon is a lifeless ball that has no atmosphere and no water. Without water or air, there can be no food. Parts of the moon are hot enough to boil the blood if a person does not wear a protective space suit. On the other hand, in the shadows of hills on the moon, a person could freeze to death at temperatures of –274 degrees Fahrenheit.

Subject _____

Supporting detail 1 _____

Supporting detail 2 _____

Supporting detail 3 _____

Supporting detail 4 _____

Supporting detail 5 _____

Type of supporting details _____

Implied main idea _____

Mark each sentence V or I.

_____   1. Plants cannot grow on the moon.

_____   2. Space suits keep people from freezing when they are on the moon.

_____   3. People cannot breathe on the moon without using special equipment.

_____   4. Some plants can live at temperatures as low as –274 degrees Fahrenheit.

_____   5. The moon has snow.

_____   6. Scientists believe that the moon looks like what the Earth did during the time of cave dwellers.

Exercise 13

In 1610, egg whites were used to build a bridge that still stands in Peru. One house in Massachusetts is made of newspapers. In Japan, it was common for farmers to use the hulls from rice to make a paste that was then molded into building blocks for their houses. Several houses throughout the world have been made from the bottoms of bottles cemented together.

Subject _____

Supporting detail 1 _____

Supporting detail 2 _____

Supporting detail 3 _____

Supporting detail 4 _____

Type of supporting details _____

Implied main idea _____

_____

Mark each sentence V or I.

_____ 1. Egg whites are still used for building bridges in Peru.

_____ 2. People will use any materials available to build what they need.

_____ 3. Only poor people use strange building materials to make things.

_____ 4. Egg whites can serve as strong glue.

_____ 5. Today, we can still use egg whites and rice hulls for building things if we need to.

_____ 6. The egg whites mentioned in the paragraph seemed to be destroyed by bad weather.

Exercise 14

Most plant roots take in liquids for plants to live on. Some roots also select vitamins and minerals that the particular plant needs to maintain life. In some plants, such as radishes and turnips, the roots store food. So you see, roots serve several different purposes that are vital to the life of a plant. In addition to providing food and water for the plant, the roots help "anchor" the plant in place. This is especially important on steep hillsides, where rain could wash away plants with shallow roots. The anchoring effect is also important in areas of heavy wind, such as on ocean cliffs.

Subject _____

Main idea _____

_____

Supporting detail 1 _____

Supporting detail 2 _____

Supporting detail 3 _____

Minor detail 1 _____

Minor detail 2 _____

Supporting detail 4 _____

    Minor detail 1 _____

    Minor detail 2 _____

Type of supporting details _____

Exercise 15

Homeless people deserve government help. It is the obligation of a humane society to make sure that all its citizens have an opportunity for a decent life. Those who can work should be given emergency food and shelter and helped to find employment. Those who are unable to work should be helped to find a stable living situation. If they can care for themselves, they can live independently with public assistance. If they are too old, sick, or disabled to care for themselves, they should be helped to find a suitable group-living situation.

Subject _____

Thesis _____

Argument _____

_____

    Minor detail 1 _____

_____

    Minor detail 2 _____

_____

        A _____

        B _____

Type of supporting details _____

Exercise 16

We should not sacrifice our tax dollars to help the homeless. Very few of them are willing to work; the majority are lazy bums. Those who really want to help themselves can always find a way to earn a living. If the government supports the homeless, then they will lose all motivation to do anything for themselves.

Subject _____

Thesis _____

_____

Argument 1 _____

   Minor detail _____

_____

Argument 2 _____

_____

Type of supporting details _____

Exercise 17

When the Spanish, under Commander Hernando Cortes, arrived in Mexico, the cacao bean, from which chocolate is made, was used for money. The Aztecs of Mexico and the Incas of Peru thought that chocolate was a drink fit only for royalty. When Cortes introduced hot chocolate sweetened with cane sugar and vanilla to Spain, it was available only in the Spanish court.

Subject _____

Supporting detail 1 _____

Supporting detail 2 _____

_____

Supporting detail 3 _____

Type of supporting details _____

Implied main idea _____

Mark each sentence V or I.

_____ 1. The Aztecs didn't know how valuable chocolate was.

_____ 2. Cortes loved to eat chocolates.

_____ 3. Cacao trees grew in Europe at one time.

_____ 4. When Cortes brought chocolate back to Spain, the king and queen were pleased.

_____ 5. Chocolate was once more valuable than gold.

_____ 6. Chocolate immediately became a favorite drink throughout Europe.

Exercise 18

Large eggs are not the best value. The size of eggs is often determined by their water content, so small eggs can be a better choice. The nutritional content of small eggs is the same as that of large eggs, and the price is about

25 percent less. Even medium eggs offer buyers more for their money; they have the same nutritional value as large eggs, and they are about 12 percent cheaper.

Subject _____

Main idea _____

_____

Supporting detail 1 _____

   Minor detail 1 _____

   Minor detail 2 _____

Supporting detail 2 _____

_____

   Minor detail 1 _____

   Minor detail 2 _____

Type of supporting details _____

Mark each sentence V or I.

_____ 1. All eggs have the same nutritional value.

_____ 2. Small eggs are the best buy.

_____ 3. Large eggs weigh more than small or medium eggs.

_____ 4. Small and medium eggs cost the same.

_____ 5. Nutritionally, the size of an egg doesn't matter.

_____ 6. Jumbo eggs are a better value than large eggs.

Exercise 19

Women in the military should not serve in combat positions. The most important reason is the effects on families. It isn't fair to small children for their mothers to have long absences or to risk death. Another reason is that women cause problems for the military. They often marry military men, and then they want to be assigned to the same combat zones as their husbands. They get pregnant, which means they need medical care, they can't fight, and eventually they need child care.

Subject _____

Thesis _____

_____

Argument 1 _____

  Minor detail _____

  _____

Argument 2 _____

  Minor detail 1 _____

  _____

  Minor detail 2 _____

    A _____

    B _____

    C _____

Type of supporting details _____

Exercise 20

Women in the military can never be treated as equals unless they have the same assignments as men. If they have less risky assignments but receive the same status and pay, then the men will resent them. If they have less risky assignments and also receive less status and pay, then they will be limited in their ability to advance in their careers.

Subject _____

Thesis _____

_____

Argument 1 _____

_____

Argument 2 _____

_____

Type of supporting details _____

Exercise 21

No doctor is perfect. Like everybody else, they each have their strengths and weaknesses. Maybe your doctor lacks a good bedside manner, but you feel that she is knowledgeable about the most recent research. However, most experts agree that there are three clues that tell you it's time to switch doctors. The first clue is if your doctor doesn't seem interested in listening to you. The second clue is if your doctor puts you down, judges you, or behaves disrespectfully to you or others. The third clue is if you think your doctor does not use good medical judgment; for example, she fails to tell you about the side effects or risks of your treatment.

Subject _____

Main idea _____

_____

Supporting detail 1 _____

Supporting detail 2 _____

_____

Supporting detail 3 _____

_____

Type of supporting details _____

Mark each sentence V or I.

_____   1. Expensive doctors are better than cheap ones.

_____   2. The best doctor is the one who has the best education.

_____   3. Some doctors are better than others.

_____   4. You can decide whether your doctor is good enough.

_____   5. The American Medical Association screens doctors carefully, so you don't have to.

_____   6. You should not put up with rudeness from your doctor.

Exercise 22

Some students have found a way to cut college costs: Don't go to class. Over one million students now take courses online, and the numbers are expected to triple in the next year or two. The tuition may be the same, but you do not pay for room and board. Plus you can access the courses 24 hours a day, seven days a week, including weekends and holidays. This means it's easier to work while taking classes, and that too makes your education more affordable.

Subject _____

Main idea _____

Supporting detail 1 _____

Supporting detail 2 _____

Type of supporting details _____

Mark each sentence V or I.

_____ 1. Online courses are not as good as traditional courses.

_____ 2. Compared to traditional courses, online courses are more convenient.

_____ 3. Online courses could offer advantages to students who have young children.

_____ 4. More and more students are expected to sign up for online classes.

_____ 5. You have to be very skilled with computers to take classes online.

_____ 6. One day traditional classes will no longer exist.

Exercise 23

Nearly everybody has moles, usually between ten and forty of them. Most moles are harmless. However, there are danger signs that you can remember by thinking "A B C D." "A" stands for asymmetry, which means irregular shape. "B" stands for border, meaning that the edges of the mole are ragged or irregular. "C" stands for color, meaning that the mole has changed color or has several colors. "D" stands for diameter, meaning that the mole is wider than a pencil eraser. These signs don't necessarily mean that the mole is cancerous, only that you should have it checked.

Subject _____

Main idea _____

Supporting detail 1 _____

Supporting detail 2 _____

Supporting detail 3 _____

Supporting detail 4 _____

Type of supporting details _____

Mark each sentence V or I.

_____ 1. A raised mole is likely to be cancerous.

_____ 2. Hairy moles are more dangerous than hairless ones.

_____ 3. Large moles are more likely to be cancerous than small ones.

_____ 4. It's a good idea to have all your moles checked.

_____ 5. Women usually have more moles than men do.

_____ 6. A change in a mole's color is a danger sign.

Exercise 24

Violent crimes are increasing. Rapes are up. Hate crimes are up. There are many reasons, but one of them is the increasing use of hateful and violent lyrics in popular music. Words have power to cause people to act, for good or for bad. Think of the _Declaration of Independence_ and the American Revolution. Think of the _Communist Manifesto_ and the Communist Revolution. Words that promote hate and violence can cause people to act in hateful and violent ways. For example, lyrics that degrade women can promote degrading behavior toward women. This is a threat to the whole society, and society has a right to set limits. The courts have the right to censor song lyrics.

Subject _____

Thesis _____

Argument _____

_____

Type of supporting details _____

Exercise 25

Censorship of popular music isn't new. In the 1950s, the Ku Klux Klan banned the records of Chuck Berry, Little Richard, and others because they thought the music was a bad influence on white youth. Today, right-wing maniacs have appointed themselves the guardians of "family values." They think they should be the ones to decide what's right and wrong for all of us. The idea that other points of view deserve respect is completely foreign to them. Song lyrics are only words, and words cannot hurt people. What hurts people is allowing one group to decide what the rest of us can say, think, and do. That is why the founders of our nation wrote, "Congress shall make no law abridging . . . freedom of speech." The courts do not have the right to censor song lyrics.

Subject _____

Thesis _____

Argument _____

_____

Type of supporting details _____

UNIT II

Introduction to the Active Critical Thinking (ACT) Method

In Unit II you will use your skills in basic vocabulary and comprehension to read longer selections. You will also start to use the six-step ACT (Active Critical Thinking) method.

Preread

Before you read each selection in Unit II, you will preview it in three ways:

1. You will go over the difficult words in advance so that they do not interfere with your comprehension when you read the selection. Each reading selection in this book starts with a Vocabulary Preview. We have identified, defined, and given examples of the most difficult words. You should read the preview and make sure that you can pronounce each word and use it correctly in a sentence.

2. You will preview the content to understand the subject and main idea before reading. This will increase your comprehension and speed. Psychologists have found that the brain works something like a library. A library stores information by filing it in categories. In order for your mind to store (learn) and retrieve (remember) information, you also need to file it in categories. Prereading the selection gives you the categories in advance. You will learn to use the structure of the reading selections, including headings and subheadings, illustrations, and different typefaces, to quickly pick out subject and main idea.

3. Next, you will think about what you already know about the subject. In psychology, this is called "activating your schema." The idea is that you already know something about most subjects. When you read, you should use your experience—what you already know—to help you put what you are reading into the right category in your mind. Using your experience will help you realize that A is like B, that C is a result of D, and that E and F cannot both be true, for instance. The more experience you can bring to your reading, the deeper your comprehension will be. We will also ask you to think about what you don't know about the subject, and you will think of some questions that might be answered by reading the selection. This will activate your curiosity and deepen your comprehension.

The prereading step helps you with the A (for Active) in the ACT method. An active reader interacts with the reading material, using what he or she already knows as well as the curiosity for what he or she doesn't yet know. Active reading raises comprehension. It also prevents you from finding yourself in the situation in which you have no idea what was in the ten pages you just finished "reading."

Read

In this book, you will be asked to read before underlining or highlighting. The reason is that you will not know what you need to underline until after you have read the selection. We will deal with underlining later in the book. For now, just use your active reading techniques to comprehend.

Analyze What You Read

This is where study techniques come in. The study technique we practice in Unit II is called making graphic organizers. A graphic organizer is a type of picture. It can be an outline, a chart, an idea map, or any other type of drawing. Because of the way the brain works, we cannot remember large blocks of words, but we can remember pictures.

Remember What's Important

The reason you memorize information is so that you can recall it when you need it. In college, you will usually need it for tests. The best way to memorize is *not* to reread your textbook or listen to taped lectures. The most effective way is to test yourself on what you want to remember until you reach the level of memory you need. In Unit II, you will put everything you are trying to remember into your graphic organizer. Then you will memorize the graphic organizer.

Make Use of What You Read

You memorize information so that you can use it. If you won't be using the information, you may not need to remember it. But in college, you are usually required to do something with the information you read. You may have a test, a paper, an oral report, or a class discussion. In this book, we supply questions that can be used as tests, for both comprehension and vocabulary.

Evaluate Your Active Critical Thinking Skills

Once you are evaluated in Step 5, you will find out how well you did. You may get a grade on a test or paper or comments about oral reports or discussions. In Step 6 you will take that feedback and use it to improve your reading and study techniques. For example, if you aren't happy with a test grade, you should review the six steps in ACT. Did you read the material actively and understand it? Did you analyze what was important for the test? Did you test yourself enough to remember it? With the ACT method, a poor grade should not be a reason to become discouraged. You should see it as a chance to figure out what needs improvement so that you will do better next time. To make your evaluation step easier, an Evaluation Checklist is provided on p. 417.

1   Listening: To Tell Fact From Opinion

Vocabulary Preview

observation (äb′zər vā′shən): a comment or remark based on something noticed

> *Example:* After seeing the gray sky, I made the observation that it looked as if it might rain.

hypothesis (hī päth′ə sis, hi-): *pl.* **hypotheses:** an unproven theory, etc., tentatively accepted to explain certain facts; an explanation that accounts for a set of facts that can be tested by further investigation

> *Example:* Scientists do experiments to test hypotheses.

speculative (spek′yə lə′tiv): guessing about future happenings; predicting events from incomplete evidence

> *Example:* Betting on race horses requires speculative ability.

sounder (soun′dər): based on more valid reasoning; stronger

> *Example:* Susan's argument was sounder than Jane's, so I believed Susan.

theory (thē′ə rē, thir′ē): an accepted explanation of a set of observations

> *Example:* No theory of how the universe was formed has yet to be proven.

cat, āte, fäther; pen, ēvil; if, kīte; nō, ôr, fōōd, book; boil, house; up, turn; chief, shell; thick, *the*; zh, treasure; ŋ, sing; ə for *a* in *about*; ' as in *able* (ā′b′l)

Preread

Preview the following reading selection starting on p. 70 by reading the title, the headings, and the first sentence of each paragraph. Answer the following questions without looking back at the reading.

1. What is the subject of the reading?

_____

2. Circle the answer that best summarizes the main idea of the reading selection.

    a. Facts are more important than opinions.

    b. You should be aware of the difference between fact and opinion.

    c. Most people confuse fact and opinion.

    d. Opinions are more important than facts.

3. Take a moment to think about facts and opinions. Think about what you know, what you don't know, and what you might find out from reading

the selection. Make up three questions that might be answered by reading the selection.

a. _____

b. _____

c. _____

Read

Read the selection without underlining.

◆ *Listening: To Tell Fact From Opinion*

Shirley Haley-James and John Warren Stewig

You spend a good part of your day listening to other people— teachers, friends, parents, radio and TV announcers. Sometimes they tell you facts; other times they offer their opinions. Can you tell the difference? If you cannot, you will have a hard time knowing what to believe.

Fact

A fact is a statement that can be proved. You can prove it yourself, or you can use a reliable authority. Here are some examples of facts and how they can be proved.

Statements of fact	Sources of proof
Abraham Lincoln was assassinated.	History book
Mr. Guthrie teaches math.	Experience
Jeff won the election.	Number of votes
Your kitchen table is fifty-two inches long.	Measurement

Laws and observations are also forms of fact. A law may be based on science (the law of gravity) or an established government authority (the speed limit). You can prove an observation, such as "Some stars are brighter than others," by pointing it out yourself or by testing it scientifically.

Opinion

An opinion cannot be proved. It is based only on someone's thoughts, feelings, or judgment.

Opinions: Abraham Lincoln was a great man.

Mr. Guthrie works his students too hard.

Jeff is the better candidate.

You should have a larger table.

Some people may think that these statements are true; others may disagree. Listen for words like *good, nice, bad, wonderful,* and *should.* They can help you identify opinions.

Some opinions, however, are sounder than others. While they cannot be proved, they can be backed up with facts. Someone who tells you that Jeff is the better candidate can support this opinion by giving facts about Jeff's experience and past actions. Historians who believe Lincoln was great can support their opinion with facts about his achievements.

A hypothesis is a form of opinion. It is a reasonable guess made to explain an observation. Each hypothesis must be tested to make sure it is a good guess.

Hypotheses: Objects move only when they are pushed or pulled.

The car stopped because it ran out of gas.

Green food makes me sneeze.

You can test the last hypothesis by seeing if you really do sneeze whenever you eat something green. If you also sneeze when you eat something yellow, you may have to change your hypothesis.

A theory is also an opinion, but it is not a guess. A theory is an accepted explanation of a set of observations. A theory often includes several hypotheses that belong together and have been tested successfully. If a theory is good, it can be used to explain other things.

Theories: Heat results from the movement of tiny particles.

All the forces of nature are interrelated.

Here are examples of some other kinds of opinions.

Speculative Statement: Alison Packer is going to win the seat in the state legislature.

Value Judgment: She is the best candidate.

Exaggeration: Alison Packer will get billions of votes.

Belief: She will change the government as she has
                       promised.

When you listen to someone—in a lecture, a commercial, an election campaign, or even just conversation—be aware of the difference between a fact and an opinion. Do not be persuaded by an opinion unless the speaker supports it with facts.

550 words

Analyze What You Read

Application: Fact Versus Opinion

The reading described the difference between fact and opinion. A fact is something that can be proved by you or by a reliable source. An opinion is based only on someone's thoughts, feelings, or judgment. Mark the following statements from the reading F if they are facts or O if they are opinions.

_F_   1. "You spend a good part of your day listening to other people."

_F_   2. "You can prove an observation."

_F_   3. "Abraham Lincoln was assassinated."

_F_   4. "Some opinions, . . . can be backed up with facts."

_O_   5. "You should have a larger table."

_F_   6. "Historians who believe Lincoln was great can support their opinion with facts about his achievements."

_O_   7. "Some stars are brighter than others."

_O_   8. "She is the best candidate."

_O_   9. "Some people think that these statements are true; others may disagree."

_O_ 10. "She will change the government as she has promised."

Graphic Organizer

It's often easier to understand and remember what we read when we put it into some kind of picture. Following is a chart that helps you compare facts with opinions. Look back at the reading and fill in the blanks. First, fill in the definitions of fact and opinion. Next, give an example of a fact and an opinion. Finally, give two forms of facts and two forms of opinions that were found in the reading selection.

	Fact	Opinion
Definition		
Example		
Two Forms		

Remember What's Important

1. To prepare for a Comprehension Check, memorize the chart. Test yourself or have someone test you on the difference between fact and opinion. Keep testing until you think you can remember everything you need to know.

How to Answer Essay Questions: Each of the Comprehension Checks in this book contains an essay question. Writing an essay is easy when you use a graphic organizer, but difficult when you don't. Before you write the essay, draw the graphic organizer that you memorized from your study guide. Sometimes the question requires you to use the whole graphic organizer, and sometimes you will need only part of the graphic organizer to answer the question. For example, the essay for this reading selection might ask you to give definitions, examples, and forms for fact and opinion, or it might just ask for examples. Write the essay from your graphic organizer and use signal words such as *first*, *most important*, and *finally* so that your essay is organized and easy to read.

2. To prepare for a Vocabulary Check, make flash cards as described on pp. 15–16 for each of the words in the Vocabulary Preview that you don't know. Test yourself or have someone test you until you can remember them.

Make Use of What You Read

When you are ready, complete the Comprehension Check on p. 323 and the Vocabulary Check on p. 324. Do them from memory, without looking back at the book or at your notes.

Evaluate Your Active Critical Thinking Skills

After your tests have been graded, record your scores on the Progress Chart, p. 416, and answer the questions on the Evaluation Checklist on p. 417.

Vocabulary Skills Review

For explanation see pp. 13–14

Dictionary Definitions

Most words have more than one meaning. Following are dictionary entries for four words used in the reading. Above each entry is the sentence in which the word is used. In the space, write the number of the definition that fits the way the underlined word is used. To make it easier for you to find the answer, the part of speech of the correct definition is written under the blank.

_____ 1. "You spend a good <u>part</u> of your day listening to other people—
    n.   teachers, friends, parents, radio and TV announcers."

part (pärt) *n.* [< L. *pars*] **1.** a portion, segment, etc. of a whole [a *part* of a book] **2.** an essential, separable element [automobile *parts*] **3.** a portion or share; specif., *a)* duty [to do one's *part*] *b)* [*usually pl.*] talent; ability [a man of *parts*] *c)* a role in a play *d)* any of the voices or instruments in a musical ensemble, or the score for this **4.** a region; esp., [*usually pl.*] a district **5.** one of the sides in a conflict, etc. **6.** a dividing line formed in combing the hair —*vt.* **1.** to break or divide into parts **2.** to comb (the hair) so as to leave a part **3.** to break or hold apart —*vi.* **1.** to break or divide into parts **2.** to separate and go different ways **3.** to cease associating **4.** to go away; leave (with *from*) —*adj.* partial

_____ 2. "Some <u>stars</u> are brighter than others."
    n.

star (stär) *n.* [OE. *steorra*] **1.** *a)* any heavenly body seen as a small fixed point of light, esp. a far-off sun *b)* a star or stars regarded as influencing one's fate **2.** a conventionalized figure with five or six points, or anything like this **3.** an asterisk **4.** one who excels, as in a sport **5.** a leading actor or actress —*vt.* **starred, star′ring 1.** to mark with stars as a decoration, etc. **2.** to present (an actor or actress) in a leading role —*vi.* **1.** to perform brilliantly **2.** to perform as a star —*adj.* **1.** having great skill; outstanding **2.** of a star —**star′less** *adj.*

_____ 3. "A theory is an accepted explanation of a <u>set</u> of observations."
    n.

set (set) *vt.* **set, set′ting** [OE. *settan*] **1.** to cause to sit; seat **2.** to put in a specified place, condition, etc. [*set* books on a shelf, *set* slaves free] **3.** to put in proper condition; fix (a trap for animals), adjust (a clock or dial), arrange (a table for a meal), fix (hair) in a desired style, etc., put (a broken bone, etc.) into normal position, etc. **4.** to make settled, rigid, or fixed [pectin *sets* jelly] **5.** to mount (gems) **6.** to direct **7.** to appoint; establish; fix (boundaries, the time for an event, a rule, a quota, etc.) **8.** to furnish (an example) for others **9.** to fit (words *to* music or music *to* words) **10.** to arrange (type) for printing *–vi.* **1.** to sit on eggs: said of a fowl **2.** to become firm, hard, or fixed [the cement *set*] **3.** to begin to move (*out, forth, off,* etc.) **4.** to sink below the horizon [the sun *sets*] **5.** to have a certain direction; tend *–adj.* **1.** fixed; established [a *set* time] **2.** intentional **3.** fixed; rigid; firm **4.** obstinate **5.** ready [get *set*] *–n.* **1.** a setting or being set **2.** the way in which a thing is set [the *set* of his jaw] **3.** direction; tendency **4.** the scenery for a play, etc. **5.** a group of persons or things classed or belonging together **6.** assembled equipment for radio or television reception, etc. **7.** *Tennis* a group of six or more games won by a margin of at least two

_____   4. "All of the forces of nature are interrelated."
n.

force (fôrs) *n.* [< L. *fortis,* strong] **1.** strength; power **2.** physical coercion against a person or thing **3.** the power to control, persuade, etc.; effectiveness **4.** military power **5.** any group of people organized for some activity [a sales *force*] **6.** energy that causes or alters motion *–vt.* **forced, forc′ing 1.** to make do something by force; compel **2.** to break open, into, or through by force **3.** to take by force; extort **4.** to impose as by force (with *on* or *upon*) **5.** to produce as by force [she *forced* a smile] **6.** to cause (plants, etc.) to develop faster by artificial means

For explanation see pp. 8–10

Pronunciation Guide

For practice in using the pronunciation guide, do the following exercises.

cat, āte, fäther; pen, ēvil; if, kīte; nō, ôr, fōōd, book; boil, house; up, tʉrn; chief, shell; thick, *the*; zh, treasure; ŋ, sing; ə for *a* in *about*; ' as in *able* (ā′b′l)

1. Translate these famous places into English spelling.

   a. *thə* grand kan′yən

   _____

   b. yel′ō stōn nash′ə n'l pärk

   _____

   c. nī ag′rə fôlz

   _____

   d. *thə* stach′ōō əv lib′ər tē

   _____

e. *thə* gōld′ən gāt brij

2. Say each of the following words out loud and listen for the sounds. Then circle the words that contain short vowel sounds (a as in c*a*t, e as in p*e*n, i as in *i*f, o as in h*o*t, and u as in *u*p).

fact   judgment   radio   guess   feel

3. Say each of the following words out loud and listen for the sounds. Then circle the words that contain the schwa sound (ə).

statement   idea   value   opinion   bad

4. Say each of the following words out loud and listen for the sounds. Then circle the words that contain long vowel sounds (*ā* as in *a*te, *ē* as in *e*vil, *ī* as in k*i*te, *ō* as in n*o*, and y$\overline{oo}$, the *u* in m*u*le).

opinion   source   sound   science   hypothesis

2   A League of Her Own

Vocabulary Preview

hypnotic (hip nät′ik): causing hypnosis or a trance

Example: Watching the flames in a fireplace can be <u>hypnotic</u>.

slogan (slō′gən): a catchword or rallying motto distinctly associated with a political party or other group

Example: The party's <u>slogan</u> was "Safe Streets."

distinctive (di stiŋk′tiv): making distinct or outstanding

Example: The zebra has <u>distinctive</u> markings.

tragic (traj′ik): like or characteristic of tragedy; bringing great harm, suffering, etc.

Example: Children playing with matches can have <u>tragic</u> consequences.

empowering (em pou′ər iŋ, im-): giving ability to; enabling; permitting

Example: Having enough money to do what you want is <u>empowering</u>.

committed (kə mit′id): dedicated; bound by a promise or loyalty

Example: I am <u>committed</u> to the cause of animal rights.

stereotypical (ster′ē ə tip′ik′l, stir′-): having the nature of a type; not original or individualized

Example: The <u>stereotypical</u> American family, with a working father and a housewife mother, is becoming more and more rare.

commanding (kə mand′iŋ): powerful and authoritative

Example: Officers in the military wear uniforms and decorations that make them more <u>commanding</u>.

efficient (e fish′ənt, i-; often, ē-, ə-): producing a desired effect, product, etc. with a minimum of effort, expense, or waste; working well

Example: Generally, companies that are <u>efficient</u> make more money.

validate (val′ə dāt′): to prove to be valid or well-grounded on principles or evidence; to make more able to withstand criticism or objection, as an argument; to strengthen

Example: Several eyewitnesses were able to <u>validate</u> her story.

cat, āte, fäther; pen, ēvil; if, kīte; nō, ôr, fo͞od, book; boil, house; up, turn; chief, shell; thick, *the*; zh, treasure; ŋ, sing; ə for *a* in *about*; ′ as in *able* (ā′b′l)

Preread

Preview the following reading selection beginning on this page by reading the title, the author, and the first sentence of each paragraph. Answer the following questions without looking back at the reading selection.

1. What is the subject?

   _____

2. Circle the statement that best summarizes the main idea.

   a. The WNBA needs financial support.

   b. Women show better sportsmanship than men do.

   c. WNBA fans are unique.

   d. Women are powerful.

3. Now take a moment to think about the WNBA. Think about what you know, what you don't know, and what you might find out from reading the selection. Make up three questions that might be answered by reading the selection.

   a. _____

   b. _____

   c. _____

Read

Read the selection without underlining.

◆ *A League of Her Own*

Rosie O'Donnell

Long before the first game was played, the colorful ball was designed, or the hypnotic slogan "We Got Next" was invented, the WNBA had hard-core fans who were already distinctive. All of us loved basketball, but we loved it on a much different level. People go to NBA games and they can figure out pretty fast that Michael Jordan is the most valuable player because he's the best. WNBA fans don't think that way. Our MVP was Sheryl Swoopes, not because she led the league in scoring or acrobatics, but because she had a baby and six weeks later, she was back on the court playing basketball. When Sheryl Swoopes came to New York, we cheered. I consider myself one of the biggest New York Liberty fans in the world, but I loved Sheryl. I know it was the same everywhere. Sheryl gets ready to go in the game and every mom in the crowd stands up and cheers: "Hey Sheryl! Go girl! Can you believe how good she looks! She had a baby! Go Sheryl! You still nursing? Sheryl, you look great!"

WNBA fans are unique. You go to men's games and you see that the home fans hate the other team. Not us. Haixia Zheng comes to New York, scores a basket for the Los Angeles Sparks, and has the biggest smile on her face. Everyone stands up and cheers because she's smiling. That's the part that is so different from all other sports. The fans are so supportive of all the women who are out there competing on the court. There was a spirit of love that went from the crowd to the players and back to the crowd last year, and it was something that you can't find anywhere else in professional sports.

When the WNBA was first announced, my reaction was: It's about time. I thought it was tragic that the greatest female basketball players in our country could not use their God-given talent at home, and either had to go overseas to play or had to become a coach and teach other women to play. Women have gotten a raw deal in terms of team professional sports. The only way professional women athletes could make money was to play an individual sport like tennis or golf. Sport mirrored a society where women are always taught to compete against each other. Who's better? Who's better looking? Who's got the best figure? You have to beat the individual.

Men, however, are taught more about teamwork because they have those professional role models in team sports, where you have to support each other in order to succeed. The mentality that comes from having to be a part of a team where everyone is supportive of each other is good for women on the whole, and that is the reason that the WNBA is such a strong attraction for women and young girls. It is about basketball and the tremendous amount of talent that these women have. But it also is about empowering women and young girls and the celebration of being a female.

From the time the WNBA came into existence, I was committed to doing everything I could to support the league, whether it was buying season tickets, shouting encouragement from the stands, or having WNBA players on The Rosie O'Donnell Show. I had a lot of them on last year, and I plan to have a lot of them on this year. Luckily, I have the ability to invite guests who move and inspire me. I wanted to show all the people watching my show that women had a league of their own (I'm kind of fond of that phrase), they were playing great basketball, and they were very entertaining.

I'll always remember the opening game in Madison Square Garden. It was so special seeing this entire arena filled with families and young girls.

When the lights went down and the players were being introduced, it brought tears to my eyes. It really did. I got all choked up because I was a kid who played a lot of sports and that's what I would dream as a child. Now the young girls will grow up some day and tell their children about what it was like to go to WNBA games during the first year. I will be able to be the stereotypical grandmother and tell my grandkids, "You know, when Grandma was little, there was no WNBA."

The WNBA has made basketball even more special to me. I love to watch and I love to play. I play in the New York women-professionals league in New York City, and we have a three-month season with one game each week. We won the championship last year, and people usually want to know my contributions. I tell them that as far as basketball goes, I'm a good softball player.

But one of the great things about the WNBA is that it has allowed women to be dreamers. I caught the fever big, and don't be surprised if this year or next, I try out for a team. I love the Liberty, and Cynthia Cooper was very enjoyable when she was on my show, but I think I am going to try out for the Charlotte Sting. I like their uniforms. The teal is very nice, I like the nickname, and I've always had great respect for the bee family. The queen bee is a powerful and commanding female figure who runs a highly efficient community.

The WNBA has already been powerful and efficient, and I think it will be for many years to come. Last year, it was a joy not only to watch its birth, development, and success, but also to be so close to a compelling group of female athletes who, like the queen bee, validated an old saying:
◆   Never underestimate the power of a woman.

1000 words

Analyze What You Read

STEP 3

Following is an outline of the reading selection. Fill in the missing support.

Graphic Organizer

A League of Her Own

  I. Women fans are different.

      A. They respect different things.

          Examples: 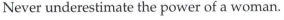 _____

          _____

          _____

B. Their emotions are different.

　　Examples: _____

II. Women athletes in the United States have previously only been able to make money in individual sports.

　　Examples: _____

III. Sports mirrored a society in which women were taught to compete against each other.

　　Examples: _____

IV. Team sports are good for women.

　　Reasons: _____

V. Rosie O'Donnell supports the WNBA.

　　Examples: _____

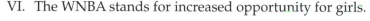

_____

_____

_____

VI. The WNBA stands for increased opportunity for girls.

VII. The WNBA has allowed girls and women to be dreamers.

Remember What's Important

1. To prepare for a Comprehension Check, memorize the outline. Test yourself or have someone test you until you can remember everything you need to know. If necessary, review *How to Answer Essay Questions* on p. 73.

2. To prepare for a Vocabulary Check, make flash cards as described on pp. 15–16 for each of the words in the Vocabulary Preview that you don't know. Test yourself or have someone test you until you can remember them.

Make Use of What You Read

When you are ready, complete the Comprehension Check on p. 325 and the Vocabulary Check on p. 327. Do them from memory, without looking back at the book or at your notes.

Evaluate Your Active Critical Thinking Skills

After your tests have been graded, record your scores on the Progress Chart, p. 416, and answer the questions on the Evaluation Checklist on p. 417.

Vocabulary Skills Review

For explanation see pp. 3–5

Context Clues

Use the context of each sentence to figure out the meaning of the italicized word. *Do not use a dictionary.* Circle the letter of the best definition, and then write in the type of clue: definition, contrast, example, experience.

1. Opinion on the death penalty is divided; some people are strongly in favor of it, and others are working to *abolish* it.

   a. increase   b. end   c. keep   d. require

   Type of clue: _____

2. A *doctorate* is the highest degree awarded by a university.

   a. a type of diploma   b. an award

   c. the highest university degree   d. a professional degree

   Type of clue: _____

3. "Thirty days hath September, April, June, and November" is a *mnemonic* device that helps us remember the number of days in the months.

   a. legal   b. boring   c. difficult   d. memory

   Type of clue: _____

4. If you want to ask someone for a favor, it's a good idea to wait until they are in a *receptive* mood.

   a. favorable   b. negative   c. nervous   d. hostile

   Type of clue: _____

5. *Sadistic* people enjoy hurting others.

   a. nice   b. normal   c. kind   d. cruel

   Type of clue: _____

6. Depending on the speaker, a lecture can range anywhere between fascinating and *stultifying.*

   a. informative   b. exciting   c. boring   d. new

   Type of clue: _____

7. *Speculative* investments, such as penny stocks, are more suitable for young people who have time to recover from a loss than for elderly people who don't.

   a. safe   b. risky   c. expensive   d. financial

   Type of clue: _____

8. The word *caption,* meaning heading, comes from the Latin word *capit,* meaning head.

   a. footnote   b. Latin   c. heading   d. direction

   Type of clue: _____

9. A "white lie" is a *deception* meant to protect someone other than oneself.

   a. conversation   b. contrast   c. saying   d. lie

   Type of clue: _____

10. You can *entice* a dog with a bone, a cat with a fish, and a rabbit with a carrot.

   a. tempt   b. punish   c. destroy   d. buy

   Type of clue: _____

Parts of Speech

For explanation see pp. 10–12

For each word below, write its part of speech. Then change it to the new part of speech. Write a sentence using the new word. Use your dictionary if you need help.

Word	Part of speech	New part of speech	New word
1. validate		adjective	
Sentence:			
2. efficient		adverb	
Sentence:			
3. distinctive		verb	
Sentence:			
4. stereotypical		verb	
Sentence:			

continued

Word	Part of speech	New part of speech	New word
5. tragic		noun	
Sentence:			
6. hypnotic		verb	
Sentence:			

Comprehension Skills Review: Fact versus Opinion

Reading 1 described the difference between fact and opinion. A fact is something that can be proved by you or by a reliable source. An opinion is based only on someone's thoughts, feelings, or judgment. Mark the following statements from the second reading selection F if they are facts and O if they are opinion.

_____ 1. "WNBA fans are unique."

_____ 2. "Sheryl Swoopes . . . had a baby and six weeks later, she was back on the court playing basketball."

_____ 3. ". . . I have the ability to invite guests who move and inspire me."

_____ 4. "The mentality that comes from having to be a part of a team where everyone is supportive of each other is good for women on the whole . . ."

_____ 5. "The teal is very nice . . ."

_____ 6. "We won the championship last year . . ."

_____ 7. ". . . it brought tears to my eyes."

_____ 8. "There was a spirit of love that went from the crowd to the players and back."

3   How to Write a Business Letter

Vocabulary Preview

asinine (as′ə nīn′): stupid, silly
Example: Wearing a lampshade on his head at the Christmas party made him look asinine.

stultifying (stul′tə fī′iŋ): foolish or boring
Example: Instructors who read their notes present stultifying lectures.

mundane (mun dān′, mun′dān): ordinary, commonplace
Example: Mundane activities, such as washing clothes, are not exciting.

receptive (ri sep′tiv): able or willing to listen to ideas
Example: An opinionated person is not very receptive to ideas that he doesn't believe.

cliché (klē shā′): an overused expression
Example: "A penny saved is a penny earned" is a cliché.

jargon (jär′gən): the special vocabulary of an activity or group
Example: BLT is jargon used by waitresses when they order a bacon, lettuce, and tomato sandwich.

flippant (flip′ənt): not respectful about serious subjects
Example: A flippant remark to your teacher might get you thrown out of class.

emphasis (em′fə sis): forcefulness of expression that gives special importance to something
Example: We raise our voices for emphasis when we are talking.

pretense (pri tens′, prē′tens): a claim to possess skills or qualities usually not supported by facts
Example: Most of us make no pretense of being outstanding artists just because we like to paint.

invariably (in ver′ē ə blē): always; without change or exception
Example: Invariably, it will rain the day you wash your car.

gospel (gäs′pəl): anything claimed or accepted as absolute truth; also **gospel truth**
Example: Some people accept the opinions of their religious leaders as gospel.

inflated (in flāt′id): increased beyond proper limits
Example: Because the value of money is inflated, we can buy only one loaf of bread for the same price that we could buy three loaves ten years ago.

annihilate (ə nī′ə lāt′): to totally destroy
Example: Hunters in North America almost annihilated the buffalo by killing many animals at once.

ego (ē′gō): conceit, exaggerated feelings of self-worth

Example: His <u>ego</u> kept him from admitting that he needed help in fixing his car.

illegible (i lej′ə b'l): impossible to read

Example: Doctors are famous for having such <u>illegible</u> handwriting that only a druggist can read it.

cat, āte, fäther; pen, ēvil; if, kīte; nō, ôr, fōōd, book; boil, house; up, tᵿrn; chief, shell; thick, *the*; zh, treasure; ŋ, sing; ə for *a* in *about*; ′ as in *able* (ā′b'l)

Preread

Preview the following reading selection by reading the title, the headings, and everything that's underlined. Answer the following questions without looking back at the reading.

1. What is the subject?

   _____

2. Circle the statement that best summarizes the main idea.

   a. There are techniques for writing a good business letter.

   b. The most important thing is to know what you want.

   c. Writing is a necessary life skill.

   d. Write from the reader's point of view.

3. Now take a moment to think about writing business letters. Think about what you know, what you don't know, and what you might find out from reading the selection. Make up three questions.

   a. _____

   b. _____

   c. _____

Read

Read the selection without underlining.

◆ *How to Write a Business Letter*

Malcolm Forbes

A good business letter can get you a job interview, get you off the hook, or get you money.

It's totally asinine to blow your chances of getting *whatever* you want—with a business letter that turns people off instead of turning them on.

The best place to learn to write is in school. If you're still there, pick your teachers' brains; if not, big deal. I learned to ride a motorcycle at 50 and fly balloons at 52. It's never too late to learn.

Over 10,000 business letters come across my desk every year. They seem to fall into three categories: stultifying if not stupid, mundane (most of them), and first rate (rare). Here's the approach I've found that separates the winners from the losers (most of it's just good common sense). It starts *before* you write your letter:

Know What You Want

If you don't, write it down—in one sentence. "I want to get an interview within the next two weeks." It's that simple. List the major points you want to get across—it'll keep you on course.

If you're *answering* a letter, check the points that need answering and keep the letter in front of you while you write. This way you won't forget anything—*that* would cause another round of letters.

And for goodness' sake, answer promptly if you're going to answer at all. Don't sit on a letter—*that* invites the person on the other end to sit on whatever you want from *him*.

Plunge Right In

Call him by name—not "Dear Sir, Madam, or Ms." "Dear Mr. Chrisanthopoulos"—and be sure to spell it right. That'll get him (thus, you) off to a good start.

(Usually, you can get his name just by phoning his company—or from a business directory in your nearest library.)

Tell what your letter is about in the first paragraph. Use one or two sentences. Don't keep your reader guessing or he might file your letter away—even before he finishes it. In the round file.

If you're answering a letter, refer to the date it was written, so the reader won't waste time hunting for it.

People who read business letters are as human as thee and me. Reading a letter shouldn't be a chore. *Reward* the reader for the time he gives you.

Write So He'll Enjoy It

Write the entire letter from his point of view. What's in it for *him?* Beat him to the draw—surprise him by answering the questions and objections he might have.

Be positive. He'll be more receptive to what you have to say.

Be nice. Contrary to the cliché, genuinely nice guys most often finish first or very near it. I admit it's not easy when you've got a gripe. To be agreeable while disagreeing—that's an art.

Be natural. Write the way you talk. Imagine him sitting in front of you—what would you *say* to him?

Business jargon too often is cold, stiff, unnatural.

Suppose I came up to you and said, "I acknowledge receipt of your letter and I beg to thank you." You'd think, "Huh? You're putting me on."

The acid test—read your letter *out loud* when you're done. You might get a shock—but you'll know for sure if it sounds natural.

Don't be cute or flippant. The reader won't take you seriously. This doesn't mean you've got to be dull. You prefer your letter to knock 'em dead rather than bore 'em to death.

Three points to remember:

Have a sense of humor. That's refreshing *anywhere*—a nice surprise in a business letter.

Be specific. If I tell you there's a new fuel that could save gasoline, you might not believe me. But suppose I tell you this:

> "Gasohol"—10% alcohol, 90% gasoline—works as well as straight gasoline. Since you can make alcohol from grain or corn stalks, wood or wood waste, coal—even garbage, it's worth some real follow-through.

Now you've got something to sink your teeth into.

Lean heavier on nouns and verbs, lighter on adjectives. Use the active voice instead of the passive. Your writing will have more guts.

Which of these is stronger? Active voice: "I kicked out my money manager." Or, passive voice: "My money manager was kicked out by me." (By the way, neither is true. My son, Malcolm Jr., manages most Forbes money—he's a brilliant moneyman.)

Give It The Best You've Got

When you don't want something enough to make *the* effort, making *an* effort is a waste.

Make your letter look appetizing—or you'll strike out before you even get to bat. Type it—on good-quality 8½" x 11" stationery. Keep it neat. And use paragraphing that makes it easier to read.

Keep your letter short—to one page, if possible. Keep your paragraphs short. After all, who's going to benefit if your letter is quick and easy to read?

You.

For emphasis, underline important words. And sometimes indent sentences as well as paragraphs.

Like this. See how well it works? (But save it for something special.)

Make it perfect. No typos, no misspellings, no factual errors. If you're sloppy and let mistakes slip by, the person reading your letter will think you don't know better or don't care. Do you?

Be crystal clear. You won't get what you're after if your reader doesn't get the message.

Use good English. If you're still in school, take all the English and writing courses you can. The way you write and speak can really help —or *hurt.*

If you're not in school (even if you are), get the little 71-page gem by Strunk & White, *Elements of Style.* It's in paperback. It's fun to read and loaded with tips on good English and good writing.

Don't put on airs. Pretense invariably impresses only the pretender.

Don't exaggerate. Even once. Your reader will suspect everything else you write.

Distinguish opinions from facts. Your opinions may be the best in the world. But they're not gospel. You owe it to your reader to let him know which is which. He'll appreciate it and he'll admire you. The dumbest people I know are those who Know It All.

Be honest. It'll get you further in the long run. If you're not, you won't rest easy until you're found out. (The latter, not speaking from experience.)

Edit ruthlessly. Somebody ~~has~~ said that words are ~~a lot~~ like inflated money—the more ~~of them that~~ you use, the less each one ~~of them~~ is worth. ~~Right on.~~ Go through your entire letter just as many times as it takes. ~~Search out and~~ Annihilate all unnecessary words, and sentences—even ~~entire~~ *paragraphs.*

Sum It Up and Get Out

The last paragraph should tell the reader exactly what you want *him* to do—or what *you're* going to do. Keep it short and sweet. "May I have an appointment? Next Monday, the 16th, I'll call your secretary to see when it'll be most convenient for you."

Close with something simple like, "Sincerely." And for heaven's sake sign legibly. The biggest ego trip I know is a completely illegible signature.

Good luck.

I hope you get what you're after.

Sincerely,

Malcolm S. Forbes

1200 words

Analyze What You Read

Application

1. Write a sample business letter requesting your college transcripts.

_____

_____

_____

2. Edit the following paragraph as Malcolm Forbes might.

People who are good readers change their reading speed of material according to how difficult they might think the material is and according to what their purpose is in reading the material. For example, in this case, if you have to try to remember the facts which are found in a college textbook chapter in a book for a test, you should read the material slowly. On the other hand, if you are reading something like a newspaper for just general information on a subject, you should try to read the material faster than you would in the first case.

Graphic Organizer

In Reading 1, you used a chart to organize the ideas. This time you will use an outline.

1. We have filled in the main points. Go back to the reading and find each one. Some of them have been paraphrased.

2. Write the Roman numeral from the outline in the margin next to where the point is located in the reading.

3. Then locate the subpoints and write the capital letter from the outline next to each subpoint in the reading.

4. Then write the subpoints in the blanks below.

How To Write a Business Letter

   I. There are three benefits that come from writing a good business letter.

     A. _____

     B. _____

     C. _____

  II. Business letters fall into three categories.

     A. _____

     B. _____

     C. _____

 III. Organize what you want to say before writing.

     A. _____

     B. _____

       _____

 IV. Start off clearly and directly.

     A. _____

     B. _____

     C. _____

  V. There are eight things that make a letter more enjoyable to read.

     A. _____

     B. _____

     C. _____

     D. _____

     E. _____

     F. _____

     G. _____

     H. _____

       _____

VI. To write the best possible business letter, you must do eleven things.

A. _____

B. _____

C. _____

D. _____

E. _____

F. _____

G. _____

H. _____

I. _____

J. _____

K. _____

VII. End the letter properly.

A. _____

_____

B. _____

Remember What's Important

1. To prepare for a Comprehension Check, memorize the outline. Test yourself or have someone test you until you can remember everything you need to know. If necessary, review *How to Answer Essay Questions* on p. 73.

2. To prepare for a Vocabulary Check, make flash cards as described on pp. 15–16 for each of the words in the Vocabulary Preview that you don't know. Test yourself or have someone test you until you can remember them.

Make Use of What You Read

When you are ready, complete the Comprehension Check on p. 329 and the Vocabulary Check on p. 331. Do them from memory, without looking back at the book or at your notes.

Evaluate Your Active Critical Thinking Skills

After your tests have been graded, record your scores on the Progress Chart, p. 416, and answer the questions on the Evaluation Checklist on p. 417.

Vocabulary Skills Review

For explanation see pp. 13–14

Dictionary Definitions

Most words have more than one meaning. Following are dictionary entries for five words used in the reading. Above each entry is the sentence in which the word is used. In the space, write the number of the definition that fits the way the underlined word is used. To make it easier for you to find the answer, the part of speech of the correct definition is written under the blank.

_____   1. "Keep it <u>short</u> and sweet."
adj.

short (shört) *adj.* [OE. *scort*] **1.** not measuring much from end to end **2.** not great in range or scope **3.** not tall **4.** brief; concise **5.** not retentive [a *short* memory] **6.** curt; abrupt **7.** less than a sufficient or correct amount **8.** crisp or flaky, as pastry rich in shortening **9.** designating a sale of securities, etc. which the seller does not yet own but expects to buy later at a lower price –*n.* **1.** something short **2.** [*pl.*] *a)* short trousers *b)* a man's undergarment like these **3.** *same as: a)* SHORTSTOP *b)* SHORT CIRCUIT –*adv.* **1.** abruptly; suddenly **2.** briefly; concisely **3.** so as to be short in length –*vt., vi.* **1.** to give less than what is needed or usual **2.** *same as: a)* SHORTCHANGE *b)* SHORT-CIRCUIT –fall (or come) short to fail to reach, suffice, etc. –in short briefly –run short to have less than enough –short of less than or lacking –**short′ness** *n.*

_____   2. "If you're <u>still</u> there pick your teachers' brains; if not, big deal."
adv.

still (stil) *adj.* [OE. *stille*] **1.** without sound; silent **2.** not moving; stationary **3.** tranquil; calm **4.** designating or of a single photograph taken from a motion-picture film –*n.* **1.** silence; quiet **2.** a still photograph –*adv.* **1.** at or up to the time indicated **2.** even; yet [*still* colder] **3.** nevertheless; yet [rich but *still* unhappy] –*conj.* nevertheless; yet –*vt., vi.* to make or become still –**still′ness** *n.*

_____   3. "List the major points you want to get across—it'll keep you
n.   on <u>course</u>."

course (kôrs) *n.* [< L. *currere,* to run] **1.** an onward movement; progress **2.** a way, path, or channel **3.** a regular mode of procedure or conduct [our wisest *course*] **4.** a series of like things in order **5.** a part of a meal served at one time **6.** *Educ. a)* a complete series of studies *b)* any of the studies –*vi.* **coursed, cours′ing 1.** to run or race **2.** to hunt with hounds –in due course in the usual sequence (of events) –in the course of during –of course **1.** naturally **2.** certainly

_____   4. "List the <u>major</u> points you want to get across."
adj.

ma•jor (mā′jər) *adj.* [L. compar. of *magnus,* great] **1.** greater in size, importance, amount, etc. **2.** *Music* higher than the corresponding minor by a half tone –*vi. Educ.* to specialize (*in* a field of study) –*n.* **1.** *U.S. Mil.* an officer ranking just above a captain **2.** *Educ.* a principal field of study

_____   5. "This way you won't forget anything—*that* would cause another
n.   <u>round</u> of letters."

round (round) *adj.* [< L. *rotundus,* rotund] **1.** shaped like a ball, circle, or cylinder **2.** plump **3.** full; complete [a *round* dozen] **4.** expressed by a whole number or in tens, hundreds, etc. **5.** large; considerable [a *round* sum] **6.** brisk; vigorous [a *round* pace] –*n.* **1.** something round, as the rung of a ladder **2.** the part of a beef animal between the rump and the leg **3.** movement in a circular course **4.** a series or succession [a <u>round</u> of parties] **5.** [*often pl.*] a regular, customary circuit, as by a watchman **6.** a single shot from a gun, or from several guns together; also, the ammunition for this **7.** a single outburst, as of applause **8.** a single period of action, as in boxing **9.** a short song which one group begins singing when another has reached the second phrase, etc. –*vt.* **1.** to make round **2.** to make plump **3.** to express as a round number **4.** to complete; finish **5.** to go or pass around –*vi.* **1.** to make a circuit **2.** to turn; reverse direction **3.** to become plump –*adv.* **1.** in a circle **2.** through a recurring period of time [to work the year *round*] **3.** from one to another **4.** in circumference [ten feet *round*] **5.** on all sides **6.** about; near **7.** in a roundabout way **8.** here and there **9.** with a rotating movement **10.** in the opposite direction –*prep.* **1.** so as to encircle **2.** on all sides of **3.** in the vicinity of **4.** in a circuit through. In the U.S. *round* (*adv. & prep.*) is generally superseded by *around* –in the round **1.** in an arena theater **2.** in full, rounded form: said of sculpture **3.** in full detail round –about in or to the opposite direction –round up to collect in a herd, group, etc. –**round′ness** *n.*

Confused Words

Some pairs of words are confused in writing because they look very similar or because they sound alike. Use the dictionary entry to help you choose the correct word to fill in the blank.

1. To get a good job, you must be able to _____ the

   _____ kind of letter.

right (rīt) *adj.* [< OE. *riht*, straight] **1.** with a straight or perpendicular line **2.** upright; virtuous **3.** correct **4.** the right hand **5.** designating the side meant to be seen. **6.** mentally or physically sound **7.** *a)* designating or of that side toward the east when one faces north *b)* designating or of the corresponding side of something *c)* closer to the right side of one facing the thing mentioned –*n.* **1.** what is right, just, etc. **2.** a power, privilege, etc. belonging to one by law, nature, etc. **3.** the right side **4.** the right hand **5.** [*often* R-] *Politics* a conservative or reactionary position, party, etc. (often with *the*) –*adv.* **1.** straight; directly [go *right* home] **2.** properly; fittingly **3.** completely **4.** exactly [*right* here] **5.** according to law, justice, etc. **6.** correctly **7.** on or toward the right side **8.** very: in certain titles [the *right* honorable] –*vt.* **1.** to put upright **2.** to correct **3.** to put in order

write (rīt) *vt.* **wrote, writ′ten, writ′ing** [OE. *writan*] **1.** to form (words, letters, etc.) on a surface, as with a pen **2.** to compose (literary or musical material) **3.** to communicate (with) in writing [he **wrote** (me) that he was ill] **4.** to record (information) in a computer –*vi.* to write words, books, a letter, etc.

2. If you are _____ when I get home, I'd like to

_____ why you were angry last night.

here (hir) *adv.* [OE. *her*] **1.** at or in this place: often used as an intensive [John *here* is an actor] **2.** to or into this place [come *here*] **3.** at this point; now **4.** on earth –*n.* this place –neither here nor there irrelevant

hear (hir) *vt.* **heard** (hurd), **hear′ing** [OE. *hīeran*] **1.** to be aware of (sounds) by the ear **2.** to listen to **3.** to conduct a hearing of (a law case, etc.) **4.** to be informed of; learn –*vi.* **1.** to be able to hear sounds **2.** to be told (*of* or *about*) –hear from to get a letter, etc. from –not hear of to refuse to consider **–hear′er** *n.*

3. _____ going to get the highest grade? It might be the person

_____ test is finished first.

whose (hōōz) *pron.* [OE. *hwæs*] that or those belonging to whom –*poss. pronominal adj.* of, belonging to, or done by whom or which

who's (hōōz) **1.** who is **2.** who has

Comprehension Skills Review: Fact versus Opinion

Mark the following statements from the article F if they are facts or O if they are opinions.

_____ 1. "It's totally asinine to blow your chances of getting *whatever* you want—with a business letter that turns people off instead of turning them on."

_____ 2. "The best place to learn to write is in school."

_____ 3. "I learned to ride a motorcycle at 50 and fly balloons at 52."

_____ 4. "He'll be more receptive to what you have to say."

_____ 5. "If you're not (honest) you won't rest easy until you're found out."

_____ 6. "Usually, you can get his name by phoning his company—or from a business directory in your nearest library."

_____ 7. "My son, Malcolm Jr., manages most Forbes money."

_____ 8. "Reading a letter shouldn't be a chore."

_____ 9. "To be agreeable while disagreeing—that's an art."

_____ 10. "Business jargon too often is cold, stiff, unnatural."

4   How to Read Faster

Vocabulary Preview

doctorate (däk′tər it): the highest university degree
> *Example:* Nearly every university professor has a <u>doctorate</u>.

novel (näv′əl): a book with one long story in it
> *Example:* The most popular <u>novels</u> of the day are on the best-seller list.

correspondence (kôr′ə spän′dəns): letters received or written
> *Example:* Secretaries handle <u>correspondence</u>.

nonfiction (nän fik′shən): writing that is based on facts rather than on imagination
> *Example:* History books are <u>nonfiction</u>.

successive (sək ses′iv): following in order
> *Example:* Beginning with middle age, hair usually gets grayer with each <u>successive</u> year.

cat, āte, fäther; pen, ēvil; if, kīte; nō, ôr, fo͞od, book; boil, house; up, turn; chief, shell; thick, *the*; zh, treasure; ŋ, sing; ə for *a* in *about*; ′ as in *able* (ā′b′l)

Preread

Preview the following reading selection by reading the title, the author, and the headings. This should take no longer than 15 seconds. Answer the following questions without looking back at the reading.

1. What is the subject?

   _____

2. Circle the statement that best summarizes the main idea.

   a. Everyone should always read faster.

   b. Clustering increases speed and comprehension.

   c. There are ways to read faster.

   d. Bill Cosby is a fast reader.

3. Take a moment to think about reading faster. Think about what you know, what you don't know, and what you might find out from reading the selection. Make up three questions.

   a. _____

b. _____

_____

c. _____

Read

Read the selection without underlining.

◆ *How to Read Faster*

Bill Cosby

When I was a kid in Philadelphia, I must have read every comic book ever published. (There were fewer of them then than there are now.)

I zipped through all of them in a couple of days, then reread the good ones until the next issues arrived.

Yes indeed, when I was a kid, the reading game was a snap.

But as I got older, my eyeballs must have slowed down or something! I mean, comic books started to pile up faster than my brother Russell and I could read them!

It wasn't until much later, when I was getting my doctorate, I realized it wasn't my eyeballs that were to blame. Thank goodness. They're still moving as well as ever.

The problem is, there's too much to read these days, and too little time to read every word of it.

Now, mind you, I still read comic books. In addition to contracts, novels, and newspapers. Screenplays, tax returns and correspondence. Even textbooks about how people read. And which techniques help people read more in less time.

I'll let you in on a little secret. There are hundreds of techniques you could learn to help you read faster. But I know of 3 that are especially good.

And if I can learn them, so can you—and you can put them to use *immediately.*

They are commonsense, practical ways to get the meaning from printed words quickly and efficiently. So you'll have time to enjoy your comic books, have a good laugh with Mark Twain or a good cry with *War and Peace.* Ready?

Okay. The first two ways can help you get through tons of reading material—fast—*without reading every word.*

They'll give you the *overall meaning* of what you're reading. And let you cut out an awful lot of *unnecessary* reading.

1. Preview—If It's Long and Hard

Previewing is especially useful for getting a general idea of heavy reading like long magazine or newspaper articles, business reports, and nonfiction books.

It can give you as much as half the comprehension in as little as one tenth the time. For example, you should be able to preview eight or ten 100-page reports in an hour. After previewing, you'll be able to decide which reports (or which *parts* of which reports) are worth a closer look.

Here's how to preview: Read the entire first two paragraphs of whatever you've chosen. Next read only the *first sentence* of each successive paragraph. Then read the entire last two paragraphs.

Previewing doesn't give you all the details. But it does keep you from spending time on things you don't really want—or need—to read.

Notice that previewing gives you a quick, overall view of *long, unfamiliar* material. For short, light reading, there's a better technique.

2. Skim—If It's Short and Simple

Skimming is a good way to get a general idea of light reading—like popular magazines or the sports and entertainment sections of the paper.

You should be able to skim a weekly popular magazine or the second section of your daily paper in less than *half* the time it takes you to read it now.

Skimming is also a great way to review material you've read before.

Here's how to skim: Think of your eyes as magnets. Force them to move fast. Sweep them across each and every line of type. Pick up *only a few key words in each line.*

Everybody skims differently.

You and I may not pick up exactly the same words when we skim the same piece, but we'll both get a pretty similar idea of what it's all about.

To show you how it works, I circled the words I picked out when I skimmed the following story. Try it. It shouldn't take you more than 10 seconds.

My brother Russell thinks monsters live in our bedroom closet at night. But I told him he is crazy.

"Go and check then," he said.

I didn't want to. Russell said I was chicken.

"Am not," I said.

"Are so," he said.

So I told him the monsters were going to eat him at midnight. He started to cry. My Dad came in and told the monsters to beat it. Then he told us to go to sleep.

"If I hear any more about monsters," he said, "I'll spank you."

We went to sleep fast. And you know something? They never did come back.

Skimming can give you a very good *idea* of this story in about half the words—and in *less* than half the time it'd take to read every word.

So far, you've seen that previewing and skimming can give you a *general idea* about content—fast. But neither technique can promise more than 50 percent comprehension, because you aren't reading all the words. (Nobody gets something for nothing in the reading game.)

To *read faster and understand most*—if not all—of what you read, you need to know a third technique.

3. Cluster—To Increase Speed *and* Comprehension

Most of us learned to read by looking at each word in a sentence—*one at a time.*

Like this:

My—brother—Russell—thinks—monsters . . .

You probably still read this way sometimes, especially when the words are difficult. Or when the words have an extra-special meaning—as in a poem, a Shakespearean play, or a contract. And that's O.K.

But word-by-word reading is a rotten way to read faster. It actually *cuts down* on your speed.

Clustering trains you to look at *groups* of words instead of one at a time—to increase your speed enormously. For most of us, clustering is a *totally different way of seeing what we read.*

Here's how to cluster: Train your eyes to see *all* the words in clusters of up to 3 or 4 words at a glance.

Here's how I'd cluster the story we just skimmed:

My brother Russell thinks monsters live in our bedroom closet at night. But I told him he is crazy.

"Go and check then," he said.

I didn't want to. Russell said I was chicken.

"Am not," I said.

"Are so," he said.

So I told him the monsters were going to eat him at midnight. He started to cry. My Dad came in and told the monsters to beat it. Then he told us to go to sleep.

"If I hear any more about monsters," he said, "I'll spank you."

We went to sleep fast. And you know something? They never did come back.

Learning to read clusters is not something your eyes do naturally. It takes constant practice.

Here's how to go about it: Pick something light to read. Read it as fast as you can. Concentrate on seeing 3 to 4 words at once rather than one word at a time. Then reread the piece at your normal speed to see what you missed the first time.

Try a second piece. First cluster, then reread to see what you missed in this one.

When you can read in clusters without missing much the first time, your speed has increased. Practice 15 minutes every day and you might pick up the technique in a week or so. (But don't be disappointed if it takes longer. Clustering *everything* takes time and practice.)

So now you have 3 ways to help you read faster. <u>Preview</u> to cut down on unnecessary heavy reading. <u>Skim</u> to get a quick, general idea of light reading. And <u>cluster</u> to increase your speed *and* comprehension.

With enough practice, you'll be able to handle *more* reading at school or work—and at home—*in less time*. You should even have enough time to read your favorite comic books—<u>and</u> *War and Peace*!

1300 words

Analyze What You Read

Application

Cluster the following paragraphs by circling groups of words as in Bill Cosby's article.

   <u>Here's how to preview:</u> Read the entire first two paragraphs of whatever you've chosen. Next read only the *first sentence* of each successive paragraph. Then read the entire last two paragraphs.

   Previewing doesn't give you all the details. But it does keep you from spending time on things you don't really want—or need—to read.

   Notice that previewing gives you a quick, overall view of *long, unfamiliar* material. For short, light reading, there's a better technique.

Graphic Organizer

You have already filled out a chart and an outline. Now you are going to fill out an *idea map*. The rectangles on the map on the next page are like Roman numerals on an outline. They represent the most important ideas. The triangles on the map are like capital letters on an outline. They represent minor ideas. We have filled in the minor ideas.

1. Go back to the reading and find each one. Draw a triangle next to it.

2. Next, find the major ideas and draw a rectangle next to each one.

3. Then fill in the rectangles on the map.

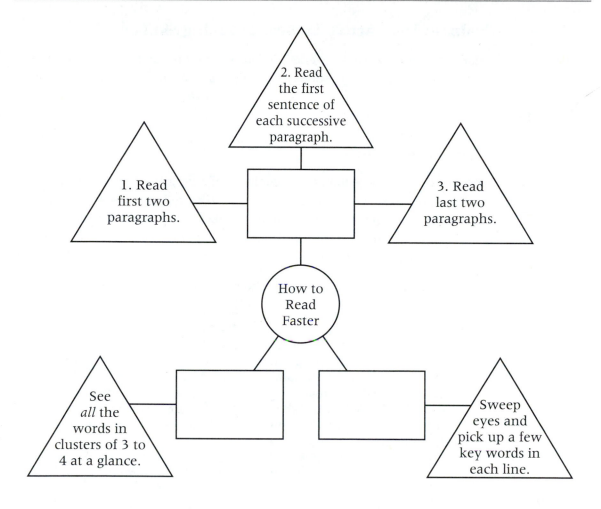

Remember What's Important

1. To prepare for a Comprehension Check, memorize the idea map. Test yourself or have someone test you until you can remember everything you need to know. If necessary, review *How to Answer Essay Questions* on p. 73.

2. To prepare for a Vocabulary Check, make flash cards as described on pp. 15–16 for each of the words in the Vocabulary Preview that you don't know. Test yourself or have someone test you until you can remember them.

Make Use of What You Read

When you are ready, complete the Comprehension Check on p. 333 and the Vocabulary Check on p. 335. Do them from memory, without looking back at the book or at your notes.

STEP
6

Evaluate Your Active Critical Thinking Skills

After your tests have been graded, record your scores on the Progress Chart, p. 416, and answer the questions on the Evaluation Checklist on p. 417.

Vocabulary Skills Review

For explanation see pp. 13–14

Dictionary Definitions

Most words have more than one meaning. Following are dictionary entries for five words used in the reading. Above each entry is the sentence in which the word is used. In the space, write the number of the definition that fits the way the underlined word is used. To make it easier for you to find the answer, the part of speech of the correct definition is written under the blank.

_____ 1. "I zipped through all of them in a couple of days, then reread
n.   the good ones until the next <u>issues</u> arrived."

is•sue (ish′o͞o) *n.* [< L. *ex-*, out *ire*, go] **1.** an outgoing; outflow **2.** an outlet; exit **3.** a result; consequence **4.** offspring **5.** a point under dispute **6.** a sending or giving out **7.** all that is put forth at one time [an *issue* of bonds, a periodical, etc.] **8.** *Med.* a discharge of blood, etc. –*vi.* **-sued, -su•ing 1.** to go or flow out; emerge **2.** to result (*from*) or end (*in*) **3.** to be published –*vt.* **1.** to let out; discharge **2.** to give or deal out, as supplies **3.** to publish **–at issue** in dispute **–take issue** to disagree

_____ 2. "In addition to <u>contracts</u>, novels, and newspapers."
n.

con•tract (kän′trakt *for n. & usually for vt. 1 & vi. 1;* kən trakt′ *for v. generally*) *n.* [< L. *com-*, together *trahere*, draw] **1.** an agreement, esp. a written one enforceable by law, between two or more people –*vt.* **1.** to undertake by contract **2.** to get or incur (a debt, disease, etc.) **3.** to reduce in size; shrink **4.** to shorten (a word or phrase) –*vi.* **1.** to make a contract **2.** to become smaller

_____ 3. "The first two ways can help you get through tons of reading
n.   material—fast—*without reading every word.*"

ma•te•ri•al (mə tir′ē əl) *adj.* [< L. *materia*, matter] **1.** of matter; physical [a *material* object] **2.** of the body or bodily needs, comfort, etc.; not spiritual **3.** important, essential, etc. –*n.* **1.** what a thing is, or may be made of; elements or parts **2.** cloth; fabric **3.** [*pl.*] tools, etc. needed to make or do something

adj.   4. "Previewing is especially useful for getting a general idea of heavy reading like long magazine or newspaper articles, business reports, and nonfiction books."

heav•y (hev'ē) _adj._ **-i•er, -i•est** [OE. _hefig_] **1.** hard to lift because of great weight **2.** of more than the usual, expected, or defined weight **3.** larger, greater, or more intense than usual [a _heavy_ blow, a _heavy_ vote, _heavy_ applause] **4.** to an unusual extent [a _heavy_ drinker] **5.** hard to do [_heavy_ work] **6.** sorrowful [a _heavy_ heart] **7.** burdened with sleep [_heavy_ eyelids] **8.** hard to digest [a _heavy_ meal] **9.** clinging; penetrating [a _heavy_ odor] **10.** cloudy; gloomy [a _heavy_ sky] **11.** using massive machinery to produce basic materials, as steel _–adv._ in a heavy manner _–n., pl._ **-ies** _Theater_ a villain **–heav'i•ly** _adv._ **–heav'-i•ness** _n._

_v._   5. "Skim—if it's short and simple."

skim (skim) _vt., vi._ **skimmed, skim'-ming** [ME. _skimen_] **1.** to remove (floating matter) from (a liquid) **2.** to glance through (a book, etc.) rapidly **3.** to glide lightly (over)

For explanation see pp. 8–10

Pronunciation Guide

For practice in using the pronunciation guide, do the following exercises.

cat, āte, fäther; pen, ēvil; if, kīte; nō, ôr, fōōd, book; boil, house; up, turn; chief, shell; thick, _the_; zh, treasure; ŋ, sing; ə for a in _about_; ' as in _able_ (ā'b'l)

1. Translate these famous fictional characters into English spelling.

   a. kount drak'yōō lə

   _____

   b. mik'ē mous'

   _____

   c. kap'tən hook'

   _____

   d. sōō'pər man

   _____

2. Say each of the following words out loud and listen for the sounds. Then circle the words that contain short vowel sounds (a as in c_a_t, e as in p_e_n, i as in _if_, ä as the _o_ sound in h_o_t, and u as in _u_p).

   kite   tube   seen   fit   shop   tack

Comprehension Skills Review: Fact versus Opinion

Mark the following statements from the article F if they are facts or O if they are opinions.

_____ 1. "I zipped through all of them [comic books] in a couple of days."

_____ 2. ". . . when I was a kid, the reading game was a snap."

_____ 3. ". . . books started to pile up faster than my brother Russell and I could read them."

_____ 4. "For short, light reading, there's a better technique."

_____ 5. "Nobody gets something for nothing in the reading game."

_____ 6. "Learning to read clusters is not something your eyes do naturally."

_____ 7. ". . . you should be able to preview eight or ten 100-page reports in an hour."

_____ 8. "Word-by-word reading is a rotten way to read faster."

_____ 9. "To show you how it works, I circled the words I picked out when I skimmed the following story."

_____ 10. "And if I can learn them, so can you. . . ."

5　Propaganda

Vocabulary Preview

connotation　(kän′ə tā′shən):　idea or notion suggested by or associated with a word or phrase in addition to its definition

Example: The word *politician* has a different connotation from the word *statesman.*

sophisticated　(sə fis′tə kāt′id):　knowledgeable about worldly things

Example: Famous or wealthy people are usually thought of as being sophisticated.

endorse　(in dôrs′):　publicly approve of, as in advertising a product, a service, and so forth, often in return for a fee

Example: Famous athletes often endorse soft drinks on television.

deception　(di sep′shən):　making a person believe what isn't true; being misleading

Example: Deception includes everything from polite fibs or harmless exaggeration to outright lies and fraud.

mediocre　(mē′dē ō′kər):　neither very good nor very bad; ordinary; average

Example: Average restaurants serve mediocre food.

cat, āte, fäther; pen, ēvil; if, kīte; nō, ôr, fōōd, book; boil, house; up, turn; chief, shell; thick, *the*; zh, treasure; ŋ, sing; ə for *a* in *about*; ' as in *able* (ā′b′l)

Preread

Preview the following reading selection by reading the title, the first paragraph, and the headings. Answer the following questions without looking back.

1. What is the subject?

_____

2. Circle the statement that best summarizes the main idea.

   a. Propaganda is an attempt to influence your actions or opinions.

   b. You should learn to recognize propaganda.

   c. There are seven types of propaganda.

   d. Propaganda appeals to emotion rather than to reason.

3. Take a moment to think about propaganda. Think about what you know, what you don't know, and what you might find out from reading the selection. Make up three questions.

a. _____

b. _____

c. _____

Read

Read the selection without underlining.

◆ *Propaganda*

Janet Maker and Minnette Lenier

Propaganda is a deliberate attempt to influence your actions or opinions. Propagandists may try to make you vote a certain way, or they may try to make you spend your money on certain products. Sometimes, being influenced by propaganda doesn't hurt; sometimes it does. But the only way to stop propaganda from influencing your decisions is to learn to see through it.

There are seven common propaganda techniques:

1. Bad names

2. Glad names

3. Transfer

4. Testimonial

5. Plain folks

6. Card stacking

7. Band wagon

Bad Names

"Bad names" are words that have negative connotations. Propagandists want you to respond with hate and fear to certain other people, groups, nations, beliefs, and policies, without looking for proof. To do this they use words such as *liberal big spenders* and *right-wing extremist*.

Glad Names

"Glad names" are used by propagandists when they want you to accept and approve of certain other people or programs. They use words that have positive connotations, such as *patriotism, democracy,* and *freedom.* Using "glad names" is the opposite of using "bad names." But names don't really mean much. Many words that mean the same thing can have opposite connotations. For example, *slender* and *thrifty* are positive words, but *skinny* and *cheap* are negative. You should not be fooled by labels; instead you should look for evidence.

Transfer

Transfer is a technique meant to make you link something you like or respect with a person, a program, or a product. For instance, if a television advertisement says that doctors or dentists approve of a product or that research shows it to be superior, you are more likely to buy it. If a politician or a program can be linked with something that you approve of, such as the church, the flag, or apple pie, you are more likely to vote for it.

Testimonial

A testimonial is a technique used by so-called authorities to "testify" to the value of a product. For example, we are supposed to believe that if Shaquille O'Neal and Hakeem Olajuwon like Taco Bell, it must be pretty good. It might be reasonable to have NBA stars "testify" to the value of sporting goods, but there is no reason to consider them experts on food. Considering the salaries they earn, it is unlikely that they eat at Taco Bell at all. Famous people give testimonials as a way of earning money.

Plain Folks

"Plain folks" is a device that politicians or other leaders use to try to appear "folksy," or just like the rest of us. They kiss babies, they love their mothers, and their wives share their favorite recipes with us. In reality, they are usually wealthy, powerful, and employ cooks.

Another place the "plain folks" technique is used is in advertising. Many ads feature average-looking people—people who could be our neighbors.

Card Stacking

In "card stacking," only the best of one point of view and the worst of the other is presented. It uses deception and "stacks the cards" against the truth. We all stack the cards sometimes: when we explain to our family or friends why we did not get A's or why we weren't promoted on the job, for example. By using card stacking, a mediocre politician can appear to be a great statesman; or an ordinary laundry detergent can appear to perform miracles.

Band Wagon

The "band wagon" technique appeals to your wish to be on the winning side or your wish to follow the crowd. In using the "band wagon" approach, propagandists claim that "everybody's doing it" and that the majority knows best. Political parties always claim that their candidates are sure to win. And advertisers like to claim that their product is a best-seller.

All seven techniques have one thing in common: They appeal to your emotions rather than to your reason. They play on fears, prejudices, and selfishness, as well as on love and generosity. Emotion is not bad, and not all propaganda is bad. For example, worthwhile charities often appeal to your sympathies to get you to make contributions. However, even when the result is good, an intelligent person does not want to be fooled or used. People want to make decisions based on facts.

If you keep the seven propaganda techniques in mind, you will see them used everywhere. They are used in newspapers, magazines, television ads, television shows, and even in the news. Practice recognizing them.

800 words

Analyze What You Read

Application

Identify the following types of fallacies by writing the appropriate symbol in the blank before each statement.

BN	Bad names	PL	Plain folks
GLN	Glad names	CS	Card stacking
TR	Transfer	BW	Band wagon
TEST	Testimonial		

_____ 1. Everybody uses the anticavity toothbrush, so you should too.

_____ 2. Don't vote for my opponent; he is a yellow-bellied coward.

_____ 3. John Jones, quarterback for the Mississippi Mudders, says, "You should buy *Twilight Madness* perfume."

_____ 4. Superman would make a great politician because he believes in truth, justice, and the American way.

_____ 5. Vote for the highway bond issue. We need new highways. There are potholes on every street. Congestion will get worse in the next ten years.

_____ 6. Everyone knows that jocks are dumb, so we shouldn't bother to listen to what Stan says.

_____ 7. Buddy Goop is our man for Congress. He has a wife and kids, and he has worked all his life just like us.

_____ 8. Flames are the most popular cigarettes in the United States, so they must be better than Smoker's Delights.

_____ 9. Maribelle Swift, the famous track star, says that everybody needs milk.

_____ 10. Nine out of ten doctors recommend aspirin for a headache.

Graphic Organizer

Fill in the following chart. The definitions or descriptions should be in your own words, and you can make up your examples.

Propaganda technique	Definition or description	Example
1.		
2.		
3.		
4.		

continued

Propaganda technique	Definition or description	Example
5.		
6.		
7.		

Remember What's Important

1. To prepare for a Comprehension Check, memorize the chart. Test yourself or have someone test you until you can remember everything you need to know. If necessary, review *How to Answer Essay Questions* on p. 73.

2. To prepare for a Vocabulary Check, make flash cards as described on pp. 15–16 for each of the words in the Vocabulary Preview that you don't know. Test yourself or have someone test you until you can remember them.

Make Use of What You Read

When you are ready, complete the Comprehension Check on p. 337 and the Vocabulary Check on p. 339. Do them from memory, without looking back at the book or at your notes.

Evaluate Your Active Critical Thinking Skills

After your tests have been graded, record your scores on the Progress Chart, p. 416, and answer the questions on the Evaluation Checklist on p. 417.

Vocabulary Skills Review

Word Parts

For explanation see pp. 5–7

Following are the prefixes and roots used in the Vocabulary Preview words for the reading on propaganda. In the exercise that follows, fill in the missing word part to make each word match the definition provided. The meaning of the word part is underlined.

Prefixes	Roots	Examples
con = with, together	not = to mark, note	connotation
	soph = wise	sophisticated
en = on, upon	dors = back	endorses
de = from	cep = to take	deception
	medi = middle	mediocre

1. __ __ __ __ istry   reasoning that seems <u>wise</u> but is really faulty

2. in __ __ __ tion   beginning (literally, to <u>take</u> up)

3. __ __ dowment   that which is given or bestowed <u>on</u> someone or something; gift

4. de __ __ __ e   to <u>mark</u>; express; indicate

5. __ __ toxify   to take the poison <u>from</u>

6. re __ __ __ __ ate   to overcome learning problems (literally, to bring back to the <u>middle</u>)

7. __ __ __ vention   where people come <u>together</u>

8. __ __ __ __ o __ __ __ __ al   located in the <u>middle</u> of the <u>back</u>

For explanation see pp. 8–10

Pronunciation Guide

For practice in using the pronunciation guide, do the following exercises.

cat, āte, fäther; pen, ēvil; if, kīte; nō, ôr, fōōd, book; boil, house; up, tʉrn; chief, shell; thick, *the*; zh, treasure; ŋ, sing; ə for *a* in *about*; ' as in *able* (ā'b'l)

1. Translate these famous places in the United States into English spelling.

   a. lôs an'jə ləs, kal'ə fôr'nyə

   _____

   b. diz'nē wʉrld

   _____

   c. *th*ə wôsh'iŋ tən män'yə mənt

   _____

d. liŋ′kən, nə bras′kə

_____

e. *thə* hwīt hous

_____

2. Say each of the following words out loud and listen for the sounds. Then circle the words that contain the schwa sound (ə).

correct   **attitude**   **negative**   **brief**   **moist**

3. Say each of the following words out loud and listen for the sounds. Then circle the words that contain long vowel sounds (ā as in *ate*, ē as in *evil*, ī as in *kite*, ō as in *no*, and yōō, the *u* in *mule*).

rhyme   **text**   **call**   **place**   **meat**

4. The word *present* has two pronunciations. The pronunciations are written under the sentences. Read the sentences out loud. Then circle the pronunciation you used.

a. I received a *present* for my birthday.

prez′n't   **pri zent′**

b. I will *present* the award tomorrow night.

prez′n't   **pri zent′**

c. I was *present* at the awards last night.

prez′n't   **pri zent′**

d. If you are *present* in class when the roll is called, you should say "here."

prez′n't   **pri zent′**

Comprehension Skills Review: Valid and Invalid Inferences

Mark each inference V if it is valid and I if it is invalid. To be a valid inference, the information must be implied in the reading. If you mark V, please write the sentence from the reading that you used to make the inference on the lines provided.

_____   1. Propaganda is bad.

_____

_____

_____ 2. People who use propaganda are trying to manipulate you.

_____

_____

_____ 3. Choice of words is important in propaganda.

_____

_____

_____ 4. Advertisers regularly use some form of dishonesty.

_____

_____

_____ 5. A politician who was completely honest probably couldn't get elected.

_____

_____

_____ 6. Most people will vote for a candidate they think is the underdog.

_____

_____

_____ 7. News stories don't use propaganda.

_____

_____

_____ 8. Most people are easily influenced by propaganda.

_____

_____

_____ 9. Worthwhile charities don't use propaganda.

_____

_____

_____ 10. Many people rely on experts or on the majority more than on their own judgment.

_____

_____

6   How to Read a Newspaper

Vocabulary Preview

caption (kap′shən): a title or subtitle, as of a picture
Example: The <u>caption</u> of an illustration will tell you the subject and sometimes the main idea.

entice (en tīs′): to tempt or lure
Example: The purpose of most advertising is to <u>entice</u> people to spend money.

analysis (ə nal′i sis): a breaking of something whole into its parts so they can be examined
Example: When you put a drop of pond water under a microscope for <u>analysis</u>, you can see lots of tiny one-celled animals.

slant (slant): to tell so as to express a particular point of view
Example: The more respectable newspapers, such as the *New York Times,* avoid <u>slanted</u> news stories.

conscientious (kän′shē en′shəs): thorough, honest, and careful
Example: A <u>conscientious</u> worker tries to do the best job possible.

inverted (in vʉrt′id): upside down
Example: An <u>inverted</u> glass will not hold water.

pundit (pun′dit): a person of great learning, sometimes used humorously
Example: A restaurant reviewer is a <u>pundit</u> on the subject of eating out.

motivate (mō′tə vāt′): to cause to act
Example: Hunger will <u>motivate</u> an animal to seek food.

colleague (käl′ēg): a fellow worker
Example: Some teachers like to have lunch with their <u>colleagues</u> in the faculty lounge.

heft (heft): to try to judge the weight of by lifting
Example: You can <u>heft</u> two bags of apples to find out which is heavier.

cat, āte, fäther; pen, ēvil; if, kīte; nō, ôr, fōōd, book; boil, house; up, tʉrn; chief, shell; thick, *the*; zh, treasure; ŋ, sing; ə for *a* in *about*; ′ as in *able* (ā′b′l)

Preread

STEP 1

Preview the following selection by reading the title, the first paragraph, and the headings. Answer the following questions without looking back.

1. What is the subject?

2. What is the main idea?

_____

3. Take a moment to think about newspapers. Think about what you know, what you don't know, and what you might find out from reading the selection. Make up three questions.

a. _____

b. _____

c. _____

Read

Read the selection without underlining.

◆ *How to Read a Newspaper*

Walter Cronkite

If you're like most Americans, you try to keep up with the news by watching it on television.

That's how 65% of us get 100% of our news—from the 24-odd-minute TV news broadcast each evening.

The problem—and I know the frustration of it firsthand—is that unless something really special happens, we in TV news have to put severe time limitations on every story, even the most complicated and important ones.

Get More Than Headlines

So what we bring you is primarily a front-page headline service. To get all you need to know, you have to flesh out those headlines with a *complete account* of the news from a well-edited and thorough newspaper.

Is it really necessary to get the *whole* story? Dorothy Greene Friendly put it this way: "What the American people don't know can kill them." Amen.

News people have a responsibility. And so do *you*. Ours is to report the news fairly, accurately, completely. *Yours* is to keep yourself informed every day.

I'll never forget the quotation hanging in Edward R. Murrow's CBS office. It was from Thoreau: "It takes two to speak the truth—one to speak and one to hear."

Take a 3-Minute Overview

Here's how I tackle a paper. For starters, I take a three-minute overview of the news. No need to go to the sports section first, or the TV listings. With my overview you'll get there quickly enough. First I scan the front-page headlines, look at the pictures and read the captions. I do the same thing page by page front to back. Only *then* do I go back for the whole feast.

The way the front page is "made up" tells you plenty. For one thing, headline type size will tell you how the paper's editor ranks the stories on relative importance. A major crop failure in Russia should get larger type than an overturned truckload of wheat on the Interstate, for example.

Which Is the Main Story?

You'll find the main or lead story in the farthest upper right-hand column. Why? Tradition. Newspapers used to appear on newsstands folded and displayed with their top right-hand quarter showing. They made up the front page with the lead story there to entice readers.

You'll find the second most important story at the top far left, unless it's related to the lead story. Do you have to read *all* the stories in the paper? Gosh, no. But you should *check* them all. Maybe the one that appears at first to be the least appealing will be the one that will most affect your life.

News Is Information, Period

A good newspaper provides four basic ingredients to help you wrap your mind around the news: *information, background, analysis,* and *interpretation.*

Rule 1 of American journalism is: "*News columns are reserved only for news.*" What *is* news? It is *information* only. You can tell a good newspaper story. It just reports the news. It doesn't try to slant it. And it gives you *both* sides of the story.

Look out for a lot of adjectives and adverbs. They don't belong in an objective news story. They tend to color and slant it so you may come to a wrong conclusion.

Do look for by-lines, datelines, and the news service sources of articles. These will also help you judge a story's importance and its facts.

As you read a story you can weigh its truthfulness by asking yourself, "Who said so?" Look out for "facts" that come from unnamed sources, such as "a highly placed government official." This could tip you off that the story is not quite true, or that someone—usually in Washington—is sending up a "trial balloon" to see if something that *may* happen or be proposed gets a good reception.

Another tip: Check for "Corrections" items. A good newspaper will straighten out false or wrong information as soon as it discovers its error. A less conscientious one will let it slide or bury it.

An Upside-Down Pyramid

Reporters write news stories in a special way called the "inverted pyramid" style. That means they start with the end, the *climax* of the story, with the most important facts first, then build in more details in order of importance. This is unlike the telling or writing of most stories, where you usually start at the beginning and save the climax for last. Knowing about the newspaper's "inverted pyramid" style will help you sift facts.

A well-reported story will tell you "who," "what," "when," "where," and "how." The best newspapers will go on to tell you "why." "Why" is often missing. And that may be the key ingredient.

Many important stories are flanked by "sidebars." These are supporting stories that offer, not news, but the "why"—*background* and *analysis*—to help you understand and evaluate it.

Background offers helpful facts. *Analysis* frequently includes opinion. So it should be—and usually is—carefully labeled as such. It's generally by-lined by an expert on the subject who explains the causes of the news and its possible consequences to you.

No good newspaper will mix *interpretation* with "hard" news, either. Interpretation goes beyond analysis and tells you not just what will probably happen, but what *ought* to happen. This should be clearly labeled, or at best, reserved for the editorial page or "op-ed" (opposite the editorial) page.

Form Your Own Opinion First

I form my own opinion *before* I turn to the editorial page for the pundits' views. I don't want them to tell me how to think until I've wrestled the issue through to my own conclusion. Once I have, I'm open to other reasoning. *Resist the temptation to let them do your thinking for you.*

Here's an idea I firmly believe in and act on. When you read something that motivates you, do something about it. Learn more about it. Join a cause. Write a letter. You can *constantly* vote on issues by writing letters, particularly to your congressman or state or local representative.

To understand the news better you can also read news magazines. *Books* help fill in the holes, too. During the Vietnam War, for example, many people felt that the daily news coverage wasn't entirely satisfactory. The truth is, you could have gotten many important new facts on the war from the books coming out at the time.

Pick a TV Story and Follow It

Now that I've told you about the basics of getting under the skin of a newspaper, let newspapers get under your skin.

Tonight, pick an important story that interests you on the TV news. Dig into the story—in your newspaper. Follow it, and *continue* to follow it closely in print. See if you don't find yourself with far more understanding of the event.

And see if you don't have a far more sensible opinion as to the "whys" and "wherefores" of that event, even down to how it will affect you—and maybe even what should be done about it.

Keep up with the news the way my colleagues and I do—on TV *and* in the newspapers.

Learn to sift it for yourself, to heft it, to value it, to question it, to ask for it *all*. You'll be in better control of your life and your fortunes.

And that's the way it is.

1200 words

Analyze What You Read

Application

Whether writing for a newspaper, a magazine, or a book, authors write articles or chapters for a variety of purposes, such as to entertain, to inform, or to persuade. There are three basic purposes for newspaper articles: (1) News stories are written to inform. (2) Feature articles, advice and gossip columns, and so on are written to entertain. (3) Editorials, many national columns, and letters to the editor are written to persuade or to express opinion. Classify the following newspaper titles by writing the number for each under the appropriate headings below.

1. Hurdle Cleared in Arms Talks

2. Pickup Kills Two on Sidewalk

3. Murder Case Eludes Solution

4. Conservatives Must Oppose Clinton Kowtowing to Liberals

5. Great Tie Robbery Leaves 'Em in Knots

6. Dear Abby

To inform	To entertain	To express opinion or to persuade
_____	_____	_____
_____	_____	_____
_____	_____	_____
_____	_____	_____
_____	_____	_____

Graphic Organizer

Walter Cronkite organizes his article under seven headings. We have converted the seven headings to questions. Write the answers in the spaces provided. You may look back at the article.

Questions	Answers
1. What is meant by "Get More Than Headlines"?	
2. How do you do a three-minute overview?	
3. How do you tell which is the main story?	
4. What is meant by "News is Information, Period"?	

continued

Questions	Answers
5. Explain the upside-down pyramid.	
6. Why should you form your own opinion first?	
7. Explain what Cronkite means when he says to pick a TV story and follow it.	

Remember What's Important

1. To prepare for a Comprehension Check, memorize the chart. Test yourself or have someone test you until you can remember everything you need to know. If necessary, review *How to Answer Essay Questions* on p. 73.

2. To prepare for a Vocabulary Check, make flash cards as described on pp. 15–16 for each of the words in the Vocabulary Preview that you don't know. Test yourself or have someone test you until you can remember them.

Make Use of What You Read

When you are ready, complete the Comprehension Check on p. 341 and the Vocabulary Check on p. 343. Do them from memory, without looking back at the book or at your notes.

Evaluate Your Active Critical Thinking Skills

After your tests have been graded, record your scores on the Progress Chart, p. 416, and answer the questions on the Evaluation Checklist on p. 417.

Vocabulary Skills Review

For explanation see pp. 5–7

Word Parts

Following are prefixes, suffixes, and roots used in the Vocabulary Preview words for the selection on reading newspapers. In the exercise below, fill in the missing word part to make each word match the definition provided. The meaning of the word part is underlined.

Prefixes	**Roots**	**Suffixes**
	cap, capit = head	tion, ion = noun ending
in = to, into, toward	vert, vers = turn	ate = verb ending
con, com = with, together	mot = move	ious = adjective ending

1. de __ __ __ e   to <u>move</u> down; to lower in rank

2. un __ __ __ __ __ tific   lacking <u>knowledge</u> of science

3. __ __ jec __ __ __ __   liquid put <u>in</u> the body with a needle (noun)

4. injur __ __ __ __   causing harm (<u>adjective</u>)

5. con __ __ __ __ & __ __ __   a changing or <u>turning</u> from one form to another (<u>noun</u>)

6. de __ __ __ __ __ & __ __ __   to cut off the <u>head</u> (<u>verb</u>)

7. __ __ __ & __ __ __ ion   disturbance (<u>moving together</u>)

For explanation see pp. 8–10

Pronunciation Guide

For practice in using the pronunciation guide, do the following exercises.

cat, āte, fäther; pen, ēvil; if, kīte; nō, ôr, fo͞od, book; boil, house; up, tu̇rn; chief, shell; thick, *the*; zh, treasure; ŋ, sing; ə for *a* in *about*; ' as in *able* (ā'b'l)

1. Translate the names of the following places into English spelling.

    a. rōm, it''lē

_____

    b. tō'kē ō', jə pan'

_____

c. par′is, frans

_____

d. lē′mə, pə rōō′

_____

e. kī′rō, ē′jipt

_____

2. Say each of the following words out loud and listen for the sounds. Then circle the words that contain the schwa sound (uh).

kill   dateline   paragraph   opinion

3. Say each of the following words out loud and listen for the sounds. Then circle the words that contain long vowel sounds (ā, ē, ī, ō, ū).

daily   entertainment   comics   columns

Comprehension Skills Review: Valid and Invalid Inferences

Mark each inference V if it is valid and I if it is invalid. To be a valid inference, the information must be implied in the reading. If you mark V, please write the sentence from the reading that you used to make the inference on the lines provided.

_____   1. Most Americans don't read newspapers.

_____

_____

_____   2. TV news tells you all you need to know.

_____

_____

_____   3. Every citizen should read a daily newspaper.

_____

_____

_____   4. You should pay attention to the size of the type.

_____

_____

_____ 5. The second most important news story is on the second page.

_____

_____

_____ 6. Analysis and interpretation are the same thing.

_____

_____

_____ 7. You should always consider the source of news.

_____

_____

_____ 8. Some newspapers are better than others.

_____

_____

_____ 9. You should act on your beliefs.

_____

_____

_____ 10. Reading the newspaper will help you have a better life.

_____

_____

7

Your Financial Independence in Ten "Foolish" Steps

Vocabulary Preview

daunting (dônt, dänt′iŋ): discouraging; frightening; dismaying
Example: If you don't keep good records, filing your income tax return can be a <u>daunting</u> task.

wither (with′ər): to dry up, as from great heat; shrivel; wilt; said esp. of plants
Example: Crops <u>wither</u> when there is a drought.

substantial (səb stan′shəl): considerable; ample; large
Example: I hope I have <u>substantial</u> savings when I retire.

hazardous (haz′ər dəs): risky; dangerous; perilous
Example: The surgeon general says that smoking is <u>hazardous</u> to your health.

obstruct (əb strukt′): to hinder (progress, an activity, etc.); block; impede
Example: Telling less that the whole truth in court can <u>obstruct</u> justice.

stipulate (stip′yoo lāt′, -yə-): to include specifically in the terms of an agreement, contract, etc.; arrange definitely
Example: Many sales contracts now <u>stipulate</u> that you have three days to change your mind.

retroactive (re′trō ak′tiv): having application to or effect on things prior to its enactment [a *retroactive* law]
Example: The reduction in long distance rates is <u>retroactive</u> to last month.

finagle (fə nā′gəl): to get, arrange, or maneuver by cleverness, persuasion, etc., or esp. by craftiness, trickery, etc.
Example: I was able to <u>finagle</u> my way into the show without paying.

scrupulous (skroo′pyə ləs): extremely careful to do the precisely right, proper, or correct thing in every last detail
Example: If you are <u>scrupulous</u> about your record keeping, you don't have to be afraid of being audited by the IRS.

adhere (ad hir′, əd-): to stick fast; stay attached
Example: If you want to play the game, you have to <u>adhere</u> to the rules.

negotiable (ni gō′shē ə bəl; -shə bəl): open to negotiation; can be conferred, bargained, or discussed with a view to reaching agreement
Example: The price I have asked is <u>negotiable</u>; make me an offer.

pummel (pum′əl): to beat or hit with repeated blows, esp. with the fist
Example: Brothers and sisters often <u>pummel</u> each other until a parent steps in.

waive (wāv): to give up or forgo (a right, claim, privilege, etc.)
> *Example:* I <u>waive</u> my right to be represented by an attorney.

perpetual (pər pech′o͞o əl): lasting or enduring forever or for an indefinitely long time; eternal; permanent; continuing indefinitely without interruption; unceasing; constant
> *Example:* I have <u>perpetual</u> back pain.

leverage (lev′ər ij): increased means of accomplishing some purpose
> *Example:* If you also need something from me, then I have some <u>leverage</u> when I ask you for a favor.

grovel (gruv′əl, gräv′-): to behave humbly or abjectly, as before authority; debase oneself in a servile fashion
> *Example:* You lose your dignity when you <u>grovel</u>.

depreciating (dē prē′shē āt′iŋ, di-): reducing in value or price
> *Example:* Unless it is antique, furniture is a <u>depreciating</u> asset.

diversify (də vʉr′sə fī′, dī-): to divide up (investments, liabilities, etc.) among different companies, securities, etc.
> *Example:* Many experts recommend that you <u>diversify</u> so that some of your assets increase in value when others decrease, thus protecting yourself against major financial loss.

cryptic (krip′tik): having a hidden or ambiguous meaning; mysterious; baffling [a *cryptic* comment]
> *Example:* The <u>cryptic</u> message was not meant to be understood by others.

syndicated (sin′də kāt′id): sold through an organization that sells special articles or features for publication by many newspapers or periodicals.
> *Example: Dear Abby* is <u>syndicated</u>.

cat, āte, fäther; pen, ēvil; if, kīte; nō, ôr, fo͞od, book; boil, house; up, tʉrn; chief, shell; thick, *the*; zh, treasure; ŋ, sing; ə for *a* in *about*; ' as in *able* (ā′b'l)

Preread

Read the title and the boldface headings. Answer the following questions without looking back at the reading selection.

1. What is the subject?

_____

2. What is the main idea?

_____

3. Take a moment to think about money management. Think about what you know, what you don't know, and what you might find out from reading the selection. Make up three questions.

a. _____

b. _____

c. _____

Read

Read the selection without underlining.

◆ *Your Financial Independence in Ten "Foolish" Steps*

Tom Gardner

The Motley Fool (a name that comes directly from Shakespeare's *As You Like It*) is an educational company created to teach people how to save money and invest, and to thoroughly enjoy the process. Normally a daunting proposition, investing is becoming more important every day. That's way we've prepared these guidelines: to help you start saving money today and investing it for the decades ahead. And you know—the whole process can actually be a good deal of Foolish fun!

1. Money isn't everything, but it is something. You know it, and we know it: Those for whom money is everything are likely to close out their lives alone in a hotel room, face down in a bag of Fritos, having spent the preceding five years sorting through legal contracts. The list is long of multi-millionaires who, paralyzed by their successes, died unhappily. We hope money isn't everything in your life.

Think about your goals and dreams. If you're like many people, you probably haven't given much thought to how you'll finance them. You just assume that you'll work at your job, save what you can, and make as good a life for yourself as you can. That's reasonable, but it might also mean that many of your dreams wither on the vine. That's a shame. A little learning can increase the odds that you'll have the freedom to pursue whatever interests you the most.

Let's say you're not paying too much attention to your finances today. Saving a little here, a little there, you end up socking away $1,000 per year for the next three decades. Perhaps you drop that cash into your local bank savings account or a certificate of deposit. If so, you'll end up with something less than $70,000, assuming a growth rate of 5 percent per year. If, on the other hand, you took a little time to become a "Foolish" investor, things might turn out differently. Let's say you put aside $2,000 per year for 30 years. And that you earned 15 percent per year, because you invested carefully in stocks. Your little nest egg would have grown to $869,490! A big difference, eh—a difference of about $800,000.

Keep in mind that this is just a rough example. You could earn less than 15 percent per year—or you could earn more. You could invest more than $2,000 per year—and perhaps a lot more. You could end up with more or less than the $869,490, but we think you'll end up with a lot more than the $70,000 from your local bank if you invest Foolishly.

2. Learning this stuff is easy, but you do have to learn it. Wall Street is chock full of financial professionals who would love to manage your money for you. . . . But a smart fellow named Fred Schwed asked an important question in a book he wrote many years ago: "Where are the customers' yachts?" Think about this. You fork over your life savings into the hands of money managers, who—after substantial fees—end up living in ritzy houses and snoozing days away on their yachts. Notice who has the yachts—not you, but the managers. Something went wrong there.

This is why Fools across the country are taking control of their own financial destinies. Why leave something as vital and as all-important as your future security in the hands of someone else, especially when, with just a little learning, you can outperform the professionals? Odd as it may seem, investing and money management aren't terribly difficult. If you can add, subtract, multiply, divide and understand percentages, you already have many of the skills you'll need.

Consider this example. Coca-Cola stock has risen at an annual rate of 16.6 percent per year since the company sold shares to the public in 1919. This has proven to be one of the most successful U.S. investments over the past 10 years, 30 years, 50 years and 70 years. Coca-Cola just keeps on churning out caramelized carbonated corn syrup to enthusiastic soda pop drinkers across the planet. Let's see what would've happened if someone in your family invested $1,000 in the company back in 1919 and never sold. What would that investment be worth today?

A simple but inefficient way to do the calculation is to multiply $1,000 times 1.166 and just hit the return button on your calculator 79 times. A more complex but more efficient process (if you have an obliging calculator) is to multiply $1,000 by 1.166, click x^y, and then type 79. Either way, you'll come up with, yep, $185.9 million. Unthinkable? We agree.

An investment in a company that we all know, and that many of us love, has turned a $1,000 investment into over $180 million over the past 79 years. The lesson of saving a little money and investing it in great companies shouldn't be lost on you now.

Remember that the decisions you make about your money will determine whether you can sail the Indian Ocean when you're 52, quit your job to start a women's clothing store at 35, afford to put all six of your children through college, or take a year off from daily doings to write a book on Mark Twain. You need, at the very least, to learn the basics about managing your money. And you might as well begin learning now.

3. Borrowing loads of money is hazardous to your health. One of the bigger mistakes any of us make is needlessly running up credit card debt. As it revolves for months or years, the big banks charge us around 18 percent interest per year. Ouch.

The average American household with credit cards now has about $7,000 in debt sitting on their monthly statements (according to a December, 1997 report from the Consumer Federation). Yikes. This means that the typical cardholder ends up paying about $1,000 per year just in interest and fees—$1,000 per year . . . and what does that get you? Nothing at all. You still have that $7,000 debt. And next year, you'll end up paying another $1,000—unless you can pay off that $7,000. By paying 18 percent interest rates, you not only get nothing for your money, you obstruct all opportunities to make money off your money. The stock market has risen at an average annual rate in the 20th century of 11 percent. Those 18 percent rates on your credit cards cannot be beaten consistently by stock or mutual fund investments. By running up high-rate credit card debt, you've sold your future down the river.

4. Debt happens. Unless you had a really rich Great Aunt Harriet, whose estate pays you thousands of bucks each year, chances are you're going to have to borrow money in your life. The costs of living—food, water, shelter, sleep and looking decent—will catch up with you. Debt happens.

What you should do is prepay every bit of debt that you possibly can now, particularly any debts with high interest rates. The longer your debts sit unpaid, the more your lender will eat out of the pie of your retirement money. You want to be eating your own pies, thank you.

Note, though, that not all debt is bad. Mortgage debt, for example, is okay up to a point. The interest rate on that debt is historically reasonable and your interest payments are tax deductible. Likewise, student loans often have attractive rates. In many cases, it's not a bad thing to hang onto this kind of debt and pay it off according to the planned schedule. For example, if you're paying 8 percent on a student loan and you can earn 10 percent to 20 percent on your investments in stocks, don't pay off the student loan immediately. Let's say that you owe $200 per month on the student loan and you can afford to pay an extra $200 each month. If you pay off an extra $200 of debt, you're saving the 8 percent you'd have had to pay on it. But if you invest the $200 instead and earn 10 percent on it, you come out ahead.

Unlike Glenda, the Good Debt (low-rate and a long time to pay it off), the Wicked Debt of the West is credit card debt. This is the debt you want to get rid of—pronto. Here are some ways to start paying it off.

- **Pay more than the minimum.** You'll make the dreams of credit card companies come true if you only pay the minimum. So try to pay as much as you can each time you get your monthly bill. In fact, make a few sacrifices so that you can pay even more. Rent a movie and pop your own corn instead of heading out to the local multiplex.

- **Move your balances to a lower interest rate card.** Many credit cards lure you with a very low "teaser" rate for the first few months—after which the rate quietly rises to something like 18 percent. You probably get some solicitations in the mail to take out a new card with perhaps a 5.9 percent initial rate. It might actually make sense to get this card and transfer your current debt while you're still paying the low rate. In the meantime, the difference between 18 percent and 5.9 percent means you'll be saving some significant money, which can be applied to paying down your debt.

  Be careful though. If the interest rate after the introductory period will be higher than what you're paying now, you may have to switch again at that time. Some banks have caught on to folks who switch from card to card to take advantage of the low introductory rates. Many of these offers now stipulate that if you transfer balances from the new card within a 12-month period, the normal interest rate will be applied to all outstanding balances retroactively. That could be a bitter pill to swallow for someone short on cash, and it certainly doesn't help your debt repayment schedule. Read the fine print.

- **Finagle your friends and family.** Why pay 18 percent to a credit card issuer when your sister might lend you enough to pay off your cards and only charge you a small amount of interest? Clearly establish the interest and repayment schedule in writing to avoid misunderstandings and hard feelings. And, of course, be scrupulous about adhering to that schedule. Otherwise, you can forget about getting any good birthday presents. There are other possibilities, too. Come visit our Dig-Yourself-Out-of-Debt area, at http://www.fool.com/credit for some more ideas.

5. Wheel and deal, because much debt is negotiable. You may think your lenders are inhuman. It may seem that if they're not sitting 40 stories above Manhattan, counting coins and plotting against their enemies, they're over in the alley with tire-irons and golf clubs pummeling a poor guy down on his luck. But the reality is that lenders are people, too. What does that mean for you? Well, know that you can very likely negotiate your debt down to a smaller total payment, a lower interest rate, or both. Lenders will often listen to your pleas, and credit card lenders are among those most likely to listen. It costs them a lot more money to attract new cardholders than they lose by reducing the interest rate on your debt to keep you as a customer.

If your current credit card is charging you more than 12 percent interest, it's time to use our Foolish Rate Negotiation Dialogue (TM) below to bully your lender into lowering your interest rate.

You: "I just got this incredibly great offer from First Banc Union USA Nation's Edge Choice for a Titanium card with a fixed APR of just 5.9 percent for the rest of my living days! I don't really want to switch cards because your service has been great. But I've noticed that the interest rate you're offering me has crept up to 18.9 percent in the past year. That's way above their offer. So naturally I'm going to have to transfer my balance unless you can lower the interest rate.

Them: (The sound of typewriter keys tapping and your credit and payment history being scrutinized.)

You: "Did I mention the Titanium card's free toaster?"

Them: (The sound of fake typing as the operator tries to psych you out with silence.)

You: (The scratching sound of you filling out the First Banc Union USA Nation's Edge Choice card application.)

Them: "Uncle! We want to keep you as a customer, so we'll lower your interest rate and waive your annual fee. Okay?"

At this point they should offer you something around 12 percent. If your operator isn't feeling generous, ask to speak to a supervisor. If you've been perpetually late with your payments, though, your lender may prefer to let you walk. So be prepared to follow through with the switch. But if you have a solid record, you should have no problem negotiating a lower lending rate. And that can save you months or years in your push to pay off the debts.

The rate you're charged isn't the only thing you can renegotiate. Even if you pay off your tab each month, you can improve your situation. Is your card charging you an annual fee? Has it just shortened its "grace period"? The grace period is the time between the close of your billing period and the date your payment is due, usually between 20 to 30 days. Some outlandish cards actually eliminate this grace period altogether for customers who pay off their bills in full each month. That's right—responsible cardholders are sometimes penalized, accumulating interest charges before their bill is even mailed to them. These are the kinds of things you need to pay attention to—and renegotiate whenever possible. Or run from.

You actually have some handy leverage in this situation. Credit card companies make a few percentage points of profit from merchants on every dollar charged. If you charge a $600 automatic nail buffer on your card at Omni-Mart, Omni-Mart has to fork over anywhere from $10 to $30 to your lender. Remind your lender that he is making money from you, even if you pay off your balance each month. Get those annual fees removed and make sure you have an acceptable grace period. When your lender tries to hit you with a $30 annual fee, call and remind them that they got a pile of money off you in merchant fees, which they won't get next year if you cancel your card. Sit back while the customer service rep grovels. Treat debt as if it were negotiable. Cause [sic] much of it is.

6. A laser-disc player is not an investment. Have you heard of "depreciating assets"? These are items that lose value over time. An extreme example of a depreciating asset is your brain. As you age, you lose brain cells. And there's little you can do to stop or reverse this process. For many men, hair is also a depreciating asset. They may start their 30s with 150,000 hairs on their scalp and then end the decade with only 100,000. Ouch!

But let's focus on depreciating assets that you have more control over, like a car. On average, new cars and trucks lose more than 20 percent of their value in just their first year. If you bought a sleek convertible last year for $30,000, today it's probably worth around $24,000.

Consider the choices you have for your savings. If your beloved Aunt Zelda passes away and leaves you $50,000, maybe you'll decide to buy a car. If you buy a fancy $50,000 BMW, it will depreciate by a few thousand dollars almost as soon as you drive it off the lot. The depreciation will total about $10,000 in its first year alone. That's $10,000 up in smoke. And every year after, it will—on average—lose an additional 10 percent of value.

But what if you bought, instead, a new Toyota for $15,000? You'd only lose about $3,000 in the first year. And you'd still have about $35,000 of Aunt Zelda's money. If you invested that money and it grew at an average of 11 percent per year, you'd have more than $99,000 in 10 years. If it grew at 15 percent, you'd end up with more than $140,000. See what a good decision it was to postpone buying your dream car?

Identify all the stuff you're going to buy that will lose its value over time—cars, bicycles, stereo equipment, and so on. Then plan to spend as little money as possible on them. Today, you want to be saving as much money as possible and investing it.

7. Move long-term savings into the stock market. You say you haven't a clue about the stock market. You don't know what it all means, and what's worse, you're not the slightest bit interested in learning. Hooey! You're involved in the stock market every day. When you buy jeans from the Gap, a Diet Coke to wash down some pizza, sneakers from NIKE, and chips and salsa for your Super Bowl party—you're supporting public companies in which you can invest. Investing in stocks can simply be a matter of examining the companies around you that you're buying a lot of stuff from each day.

Many advisers suggest broadly diversifying your long-term savings into stocks as well as bonds, gold, real estate, blah blah blah. We don't buy it. Consider these numbers, taken from the book, *Stocks for the Long Run,* by Jeremy Siegel—a business professor at the Wharton School at the University of Pennsylvania. Professor Siegel studied how stocks and other investment options (such as bonds and gold) performed over almost 200 years, and he found that stocks fared considerably better. To prove his point, he looked at what happened to a single dollar invested in 1802 (only three years after George Washington died) in stocks, short-term bonds, long-term bonds and gold. The results are impressive. In 190 years, the single dollar grew to the following sizes:

Stocks:	$3,100,000.00
Long-term bonds:	6,620.00
Short-term bonds:	2,934.00
Gold:	13.40

Of course, you probably don't expect to live 190 years, right? So let's look at a shorter time period. According to the Ibbotson & Associates 1997

Yearbook, stocks outperformed everything else you could have invested in during 52 out of 52 20-year periods since 1926. Check out these average annual returns from 1926 to 1996:

Large company stocks	10.7%
Small company stocks	12.6%
Long-term corporate bonds	5.6%
U.S. Treasury bills	3.7%

Remember that this period included the crash of 1929, the Great Depression and several major recessions. Yet despite occasional periods of unpleasantness and despite the occasional wailing and gnashing of teeth by un-Foolish investors, stocks were still your best bet and still rose in value—over the long term.

That's why we like stocks for all money you can afford to put away for more than five years.

8. Understand the value of one buck. A dollar holds more value than you think. Let's say you're 20 years old. Start with $1 and add a new dollar of savings every week. At the end of each year, move that $52 into the stock market. Repeat this for every year until you're 65 years old. How much will you have saved? $51,253. That's a lot of marbles for just putting one buck away each week. Imagine if you had saved $5 a week—you'd end up with $256,266. A quarter of a million dollars!

The above examples assume that your money is growing at the historical market average of 11 percent per year. But there are ways you can be more Foolish with your investing. The Dow Dividend Approach, for example, is easy enough for a nine-year-old to figure out, and has returned an annual average of between 16 percent and 20 percent for decades. If your $5 per week grew at 16 percent, it would become $1.3 million. At 20 percent, it grows to a whopping $4.8 million. Saving small sums of money regularly and investing them can open up a world of opportunities for you.

9. Don't blindly expect the financial industry to help you. Fools find it amusing that so much of the financial industry is built upon the assumption that managing money and investing are so mysterious, so difficult, so complex and cryptic, that no mere mortal should try and manage her own money. It's in the financial industry's best interest to popularize this attitude. If Floyd Papadopolous thinks that he might make a bonehead move and see all his life's savings flushed down the toilet, he'll just trot down to his local mutual fund company and hand over his money. "Here—you take it. You know what's best. Charge me whatever."

To this, the Fool snorts, "Pshaw." No one cares more about your money than you do. Consider the incredible fact that the vast majority of mutual funds perform worse than the market in general. According to Lipper Analytical Services, for example, from 1993 through 1997, fully 91 percent of mutual funds underperformed the S&P 500, a basket of 500 of the biggest companies in the country. Who's managing those thousands of under-performing mutual funds? You got it—well-paid professionals (many of whom own yachts).

If you learn about investing, do your own thinking, and invest Foolishly, you should do very well. Even if you end up just investing in an S&P 500 index fund and not spending any time trying to beat the market. You can learn more in the years ahead, but for now—just recognize that the financial industry does not always have as its chief aim helping you. Nope, oftentimes its primary aim is helping itself.

10. Have fun and be Foolish. This may be an unusual way to end your Foolish Steps to Independence, but we can offer perhaps no better advice than this. Treat the management of your money as the fun and rewarding activity that it can be. Trick yourself into saving a little cash each month. Invite friends to help you through the typically grim process of buying a car. Have fun on the phone, negotiating down your debt with your credi-tors. For the sheer Foolishness of it, do a little research and then buy stock in a company whose products you love.

When in Fooldom, you can relax and learn while chuckling. Our mis-sion is to inform, to amuse and to enrich. We want to help you learn how to manage your own money and we provide a community where all Fools can learn more from one another, ask questions and get answers. Come visit us online at http://www.fool.com where we've got a lot to offer you. Here is just a tip of our iceberg:

How to buy a car.

How to buy a house.

How to finance an education.

How to dig yourself out of debt.

How to land a great job.

Several real-money portfolios to follow.

2,000-plus online discussion folders for individual stocks and investment strategies.

A jargon-free explanation of different investment strategies.

Lessons on how to value companies and stocks.

Ideas of interesting stocks that you might research further and perhaps invest in.

If you're not yet roaming the online world, you'll also find us: Syndicated in some 130-plus newspapers across the country, from the *L.A. Times* to the *Miami Herald.* In your local library or bookstore, where we have three best-selling books.

If you take a little time to learn how to save some money, invest it in common stocks for the long haul, and even gain Foolish pleasure from the process, we think you'll be adding monetary and non-monetary wealth to your life in the decades ahead beyond any of your expectations. Good luck out there and . . . Fool on!

3500 words

Analyze What You Read

STEP 3

Following are the ten steps discussed in the reading. Restate the main idea of each one in your own words.

Steps	Main idea
1. Money isn't everything, but it is something.	
2. Learning this stuff is easy, but you do have to learn it.	
3. Borrowing loads of money is hazardous to your health.	
4. Debt happens.	
5. Wheel and deal, because much debt is negotiable.	
6. A laser-disc player is not an investment.	

continued

Steps	Main idea
7. Move long-term savings into the stock market.	
8. Understand the value of one buck.	
9. Don't blindly expect the financial industry to help you.	
10. Have fun and be Foolish.	

Remember What's Important

1. To prepare for a Comprehension Check, memorize the outline. Test yourself or have someone test you until you can remember everything you need to know. If necessary, review *How to Answer Essay Questions* on p. 73.

2. To prepare for a Vocabulary Check, make flash cards as described on pp. 15–16 for each of the words in the Vocabulary Preview that you don't know. Test yourself or have someone test you until you can remember them.

Make Use of What You Read

When you are ready, complete the Comprehension Check on p. 345 and the Vocabulary Check on p. 347. Do them from memory, without looking back at the book or at your notes.

Evaluate Your Active Critical Thinking Skills

After your tests have been graded, record your scores on the Progress Chart, p. 416, and answer the questions on the Evaluation Checklist on p. 417.

Vocabulary Skills Review

For explanation see pp. 3–5

Context Clues

Use the context of each sentence to figure out the meaning of the italicized word. *Do not use a dictionary.* Circle the letter of the best definition, and then write in the type of clue: definition, contrast, example, experience.

1. ACT is a *strategy* for better reading.

   a. class b. method c. book d. video

   Type of clue: _____

2. A *polygraph* is used to find out whether someone is lying.

   a. heart monitor b. thermometer c. sworn statement d. lie detector

   Type of clue: _____

3. When you don't make yourself clear, people can easily *misconstrue* your meaning.

   a. understand b. read c. misunderstand d. communicate

   Type of clue: _____

4. Unfamiliar words in this exercise are written in *italic* type.

   a. dark b. regular c. slanted d. large

   Type of clue: _____

5. "Neurotic" is a term used to indicate mild mental disturbance, but *psychotic* is used to indicate a serious mental illness.

   a. mentally ill b. mentally retarded c. angry d. suspicious

   Type of clue: _____

6. Good behavior is rewarded, but bad behavior is *penalized.*

   a. encouraged b. forgotten c. ignored d. punished

   Type of clue: _____

7. Rich people usually *acquire* more possessions than poor people do.

   a. give away b. lose c. borrow d. get

   Type of clue: _____

8. Millions of people go to Yellowstone National Park to see the geothermal *phenomena* such as geysers and boiling mudpots.

   a. unusual things b. plants and animals

   c. mountains and rivers d. photos and videos

   Type of clue: _____

9. When times are good, people can spend freely, but during bad times we have to *curtail* our spending.

   a. reduce b. increase c. maintain d. raise

   Type of clue: _____

10. Most of us would feel *intimidated* by someone much bigger who wanted to fight.

a. angered　　b. thrilled　　c. frightened　　d. saddened

Type of clue: _____

Analogies

A word analogy is a puzzle in which two sets of words are compared. The two words in the first set have some kind of relationship to each other. You have to recognize the relationship in order to fill in the blank in the second set. Analogies use the mathematical symbols : which means *is to*, and : :, which means *as*. For example:

night : day : : dark : _____

This example reads: night *is to* day *as* dark *is to* _____. You must decide on the relationship between the first two words. *Night* and *day* are opposites. Therefore, the word in the blank must be the opposite of *dark*. The answer is *light*.

There are two kind of relationships in the analogies in this book. The words either mean the same thing or they are opposites. Write the letter of the correct choice in the blank provided.

1. daunt : encourage : : wither : _____

a. face　　b. ripen　　c. dry up　　d. wilt

2. substantial : large : : hazardous : _____

a. safe　　b. different　　c. new　　d. dangerous

3. obstruct : help : : scrupulous : _____

a. careless　　b. careful　　c. detailed　　d. accurate

4. adhere : stick : : waive : _____

a. keep　　b. demand　　c. give up　　d. claim

5. perpetual : never : : depreciate : _____

a. grow　　b. lessen　　c. maintain　　d. lose

Comprehension Skills Review: Valid and Invalid Inferences

Mark each inference V if it is valid and I if it is invalid. To be a valid inference, the information must be implied in the reading. If you mark V, please write the sentence from the reading that you used to make the inference on the lines provided.

_____   1. Some debt is better than other debt.

_____

_____

_____   2. The authors recommend diversification among different types of investments.

_____

_____

_____   3. The information at the Motley Fool Web site costs money.

_____

_____

_____   4. The Motley Fool is well known.

_____

_____

_____   5. A house is usually a depreciating asset.

_____

_____

_____   6. The author recommends investing in mutual funds.

_____

_____

_____   7. The key to financial independence later is preparing now.

_____

_____

_____   8. If you pay higher interest on your debts than you make on your investments, you'll never get ahead.

_____

_____

_____   9. Most people aren't smart enough to do well in the stock market.

_____

_____

_____   10. Investing is very boring.

_____

_____

8   Improve Your Memory in 7 Easy Steps

Vocabulary Preview

acronym (ak′rə nim): a word formed from the first letter (or first few letters) of several words

Example: Scuba is an <u>acronym</u> for "self-contained underwater breathing apparatus."

mediation (mē′dē ā′shən): an intermediary position or something that comes between to help join two things

Example: Children use the memory technique of <u>mediation</u> when they sing the ABC song.

sensory (sen′sə rē): having to do with the five senses

Example: If you are floating in warm water in a dark, quiet room, you have very few <u>sensory</u> impressions.

mnemonic (nē män′ik): of or helping the memory

Example: The rhyme, "In fourteen hundred ninety-two, Columbus sailed the ocean blue" is a <u>mnemonic</u> device.

retrieve (ri trēv′): to recover (information) from stored data; to get back

Example: After thinking about it for a long time, the scientist was able to <u>retrieve</u> the equation he thought he had forgotten.

cat, āte, fäther; pen, ēvil; if, kīte; nō, ôr, fōod, book; boil, house; up, tʉrn; chief, shell; thick, *the*; zh, treasure; ŋ, sing; ə for *a* in *about*; ′ as in *able* (ā′b′l)

Preread

Read the first two paragraphs and the headings that are in boldface print.

1. What is the subject?

_____

2. What is the main idea?

_____

3. Take a moment to think about memory. Think about what you know, what you don't know, and what you might find out from reading the selection. Make up three questions.

a. _____

b. _____

c. _____

STEP 2

Read

Read the selection without underlining.

◆ *Improve Your Memory in 7 Easy Steps*

Morton Hunt

Q UESTION: *Which of these statements is correct?*

- You can improve your memory by exercising it—that is, by memorizing poetry, important dates and so on.

- You can't do anything about your memory; like height, it's inherited.

ANSWER: *Neither, according to the latest psychological research.*

In fact, volunteers who memorized masses of material got *poorer* at it as their minds became cluttered. Memory isn't a muscle; exercise doesn't make it stronger. Yet you *can* improve your memory. Here are seven proven ways:

1. External Memory

This refers to all physical devices that help you remember: lists, memos, diaries and alarm clocks. Many of us are either too lazy or too proud to make the best use of such help; we forget to perform a chore because we felt we didn't need to jot it down.

One handy form of external memory is the deliberately misplaced object. When my wife needs to remember some chore first thing in the morning, she stands a pitcher or jar of jam at the foot of the stairs, where she can't miss it on her way down to breakfast. "What's that doing there?" she'll say. "Oh, yes!"

2. Chunking

This means grouping several items of information into one piece that's as easy to remember as a single item. We recall an acronym like UNICEF as a single name, not as six letters. And, to cue us in to the Great Lakes, many of us use HOMES: *H*uron, *O*ntario, *M*ichigan, *E*rie and *S*uperior.

Psychologist Laird Cermak, author of *Improving Your Memory,* urges you to make up your own chunks. His example: For a picnic, you need milk, soda, beer, salami, bologna, liverwurst, napkins, paper cups and paper plates: if you don't have a pencil handy, that's a lot to remember. Yet you can make it easy. There are three *drinks,* three *meats* and three *paper goods;* use the first letter of each category—*d, m, p*—to make a word: *damp* (bad for picnics). Remember that, and you'll recall the categories, and then the items in each.

3. Mediation

This means attaching the items of a list to some easily remembered "mediating" device, such as the jingle most adults use to recall the lengths of the months: "30 days hath September . . ."

Make up your own mediators. To remember all the things to take care of when going away for a weekend, I listed them: water *plants,* throw out spoilables in *refrigerator,* turn on *telephone* answering machine, lower *thermostat,* lock *windows,* put out *garbage,* lock *doors.* From the first letter of each item, I made up the sentence, "*P*eter *R*abbit *t*akes *T*ums *w*ith *g*ourmet *d*inners." Ridiculous, but easy to remember.

4. Associations

Visual images are one effective form of association. To remember names, think of a visual link between a person's name and some facial feature. For instance: You've just met a Mr. Clausen, who has bushy eyebrows. Think of a "keyword" (a soundalike) for his name—*claws;* then visualize a lobster claw tearing at his eyebrows. When you try to recall his name, you see his eyebrows, then remember the claw tearing at them and—aha!—*Clausen!*

Any association can work. I remember the name of Mrs. Purdy, the woman who assigns garden plots at a nearby preserve, by thinking: "If I don't get a garden plot, I'll be in a *purty* bad fix."

5. Reliving the Moment

Studies have shown that sensory impressions are associated in memory to what we're learning and later help remind us of what we learned. So if you're trying to recall a name or fact, picture the place in which you learned it, the people around you at the time, even the feeling of the seat you sat in; your chance of remembering it will be greatly increased.

And if you're trying to remember where you lost something, mentally retrace your steps. "Ah!" you may suddenly say, seeing the scene in your mind's eye. "I put the parcel on the empty chair next to me in the restaurant when the waiter handed me the menu."

6. Mnemonic Pegboards

Performers who remember scores of names called out by people in their audiences do not have unusual memories: they've previously memorized a set of words or images to which they mentally attach the names. Anyone can do it. First, memorize these 10 "pegwords" (since they rhyme with the numbers one to 10, it's easy): *one—bun; two—shoe; three—tree; four—door; five—hive; six—sticks; seven—heaven; eight—gate; nine—line; ten—hen.*

Now make up a list of 10 other words and number them. Link each one to the pegword with the same number by means of an image. Suppose your first word is *bowl;* picture a bun lying inside a bowl. If your second word is *desk,* picture a shoe parked on a desk. A minute should be enough for all 10.

You'll be amazed at how effortlessly—and for how long—you can recall the whole list.

7. Weaving It into the Web

All the above methods are useful for recalling simple lists and names. But with more complicated information, you can't merely memorize; you have to connect it to the many related items you already know. That, according to psychologists, is the best way to retrieve it later.

And now you're equipped with seven ways to increase your memory power—if you can remember what they are.

900 words

Analyze What You Read

Application

Use an association method to remember a list of four errands. On the first line, list the errands. On the second line, describe the mental picture, word association, sound association, or physical object that you are using to remember the errand.

1. Errands _____

   _____

2. Device _____

   _____

Graphic Organizer

On the following chart, write the seven ways to improve your memory and give an example of each.

Method	Example
1.	
2.	
3.	
4.	
5.	
6.	
7.	

Remember What's Important

1. To prepare for a Comprehension Check, memorize the chart. Test yourself or have someone test you until you can remember everything you need to know. If necessary, review *How to Answer Essay Questions* on p. 73.

2. To prepare for a Vocabulary Check, make flash cards as described on pp. 15–16 for each of the words in the Vocabulary Preview that you don't know. Test yourself or have someone test you until you can remember them.

Make Use of What You Read

When you are ready, complete the Comprehension Check on p. 349 and the Vocabulary Check on p. 351. Do them from memory, without looking back at the book or at your notes.

Evaluate Your Active Critical Thinking Skills

After your tests have been graded, record your scores on the Progress Chart, p. 416, and answer the questions on the Evaluation Checklist on p. 417.

Vocabulary Skills Review: Word Memory

Listed below are ten words from previous readings. Choose five and use the memory techniques discussed in this reading to remember the definition.

1. caption _____

_____

_____

2. deport _____

_____

_____

3. asinine _____

_____

_____

4. flippant _____

_____

_____

5. inflated _____

_____

_____

6. doctorate _____

_____

_____

7. conscientious _____

_____

_____

8. descendant _____

_____

_____

9. correspondence _____

_____

_____

10. endorses _____

_____

_____

Confused Words

Some pairs of words are confused in writing because they look very similar or because they sound alike, or both. Use the dictionary entry to help you choose the correct word to fill in the blank.

1. He went to the library and _____ went home.

2. Bill Gates is richer _____ Bill Clinton.

> **then** (*then*) *adv.* [ME.: see THAN] **1.** at that time [he was young *then*] **2.** soon afterward; next in time [he took his hat and *then* left] **3.** next in order [first comes alpha and *then* beta] **4.** in that case; therefore; accordingly: used with conjunctive force [if it rains, *then* there will be no picnic] **5.** besides; moreover [he likes to walk, and *then* it's good exercise] **6.** at another time or at other times: used as a correlative with now, sometimes, etc. [now it's warm, *then* freezing] –*adj.* of that time; being such at that time [the *then* director] –*n.* that time [by *then*, they were gone] **–but then** but on the other hand; but at the same time **–then and there** at that time and in that place; at once **–what then?** what would happen in that case?

> **than** (*than*; unstressed, *then*, *thən*) *conj.* [ME. *than*, *thene*, *thonne* < OE. *thenne*, *thanne*, *thonne*, orig., then: for IE. base see THAT] **1.** introducing the second element in a comparison, following an adjective or adverb in the comparative degree [A is taller *than* B; arrived earlier *than* the others] **2.** expressing exception, following an adjective or adverb [none other *than* Sam] **3.** when: used esp. after inverted constructions introduced by *scarcely, hardly, barely,* etc. [scarcely has I see her *than* she spoke to me] –*prep.* compared to: in *than whom, than which* [a writer *than whom* there is none finer]

1. Let's study at _____ house.

2. If you don't hurry, _____ going to be late.

your (yoor; often yôr; unstressed, yər) *possessive pronominal adj.* [ME. *your, eower* < OE. *eower,* gen. of *ge,* ye: see YOU] of, belonging to, or done by you: also used before some formal titles [*your* Honor, *your* Majesty]

you're {yoor, yо̅о̅r; unstressed, yər) you are

1. Everyone _____ Tiffany is going to the party.

2. I think I will _____ a job in Hong Kong.

ac•cept (ak sept′, ək-) *vt.* HAVE **1.** to take (what is offered or given); receive, esp. willingly **2.** to receive favorably; approve [to *accept* a theory] **3.** to submit to; be resigned to [he had to *accept* defeat] **4.** to believe in **5.** to understand as having a certain meaning **6.** to respond to in the affirmative [to *accept* an invitation] **7.** to admit as a student, member, etc. **8.** to agree to take the responsibilities of (a job, office, etc.) **9.** to receive (a committee report) as satisfactory according to parliamentary procedure **10.** Business to agree, as by a signed promise, to pay **11.** Law to receive with intent to retain and adopt –*vi.* to accept something offered –*SYN.* RECEIVE **–ac•cept′er** *n.*

ex•cept (ek sept′, ik-) *vt.* [ME. *excepten* < OFr. *excepter* < L. *exceptare,* to take out, except < *exceptus,* pp. of *excipere* < *ex-,* out + *capere,* to take: see HAVE] to leave out or take out; make an exception of; exclude; omit –*vi.* [Now Rare] to object; take exception: with to or against [to *except* to a remark] –*prep.* [ME. < L. *exceptus*] leaving out; other than; but [to everyone *except* me] –*conj.* **1.** [Archaic] unless **2.** [Colloq.] were it not that; only [I'd quit *except* I need the money] **–except for** if it were not for

Comprehension Skills Review: Valid and Invalid Inferences

Mark each inference V if it is valid and I if it is invalid. To be a valid inference, the information must be implied in the reading. If you mark V, please write the sentence from the reading that you used to make the inference on the lines provided.

_____   1. Memory improves with exercise.

_____

_____

_____   2. Chunking is less useful than mediation.

_____

_____

_____ 3. People often don't want to use the external things that improve memory.

_____

_____

_____ 4. Things that are out of place attract our attention.

_____

_____

_____ 5. Organizing things helps memory.

_____

_____

_____ 6. Most people already use some of the memory techniques discussed.

_____

_____

_____ 7. Memory devices can be used to remember everyday things.

_____

_____

_____ 8. Mnemonics don't have to sound logical.

_____

_____

_____ 9. Visual association aids in recalling names and faces.

_____

_____

_____ 10. Lists learned by mnemonic pegboards are quickly forgotten.

_____

_____

9 How to Become an Effective Test Taker

Vocabulary Preview

acquire (ə kwīr′): to gain by one's own efforts
Example: Skill in reading is <u>acquired</u> through practice.

enumerate (i nōō′mər āt): to name one by one
Example: The six steps of the ACT method are <u>enumerated</u> in this book.

italic (i tal′ik): a typeface in which the letters slant upward to the right
Example: One way an author has of emphasizing a particular word is to print it in <u>italics</u>.

methodically (meth äd′i klē): in an orderly, systematic manner
Example: If you finish a test before the time is up, you should <u>methodically</u> check all your answers before you turn it in.

strategy (strat′ə jē): a careful plan or method
Example: Before asking my boss for a raise, I planned my <u>strategy</u>.

penalize (pēn′ə līz): to impose a penalty on; punish
Example: Most colleges will <u>penalize</u> students who turn in assignments late.

pertinent (pʉr′t'n ənt): connected to the matter at hand
Example: When writing a term paper, you need sources of <u>pertinent</u> information.

acrostic (ə krôs′tik): a composition, usually in verse, in which certain letters in each line, such as the first or last, spell out a word, motto, etc.
Example: Many newspapers and magazines have <u>acrostics</u> instead of or in addition to crossword puzzles.

phenomenon (fə näm′ə nän): any fact or event that can be scientifically described
Example: A solar eclipse is an astronomical <u>phenomenon</u>.

demanding (di man′diŋ): difficult
Example: Getting all A's and B's in college is a <u>demanding</u> job.

cat, āte, fäther; pen, ēvil; if, kīte; nō, ôr, fōōd, book; boil, house; up, tʉrn; chief, shell; thick, *the*; zh, treasure; ŋ, sing; ə for *a* in *about*; ′ as in *able* (ā′b'l)

Preread

Read all the boldface and italic headings.

1. What is the subject?

_____

2. What is the main idea?

   _____

3. Take a moment to think about taking tests. Think about what you know, what you don't know, and what you might find out from reading the selection. Make up three questions.

   a. _____

   _____

   b. _____

   _____

   c. _____

   _____

Read

STEP 2

Read the selection without underlining.

◆ *How to Become an Effective Test Taker*

Brian K. Williams and Sharon M. Knight

The first requirement of test taking is, of course, knowledge of the subject matter. . . . You should also make it a point to *ask* your instructor what kinds of questions will be asked on tests. Beyond this, however, there are certain skills one can acquire that will help during the test-taking process. Here are some suggestions. . . .

Reviewing: Study Information That Is Emphasized and Enumerated

Because you will not always know whether an exam will be an objective or essay test, you need to be prepared for both. Here are some general tips.

■ *Review material that is emphasized:* In the lectures, this consists of any points your instructor pointed out as being significant or important, or spent a good deal of time discussing or specifically advised you to study.

In the textbook, pay attention to key terms (often emphasized in *italic* or **boldface** type), their definitions, and the examples that clarify them. Also, of course, material that has a good many pages given over to it should also be considered important.

■ *Review material that is enumerated:* Pay attention to any numbered lists, both in your lectures and in your notes, whether it is the 13 vitamins, the major schools of psychology, or the warning signs for heart disease. Enumerations often provide the basis for essay and multiple-choice questions.

■ *Review other tests:* Look over past quizzes as well as the discussion questions and review questions given at the ends of chapters in many textbooks.

Prepare by Doing Final Reviews and Budgeting Your Test Time

Learn how to make your energy and time work for you. Whether you have studied methodically or are only able to cram for an exam, here are some tips:

■ *Review your notes:* Spend the night before reviewing your notes, then go to bed without interfering with the material you have absorbed (as by watching television). Get up early the next morning and review your notes again.

■ *Find a good test-taking spot:* Make sure you go to the exam with any pencils and other materials you need. Get to the classroom early, or at least on time, and find a quiet spot. If you don't have a watch, sit where you can watch a clock. Again, review your notes and avoid talking with others, so as not to interfere with the information you have learned or increase your anxiety.

■ *Read the test directions:* Many students don't do this and end up losing points because they didn't understand precisely what was required of them. Also, listen to any verbal directions or hints your instructor gives you before the test.

■ *Budget your time:* Here is an important point of test strategy. Before you start, read through the entire test and figure out how much time you can spend on each section. The reason for budgeting your time, of course, is so that you won't find yourself with only a few minutes left and a long essay still to be written or a great number of multiple-choice questions to answer.

Write the number of minutes allowed for each section on the test booklet or on a scratch sheet and stick to the schedule. The way you budget your time should correspond to how confident you feel about answering the questions.

Objective Tests: Answer Easy Questions and Eliminate Options

Some suggestions for taking objective tests, such as multiple-choice, true-false, or fill-in, are as follows:

- *Answer the easy questions first:* Don't waste time stewing over difficult questions. Do the easy ones first and come back to the hard ones later (put a check mark opposite those you're not sure about). Your unconscious mind may have solved them in the meantime, or later items may provide you with the extra information you need.

- *Answer all questions:* Unless the instructor says you will be penalized for wrong answers, try to answer all questions. If you have time, review all questions and make sure you have recorded them correctly.

- *Eliminate the options:* Cross out answers you know are incorrect. Be sure to read all the possible answers, especially when the first answer is correct (because other answers could also be correct, so that "All of the above" may be the right choice). Be aware that the test may provide information pertinent to one question in another question on the test. Pay particular attention to options that are long and detailed, since answers that are more detailed and specific are apt to be correct. If two answers have the opposite meaning, one of the two is probably correct.

Essay Tests: First Anticipate Answers and Prepare an Outline

Because there is only a limited amount of time during the test, there are only a few essay questions that your instructor is apt to ask during the exam. The key to success is to try to anticipate beforehand what the questions might be and memorize an outline for an answer. Here are some specific suggestions.

- *Anticipate 10 possible essay questions:* Using the principles we discussed above of reviewing the lecture and textbook material that is *emphasized* and *enumerated,* you are in a position to identify 10 essay questions your instructor may ask. Write out these questions.

- *Prepare and memorize informal essay answers:* Write out each of the questions and list the main points that need to be discussed. Put supporting information in parentheses. Circle the key words in each main point, and below the question put the first letter of the key word. Make up catch phrases, using acronyms, acrostics, or word games, so that you can memorize these key words. Test yourself until you can recall the key words that the letters stand for and the main points the key words represent.

For example, if the question you make up is "What is the difference between the traditional and the modern theory of adolescence?", you might put down the following answers:

1. *Biologically generated.* Universal phenomenon (Hall's theory: hormonal).

2. *Sociologically generated.* Not universal phenomenon (not purely hormonal).

   BG SG   BIG GUY   SMALL GUY

When you receive the questions for the essay examination, read all the directions carefully, then start with the *least demanding question.* Putting down a good answer at the start will give you confidence and make it easier to proceed with the rest. Make a brief outline, similar to the one you did for your anticipated question, before you begin writing.

1000 words

Analyze What You Read

STEP 3

Application

Think about the last test you took in another class. Review the selection and decide whether you did everything that was recommended. Answer yes or no; if the question does not apply to the test you took, write N/A.

1. Did you ask the instructor what kinds of questions would be on the test? _____

2. Did you review material that was emphasized in the lectures?

   _____

3. Did you pay attention to key terms (especially those in italics or boldface), their definitions, and examples? _____

4. Did you review material that was enumerated in the lectures and your notes? _____

5. Did you review past quizzes and the discussion and review questions in your textbook? _____

6. Did you review your notes just before the test? _____

7. Did you go to the exam with the materials you need and early enough to find a good spot and review your notes? _____

8. Did you read and understand the test directions? _____

9. Did you budget your time? _____

10. On the objective questions, did you answer the easy ones first? _____

11. Did you answer all the questions? _____

12. On multiple-choice questions, did you eliminate the options? _____

13. For essay questions, did you anticipate at least 10 questions beforehand and memorize an outline (or other graphic organizer) for an answer? _____

14. Did you use mnemonic devices for key words from the graphic organizer? _____

15. For essay questions, did you read all the directions carefully, start with the least demanding, and write a brief outline (or other graphic organizer) before beginning writing? _____

Graphic Organizers

The following outline is blank.

1. Go back to the reading and write the Roman numerals from the outline in the margin next to the boldface headings.

2. Write the capital letters from the outline next to the italic headings.

3. Then use the numbers and letters to fill in the outline.

How to Become an Effective Test Taker

    I. _____

        _____

        A. _____

      B. _____

      C. _____

II. _____

      _____

      A. _____

      B. _____

      C. _____

      D. _____

III. _____

      _____

      A. _____

      B. _____

      C. _____

IV. _____

      _____

      A. _____

      B. _____

To make sure you understand the relationship between an outline and an idea map, take the information from the outline and put it on the map on p. 158. The rectangles are the same as the Roman numerals, and the triangles are the same as the capital letters on the outline.

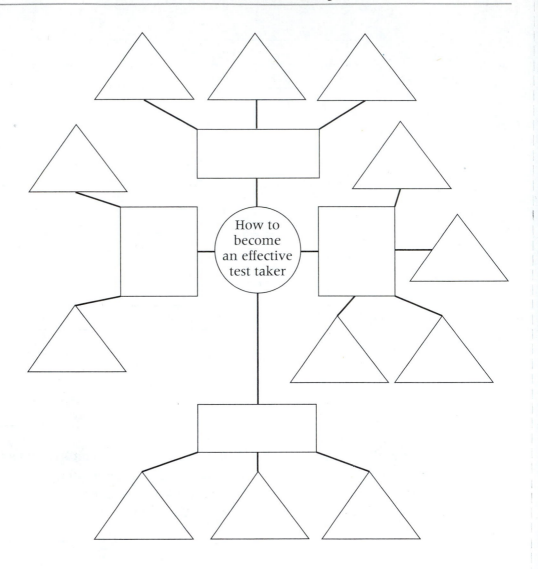

Remember What's Important

1. To prepare for a Comprehension Check, memorize the outline and/or idea map. Test yourself or have someone test you until you can remember everything you need to know. If necessary, review *How to Answer Essay Questions* on p. 73.

2. To prepare for a Vocabulary Check, make flash cards as described on pp. 15–16 for each of the words in the Vocabulary Preview that you don't know. Test yourself or have someone test you until you can remember them.

Make Use of What You Read

When you are ready, complete the Comprehension Check on p. 353 and the Vocabulary Check on p. 355. Do them from memory, without looking back at the book or at your notes.

Evaluate Your Active Critical Thinking Skills

After your tests have been graded, record your scores on the Progress Chart, p. 416, and answer the questions on the Evaluation Checklist on p. 417.

Vocabulary Skills Review

For explanation see pp. 10–12

Parts of Speech

For each preview word, write the part of speech in the space provided. Then look at the new part of speech. Use your dictionary to find the new form of the word. Then write the new word in a sentence. The first item has been done for you as an example.

Preview word	Part of speech	New part of speech	New word
1. acquire	verb	noun	acquisition
Sentence: My CD player is my favorite *acquisition*.			
2. methodically		adjective	
Sentence:			
3. strategy		adjective	
Sentence:			
4. penalize		noun	
Sentence:			
5. pertinent		verb	
Sentence:			

For explanation see p. 140

Analogies

Complete the analogies.

1. enumerate : count : : pertinent : _____

   a. related   b. expensive   c. irrelevant   d. sad

2. phenomenon : event : : penalize : _____

   a. punish   b. reward   c. pay   d. bill

3. demanding : easy : : methodical : _____

   a. neat   b. sloppy   c. angry   d. pleasant

4. acquire : get : : italic : _____

   a. boldface   b. modern   c. slanted   d. connected

5. acrostic : word puzzle : : strategy : _____

   a. dishonesty   b. honesty   c. happening   d. plan

Comprehension Skills Review: Valid and Invalid Inferences

Mark each inference V if it is valid and I if it is invalid. To be a valid inference, the information must be implied in the reading. If you mark V, please write the sentence from the reading that you used to make the inference on the lines provided.

_____   1. Most instructors will give you information about an upcoming test.

_____

_____

_____   2. You can usually predict what will be on a test.

_____

_____

_____   3. Most essay tests are easier than objective tests.

_____

_____

_____   4. Failure to read directions often causes low test scores.

_____

_____

_____   5. If the first choice looks correct, you should mark it and move on.

_____

_____

_____   6. On an essay exam, you should begin with the hardest question.

_____

_____

_____   7. You should always outline an essay before writing.

_____

_____

_____   8. On a multiple-choice test, the longest choice is usually correct.

_____

_____

_____   9. When you don't know an answer, you should leave it blank.

_____

_____

_____   10. If an essay is worth 50 percent of the grade, you should plan to spend half of your time on it.

_____

_____

10 Obtaining Information about Employment Opportunities

Vocabulary Preview

solicit (sə lis′it): to ask or seek

Example: Most charities <u>solicit</u> contributions.

credentials (kri den′shəlz): letters, certificates, or documents showing that a person has a right to the exercise of a certain position or authority

Example: You need <u>credentials</u> to qualify for certain jobs.

résumé (rez′ə mā′, rā′zə-; rā′zə mā′): a statement of a job applicant's previous employment experience, education, etc.

Example: Career counselors recommend changing your <u>résumé</u> to match the description of each job you are applying for.

minimal (min′i məl): smallest or least possible; at a minimum

Example: The cost of public transportation has to be kept <u>minimal</u> so people can get to work.

database (dāt′ə bās′, dat′ə bās′): a large collection of data in a computer, organized so that it can be expanded, updated, and retrieved rapidly for various uses

Example: It's a good idea for a merchant to keep a <u>database</u> of past customers.

reference (ref′ər əns, ref′rəns): *a)* the giving of the name of another person who can offer information or recommendation *b)* the person so indicated *c)* a written statement of character, qualification, or ability, as of someone seeking a position; testimonial

Example: You hope your last employer will give you a good <u>reference</u>.

initiate (i nish′ē āt′): start

Example: You can <u>initiate</u> your job search by signing up at your campus career center.

access (ak′ses′): to gain or have access to; esp. to retrieve data from, or add data to, a database

Example: There are Web sites where you can <u>access</u> financial information that will help you make better investment decisions.

scope (skōp): the range or extent of action, inquiry, etc., or of an activity, concept, etc.

Example: Publicity for large-budget motion pictures is international in <u>scope</u>.

comprehensive (käm′prē hen′siv): dealing with all or many of the relevant details; including much; inclusive [a *comprehensive* survey]

Example: A <u>comprehensive</u> job search includes using a career center, publications, the Internet, networking, advertising, and employment agencies.

distribute (di strib′yo͞ot, -yoot): to put (things) in various distinct places
Example: Soup kitchens <u>distribute</u> food to poor and homeless people.

significant (sig nif′ə kənt): important; large
Example: Getting a college degree requires a <u>significant</u> amount of work.

extensive (ek sten′siv, ik-): having a wide scope, effect, influence, etc.; far-reaching; comprehensive
Example: A senior management position usually requires <u>extensive</u> experience.

sector (sek′tər, -tôr′): a distinct part of society or of an economy, group, area, etc.; section; segment
Example: In a job search, you can look both in government and in the private <u>sector</u>.

personnel (pʉr′sə nel′): of or relating to the division within a business or other enterprise whose functions include hiring and training employees, and administering their benefits
Example: The Human Services Department handles <u>personnel</u> work.

advent (ad′vent′): a coming or arrival
Example: With the <u>advent</u> of word processing, few people use typewriters.

cyberspace (sī′bər spās′): the electronic system of interlinked networks of computers, bulletin boards, etc. that is thought of as being a boundless environment providing access to information, interactive communication, and, in science fiction, a form of VIRTUAL REALITY
Example: A great deal of job information is available in <u>cyberspace</u>.

diversity (də vʉr′sə tē, dī-): variety; often referring to employees of different sexes and races
Example: Affirmative action programs attempt to increase <u>diversity</u> in the workplace.

hypertext (hī′pər tekst′): *Comput.* information stored in a computer and specially organized so that related items are linked together and can be readily accessed
Example: When you write Web pages, you use HTML, or <u>Hypertext</u> Markup Language.

vigorous (vig′ər əs): acting, or ready to act, with energy and force
Example: A <u>vigorous</u> job campaign takes a lot of work.

cat, āte, fäther; pen, ēvil; if, kīte; nō, ôr, fo͞od, book; boil, house; up, tʉrn; chief, shell; thick, *the*; zh, treasure; ŋ, sing; ə for *a* in *about*; ′ as in *able* (ā′b'l)

Preread

Preview the following reading selection by reading the title and the boldface headings. Answer the questions without looking back at the reading.

1. What is the subject?

   _____

2. What is the main idea?

   _____

3. Take a moment to think about finding jobs. Think about what you know, what you don't know, and what you might find out from reading the selection. Make up three questions.

   a. _____

   b. _____

   c. _____

Read

Read the selection without underlining.

◆ *Obtaining Information about Employment Opportunities*

A. C. "Buddy" Krizan, Patricia Merrier, Carol Larson Jones, Jules Harcourt

Finding positions for which you can apply generally requires an organized effort. You must determine what jobs are available and what the job requirements are for those positions.

Many career-related positions are solicited. A **solicited position** is a specific job for which employers are seeking applicants. These jobs can be listed with career centers or advertised in newspapers or journals. They can be announced through private or government placement agencies, or listed on the Web.

A job that is available but is unlisted or unadvertised is called an unsolicited position. These positions may be an important part of your job campaign. Unsolicited positions are obtained by direct contact with a company of your choice. You will learn of the availability of many of these positions through your network of friends, relatives, instructors, and acquaintances. Joining a professional association is important for networking with other individuals in your field. This network will provide you with information on available positions as well as keep you current in your career field.

An effective job campaign requires careful, documented research. You will want to use all appropriate sources of information about the availability of jobs and about their requirements. The following sections discuss possible sources.

Career Centers

The most valuable source of information about jobs will likely be your career center. Whether you are an undergraduate student looking for your first career position or a graduate seeking a change in employment, the career center can provide many services.

Among the placement services offered by most career centers are job-related publications, listings of job openings and arrangements for on-campus company interviews with company representatives. They also provide maintenance of a credentials file, advice on the preparation of résumés and application letters, and guidance about or training for a job interview. These services are free or offered at minimal cost. The career center should be one of the first places you visit as you start your job campaign. Career centers may also be located on the Web by accessing the URL http://www.jobweb.org/catapult/homepage.htm. This Web site is a helpful starting place for information or preparing for the on-line job search and locating the job.

Of the publications available at the career center, the *Job Choices* series is one of the most helpful. This publication contains positions available across the nation. It lists the positions for which employers are seeking applicants and the educational requirements for those jobs. The employers are listed by geographical location, by occupational specialty, and by company name. From this list of employers, you can develop a list of job opportunities in your field. The person to contact within each company is listed. This enables you to develop a mailing list for your job campaign. You can also search on-line with the new employer directory of *Job Choices* at http://www.jobweb.org/search/jobs/. This Web site has a database of job postings, employer profiles, career fairs, school districts, and other Web sites for jobs.

Other job-related books include the *Occupational Outlook Handbook* and *Dictionary of Occupational Titles.* Job-related periodicals such as *Changing Times, High Technology,* or *Small Business Reporter* will also be available at the career center. Additional publications such as trade association publications, government publications, and individual company publications may be available. The highly rated CD-ROM software program *Job Power Source* can also help with your job search. This program will help you set career goals, determine your work styles, and find jobs.

Career centers list specific job openings. In colleges, they arrange for on-campus interviews with company representatives. Generally, the listings of job openings are published periodically. Career centers will post these listings on campus and may mail them to graduates. If you find a position opening that interests you, the career center can assist you. They can contact the employer and send your credentials. Sometimes they can arrange an on-campus interview.

To take advantage of your career center's services, register with that office. This registration will involve the careful, accurate, thorough, and neat completion of your credentials file. The credentials file contains information about your education and experience. In addition, it contains the letters of reference that you request be placed there.

Completing your credentials file will serve you in at least two ways. One, it will motivate you to gather and record important data about yourself. These data will be helpful to you in preparing your résumé. Two, the credentials file will be duplicated and, with your permission or at your request, provided to potential employers.

Many positions are obtained through the services of a career center. It should be your first source of information when you initiate a job search.

Newspaper and Journal Advertisements

The classified advertisement sections of newspapers and many trade journals are other sources of information about job openings. You can obtain trade or professional journals for your field at your school library or public library. You may also access classified ads from the *Boston Globe, New York Times, Los Angeles Times, Chicago Tribune, Washington Post, San Jose Mercury,* and several other newspapers at the Web site as follows: http://www.careerpath.com. Classified ads can also be found in *USA Today* at the following Web site: http://www.usatoday.com.

Although journal job advertisements generally are national in scope, newspaper job advertisements are a good source of information about specific positions in a given geographic area. Most classified advertisements of position openings also carry information about the job requirements and salary levels. By studying advertisements, you can determine what jobs are available in a geographic area, what salaries are offered, and whether you can meet the job requirements. Most newspapers have several editions, and the job opening advertisements may vary from edition to edition. If you wish to relocate to Miami, for example, be aware that the edition of the *Miami Tribune* distributed within Miami will likely contain a more comprehensive listing of job openings than the edition distributed elsewhere. If you plan to relocate to a specific area, you may want to subscribe to one or more of the papers published there.

Private or Government Employment Agencies

Private employment agencies bring together job seekers and employers. Their services will be similar to those offered by your career center. Private employment agencies are in business both to provide these specialized services and to make a profit. Therefore, either the employee or the employer will have to pay the significant fee charged. Before using a private employment agency, be sure that you understand clearly what services are provided, how much the fee will be, and who is to pay the fee.

Another category of private employment agency is the nonprofit service of professional organizations. Some professional organizations publish job opening announcements, provide a hotline with recorded job listings, assist in linking job seekers and employers at professional conferences, and maintain a credentials file service. These services are usually offered at low or no cost to members. To determine what services are available to you from professional organizations, ask a professional in your field.

Public employment agencies are also found at all levels or government: federal, state, regional and local. There is usually no charge for their services.

At the federal government level, the U.S. Office of Personnel Management administers an extensive employment service. There are hundreds of area federal employment offices throughout the United States that are sources of job opportunities within the U.S. government. You can located your nearest federal employment office by contacting any federal government agency in your area. Also, at the federal level, there are job opportunities available in the United States Army, Navy, Marines, Coast Guard, and Air Force. These branches of the military service have recruiters in most local communities. The U.S. Government's official Web site for jobs and employment information can be located at <http://www.usajobs.opm.gov>. America's Job Bank, which will also list jobs that can be found in the 50 states, can be viewed at http://www.ajb.dui.us. The home page of the White House is another site for job openings in the United States. The address is <http://www.whitehouse.gov/wh/welcome.html>.

State governments also provide employment services. These services are more extensive than the employment services provided by the federal government. They include employment opportunities both in the private sector and in the state government. Most states have regional employment offices throughout the state to serve local geographic areas. Usually, you can locate these services by looking under the name of your state in the telephone book or by contacting any state government office.

Local and regional government agencies provide employment services to link employees with positions within their agencies. Cities, counties, and regional service units are all sources of jobs. Usually, you can locate their employment or personnel offices by looking in the telephone book under the name of the government unit, city, county, or region. Many cities and Chambers of Commerce publish directories listing the names, addresses, and phone numbers of businesses in their localities. These directories often contain the names of top executives and departmental managers. They are a good source for contacting individual businesses for possible unpublished job openings.

The Internet

With the advent of the Internet, you now have a new method for seeking your career position and making worthwhile connections. The Web has now opened up a new area of job hunting for you. The Web can be used for accessing information on how to conduct a job search on the Web, how to develop an on-line résumé, how to learn about the various companies, and which companies have openings in your field.

To begin the cyberspace job search you must first have a computer with access to the Web. As mentioned earlier, a good place to start your job search is on your career center's home page, which will have links to the necessary resources. Your career center may be located through the Catapult Career Offices Home Pages: Index (cited earlier) at http://www.jobweb.org/catapult/homepage.htm or through Jobtrak, which has partnered with over 500 college and university career centers nationwide. The URL for this Web site is http://www.jobtrak.com/. Jobtrak has job listings for full-time jobs, part-time jobs, temporary jobs, and internships. Jobtrak has information on career fairs, résumé development, job searches, and top recruiters, too.

The Riley Guide Web site, which was developed by Worcester Polytechnic Institute's librarian Margaret F. Riley Dikel (the grandmother of resources for job seekers), is a site with information on employment opportunities and job resources on the Internet. This site, found at http://www.dbm.com/jobguide, has information ranging from the basic use of the Internet to incorporating the Internet into your job search to on-line job application procedures to recruiting on-line. This Web site includes all the current information on searching for positions on the Web.

Several Web sites that can be helpful with your on-line job search have been listed in the previous materials. Additional sites that can be accessed on the Web include the following:

Career Magazine. http://www.careermag.com. This Web site is an on-line career magazine with information on job openings, employers, résumé banks, job fairs, and various articles on current topics such as diversity in the workplace.

Career Mosaic. http://careermosaic.com. This Web site is popular with college students. It has a jobs database, a "Usenet" to perform searches of jobs listed in regional and occupational newsgroups, an on-line job fair, career resource center, and an international gateway to link to *Career Mosaic* sites around the world. This Web site strives to be a valuable source to both the employer and the job seeker.

E-Span: Interactive Employment Network. http://www.espan.com. E-Span has as its motto "The Right Person for the Job and the Right Job for the Person." This site offers job-search information and job listings.

JobDirect. http://www.jobdirect.com. JobDirect connects entry-level job seekers with employers who want qualified applicants. This Web site will help students find summer jobs, internships, or career positions.

Monster Board. http://www.monster.com. This is one of the most popular Web sites for job seekers. Monster Board offers a variety of hypertext links to job-search resources and connections to job listings.

Online Career Center. http://www.occ.com. Online is a nonprofit job-search home page. It is sponsored by employer organizations and includes information on companies and job listings.

The above is a listing of just a few of the Web site addresses for job searching on-line. You may contact your career center staff or Internet directory indexes for additional sites. New ones are added regularly. As you surf the Internet and the many career-related sites, remember to select sites that are current. Look out for sales pitches, check the fees for listing your résumé. Be selective in contacting that potential employer. Ask what type of confidentiality or privacy protection for your résumé is offered. The job search on the Web is just another tool to assist you in locating your career position.

Other Sources

Other possible sources of information about available jobs and their requirements are through networks with colleagues, members of your professional associations, friends, relatives, instructors, acquaintances, and past or present employers. In an aggressive, vigorous job campaign, you will want to seek assistance from all sources. You may even want to advertise your job interests and qualifications in a newspaper or journal in order to obtain job leads.

2200 words

Analyze What You Read

Application

Is there a career center on your campus? If not, find one either in your community or on the Internet. Using the career center you have chosen, answer the following questions:

1. Where is it located? _____

   _____

2. What days and hours is it open? _____

   _____

3. How much does it cost? _____

   _____

4. Do they offer testing and counseling to help you choose a career? _____

   _____

5. Does it have listings of job openings? _____

   _____

6. Which job-related publications does it have?_____

   _____

7. Can they arrange on-campus interviews for you? _____

   _____

8. Will they maintain a credentials file for you? _____

_____

9. Will they help you prepare a résumé and application letters? _____

_____

10. Will they help you prepare for a job interview? _____

_____

Graphic Organizers

Some of the information on the following outline has been filled in for you.

1. Go back to the reading selection and find all the Roman numeral headings from the outline. Write the Roman numeral from the outline in the margin next to where the information appears. Fill in any blank Roman numeral headings on the outline.

2. Go back to the reading selection and find all the capital letter headings from the outline. Write the capital letter in the margin next to where the information appears. Fill in the blank capital letter headings on the outline.

3. Go back to the reading selection and find all Arabic number headings from the outline. Fill in the blank number headings in the outline.

4. Go back to the reading selection and find all lower-case letter headings from the outline. Fill in the blank lower-case letter headings in the outline.

Obtaining Information about Employment Opportunities

I. Solicited versus unsolicited

    A. How to find solicited positions

        1. _____

        2. _____

    B. How to find unsolicited positions

        1. _____

        2. _____

II. Career centers

    A. _____

        1. *Job Choices* in print or online at http://www.jobweb.org/search/jobs/

    2. _____

    3. *Dictionary of Occupational Titles*

    4. _____

    5. *High Technology*

    6. _____

    7. Trade association publications

    8. _____

    9. Individual company publications

   10. _____

B. _____

C. _____

D. _____

    1. Contains information about education and experience and letters of reference

    2. Will help you in two ways

       a. _____

       b. _____

E. _____

F. _____

G. Career centers on the Web: http://www.jobweb.org/catapult/homepage.htm

III. _____

A. Classified ad sections of newspapers in libraries

    1. _____

    2. _____

    3. _____

    4. _____

    5. _____

    6. _____

    7. Others on Web site: http://www.careerpath.com

    8. *USA Today* or on Web site: http://usatoday.com

    9. If you plan to relocate, subscribe to a newspaper from that area.

B. Trade or professional journals in library: national in scope

IV. _____

A. Private for profit

  1. Services similar to career center; find out what they are.

  2. Employer or employee pays fee; find out who pays and how much.

B. Private nonprofit service of professional organizations: for members

  1. _____

  2. _____

  3. _____

  4. _____

C. _____

  1. _____

  2. Area federal employment offices

  3. _____

  4. U.S. Government Web site: http://www.usajobs.opm.gov

  5. _____

  6. White House: http://www.whitehouse.gov/wh/welcome.html

D. Public, state: Regional employment offices listed in telephone book

E. Public, city, county, regional service units: look in telephone book

V. _____

A. Career center

  1. Catapult Career Offices Home Pages: Index (see II above) http://jobweb.org/catapult/homepage.htm

  2. Jobtrak has full-time, part-time, temporary jobs, internships, career fairs, résumé development, job searches, and recruiters: http://www.jobtrak.com

B. _____

C. *Career Magazine.* http://www.careermag.com

D. _____

E. *E-Span: Interactive Employment Network* http://www.espan.com

F. _____

G. *Monster Board.* http://monster.com

H. _____

VI. Other sources

A. Networks: colleagues, members of professional associations, friends, relatives, instructors, acquaintances, past or present employers

B. Advertise in newspapers or journals

Remember What's Important

1. To prepare for a Comprehension Check, memorize the outline. Test yourself or have someone test you until you can remember everything you need to know. If necessary, review *How to Answer Essay Questions* on p. 73.

2. To prepare for a Vocabulary Check, make flash cards as described on pp. 15–16 for each of the words in the Vocabulary Preview that you don't know. Test yourself or have someone test you until you can remember them.

Make Use of What You Read

When you are ready, complete the Comprehension Check on p. 357 and the Vocabulary Check on p. 359. Do them from memory, without looking back at the book or at your notes.

Evaluate Your Active Critical Thinking Skills

After your tests have been graded, record your scores on the Progress Chart, p. 416, and answer the questions on the Evaluation Checklist on p. 417.

Vocabulary Skills Review

| For explanation see pp. 15–16 |

Word Memory

There are four major ways to memorize new words: (1) make the word meaningful by using it in context, (2) make associations between a familiar word and the new word, (3) use word parts, and (4) use flash cards.

1. *Use the word in context.* Write sentences that make clear the meanings of the following words.

   a. solicit _____

   _____

b. résumé _____

_____

c. database _____

_____

d. reference _____

_____

e. vigorous _____

_____

2. *Make word associations.* In the space next to each of the following words, write a familiar word that can help you remember the new one.

   a. minimal   _____

   b. personnel   _____

   c. extensive   _____

For explanation see pp. 5–7

3. *Use word parts.* Write the correct word from the following list in each blank. Make sure the words match their definitions. Use the dictionary if you need help.

Word part	**Example**
ten = stretch	tension
ven = come	prevent (come before)
sect = cut	section
vers = turn	reverse (turn back)
cred = believe, trust	incredible (not believable)
sign = mark, sign	design (marking)
scop = see	telescope (see far)

Word	**Definition**
1. ad __ __ __ t	a coming
2. di __ __ __ __ ity	turn apart (in different directions)
3. __ __ __ __ e	range (as far as can be seen)
4. __ __ __ __ entials	documents showing a person can be trusted
5. ex __ __ __ sive	stretching or reaching far
6. __ __ __ __ or	area (a piece cut out)

For explanation see pp. 15–16

4. *Make flash cards.* Find ten words from this or previous readings in this book that you are having trouble remembering. On the front of the card, write the word and its pronunciation. On the back, write the definition in your own words and use the word in a sentence. Test yourself by looking at the front of the card and trying to restate the definition and a sentence. The average person needs seven self-testing sessions to master a new word.

Comprehension Skills Review: Valid and Invalid Inferences

Mark each inference V if it is valid and I if it is invalid. To be a valid inference, the information must be implied in the reading. If you mark V, please write the sentence from the reading that you used to make the inference on the lines provided.

_____   1. Most people luck into jobs that someone in their network has told them about.

_____

_____

_____   2. Probably your career center will be your most valuable source of job information.

_____

_____

_____   3. There is a Web site that tells you how to search for a job using the Internet.

_____

_____

_____   4. The best way to get a job is to sign up with an employment agency.

_____

_____

_____   5. Conducting an effective job search will usually require research skills.

_____

_____

_____ 6. A credentials file contains information about a person's education and experience, as well as references.

_____

_____

_____

_____ 7. Job-related publications can be found in career centers.

_____

_____

_____ 8. You get unsolicited positions directly from a company, without using an employment service.

_____

_____

_____ 9. If you are looking for a job in another part of the country, you should read the newspapers from that area.

_____

_____

_____

_____

_____ 10. Your credentials file will never be given to potential employers.

_____

_____

ISSUE

Lie-Detector Tests

The two reading selections on this topic were taken from a textbook for a college speech course. They are an example of two speakers taking opposite sides on an issue.

Self-Questioning

It is important to be aware of your own beliefs and biases when you read. Answering the following questions will help you clarify your views. Write the number from the rating scale that best expresses your opinion. You will take the same survey to reevaluate your views after you have completed the two readings.

Rating Scale

1. No

2. Perhaps not

3. No opinion

4. Perhaps

5. Yes

Rate each question 1 to 5.

_____ 1. Are lie-detector tests accurate?

_____ 2. Should lie-detector tests be used by employers as part of the hiring process?

_____ 3. Should lie-detector tests be used by employers for detecting employee theft?

_____ 4. Can lie-detector tests cause serious harm?

_____ 5. Are lie-detector tests the best means of screening employees?

11 | Lie-Detector Tests Should Be Prohibited

Vocabulary Preview

polygraph (päl′i graf′): an instrument for recording simultaneously changes in blood pressure, respiration, pulse rate, etc., lie detector

Example: Polygraph evidence is not allowed in most courts.

technological (tek′nə läj′i kəl): due to developments in technology, resulting from technical progress in the use of machinery and automation in industry, agriculture, etc.

Example: Technological advances are reducing the need for unskilled workers.

intimidate (in tim′ə dāt′): to make timid; make afraid; daunt

Example: Computers intimidate many people.

curtail (kər tāl′): cut short; reduce; abridge

Example: After several court decisions upholding citizens' rights to privacy, law enforcement agencies have had to curtail their use of wiretaps and illegal searches.

misconstrue (mis′kən stroo′): to construe wrongly; misinterpret; misunderstand

Example: Because it is easy to misconstrue one's statements, you should be careful when speaking to the press.

cat, āte, fäther; pen, ēvil; if, kīte; nō, ôr, food, book; boil, house; up, turn; chief, shell; thick, *the*; zh, treasure; ŋ, sing; ə for *a* in *about*; ' as in *able* (ā′b'l)

Preread

Preview the following reading selection by reading the title and the first paragraph. Answer the questions without looking back at the reading.

1. What is the subject?

_____

2. What is the thesis (the main point the author is making about the subject)?

_____

3. Now take a moment to compare your beliefs about lie-detector tests with the author's. On a scale of 1 (no way) to 5 (definitely), how open is your mind to the author's thesis?

_____

STEP 2

Read

Read the selection without underlining. Focus on understanding the author's arguments.

◆ *Lie-Detector Tests Should Be Prohibited*

From Rudolph F. Verderber

Lie-detector or polygraph tests used either to screen job applicants or to uncover thefts by employees have become a big business. Hundreds of thousands are given each year, and the number is steadily rising. What I propose to you today is that employers should be prohibited from administering lie-detector tests to their employees either as a condition of employment or as a condition of maintaining their job. I support this proposition for two reasons. First, despite technological improvement in equipment, the accuracy of results is open to question; and second, even if the tests are accurate, use of lie-detector tests is an invasion of privacy.

First, let's consider their accuracy. Lie-detector tests just have not proved to be very accurate. According to Senator Birch Bayh, tests are only about 70-percent accurate. And equally important, even the results of this 70 percent can be misleading. Let's look at two examples of the kinds of harm that come from these misleading results.

One case involves a young girl named Linda Boycose. She was at the time of the incident a bookkeeper for Kresge's. One day she reported $1.50 missing from the previous day's receipts. A few weeks later the store's security man gave her a lie-detector test. He first used the equipment with all its intimidating wiring, and then he used persuasion to get information. He accused her of deceiving him and actually stealing the money. After this test, Boycose was so upset she quit her job—she then spent the next two years indulging in Valium at an almost suicidal level. Last year a Detroit jury found Boycose's story so convincing that it ordered the department store chain to award her $100,000. Now, almost six years later, she is still afraid to handle the bookkeeping at the doctor's office she manages.

The next example is of a supermarket clerk in Los Angeles. She was fired after an emotional response to the question "Have you ever given discount groceries to your mother?" It was later discovered that her mother had been dead for five years, thus showing that her response was clearly an emotional one.

Much of the inaccuracy of the tests has to do with the examiner's competence. Jerry Wall, a Los Angeles tester, said that out of an estimated three thousand U.S. examiners, only fifty are competent. Some polygraph operators tell an interviewee that he or she has lied at one point even if the person has not, just to see how the person will handle the stress. This strategy can destroy a person's poise, leading to inaccuracies. With these examples of stress situations and inefficient examiners, the facts point to the inaccuracy of polygraph test results.

My second reason for abolishing the use of these tests is that they are an invasion of privacy. Examiners can and do ask job applicants about such things as sexual habits and how often they change their underwear. The supposed purpose of lie-detector tests is to determine whether an employee is stealing. These irrelevant questions are an invasion of privacy, and not a way to indicate whether someone is breaking the law.

Excesses are such that the federal government has been conducting hearings on misuse. Congress is considering ways to curtail their use.

That they are an invasion of privacy seems to be admitted by the companies that use them. Employers are afraid to reveal too much information from tests because they have a fear of being sued. Because of an examiner's prying questions on an employee's background, and because government has shown such a concern about the continued use of polygraphs, we can conclude that they are an invasion of privacy.

In conclusion, let me ask you how, as an employee, you would feel taking such a test. You'd probably feel nervous and reluctant to take the test. Couldn't you see yourself stating something that would be misconstrued, not because of the truth, but because of your nervousness? Also, how would you feel about having to answer very personal and intimate questions about yourself in order to get a job?

Because lie-detector tests are inaccurate and an invasion of privacy, I believe their use should be prohibited.

700 words

Analyze What You Read

STEP 3

Identify the Thesis and Arguments

A. In the margin of the reading, write *thesis* next to the two places the speaker presents her point of view.

B. There are two major arguments:

1. Lie-detector tests are inaccurate.

2. Use of lie-detector tests is an invasion of privacy.

Go back to the reading selection and find each argument. Write *Arg. 1* or *Arg. 2* in the margin next to where each argument appears.

Identify Supporting Details

Following are details that support each argument.

A. Go back to the reading and underline each supporting detail.

B. In the blank before each detail below, write the number of the argument (1 or 2) that the detail supports. For example, detail a (Birch Bayh) supports argument 1, that the tests are not accurate.

_____ a. According to Senator Birch Bayh, the tests are only about 70-percent accurate.

_____ b. Jerry Wall says that only fifty out of three thousand testers are competent.

_____ c. The government has been conducting hearings on misuse.

_____ d. A Los Angeles supermarket clerk reacted emotionally when asked about giving groceries to her mother.

_____ e. Employers who use lie-detector tests are afraid of being sued.

_____ f. Linda Boycose was accused of stealing $1.50.

_____ g. Examiners ask irrelevant and personal questions.

C. Write the most common type of support used: facts, examples, testimony, or reasons.

_____

Evaluate Supporting Details

The supporting details listed above have some logical weakness. The weaknesses are written below. Write the letter of the supporting detail (a–g) in the blank in front of its weakness. You may have more than one letter in the same blank.

_____ 1. Testimony is given, but it is not established why the person is an expert on this topic and/or how he got his information.

_____ 2. The author cites facts to show that this is a widespread problem, but either the sample is too small, or no proof is given at all.

_____ 3. The statements about the government and employers need more data to show their significance.

Make Graphic Organizers

Fill in the blanks in the idea map.

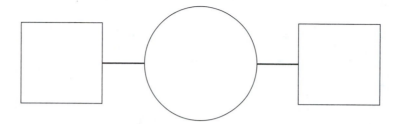

Remember What's Important

Review your marginal notes identifying the thesis and the major arguments. Review the underlining that identified the supporting details. Review the graphic organizer. Test yourself until you are sure you will remember the material. Test yourself as needed on the Vocabulary Preview words.

Make Use of What You Read

When you are ready, complete the Comprehension Check on p. 361 and the Vocabulary Check on p. 363. Do them from memory, without looking back at the book or at your notes.

Evaluate Your Active Critical Thinking Skills

After your tests have been graded, record your scores on the Progress Chart, p. 416, and answer the questions on the Evaluation Checklist on p. 417.

Vocabulary Skills Review

For explanation see pp. 10–12

Parts of Speech

For each word on the next page, write its part of speech. Then change it to the new part of speech. Write a sentence using the new word. Use your dictionary if you need help.

Preview word	Part of speech	New part of speech	New word
1. polygraph		adjective	
Sentence:			
2. technological		noun	
Sentence:			
3. intimidate		noun	
Sentence:			
4. curtail		noun	
Sentence:			
5. misconstrue		noun	
Sentence:			

Confused Words

The following words are often confused. Fill in the blanks with the correct word.

1. When you write a research paper, you must _____ your sources.

2. I recognized him by _____.

3. An architect has to make a building fit its _____.

> **sight** (sīt) *n.* [ME. *siht* < OE. *(ge)siht* < base of *seon*, to SEE[1]] **1.** the ability to see **2.** the act or fact of seeing **3.** the field of one's vision **4.** something that is seen **5.** something worth seeing [the *sights* of London] **6.** *Informal;* something unsightly [Her hair was a *sight.*] **7.** a device used in aiming, as on a gun —*v.* **1.** to see or observe within one's field of vision [*sight* land] **2.** to take aim with (a firearm)

site (sīt) *n.* [ME. < L. *situs*, position, situation < pp. of *sinere*, to put down, permit, allow < IE. base **sei-*, to cast out, let fall: see SIDE] **1.** a piece of land considered from the standpoint of its use for some specified purpose [a good *site* for a town] **2.** the place where something is, was, or is to be; location or scene [the *site* of a battle] —*vt.* **sit′ed, sit′ing** to locate or position on a site

cite (sīt) *vt.* **cit′ed, cit′ing** [ME. *citen* < OFr. *citer,* to summon < L. *citare,* to arouse, summon < *ciere,* to put into motion, rouse < IE. base **kei-* > Gr. *kinein,* to move, OE. *hatan,* to command] **1.** to summon to appear before a court of law **2.** to quote (a passage, book, speech, writer, etc.) **3.** to refer to or mention as by way of example, proof, or precedent ☆**4.** to mention in a CITATION (sense 5) **5.** [Archaic] to stir to action; arouse —*n.* [Colloq.] CITATION (sense 3) **cit′a•ble** or **cite′a•ble** *adj.*

1. The feelings of one member of a family will _____ all the

   other members.

2. The _____ of the law was to make it harder to buy guns.

   af•fect (ə fekt′; for n. 2, af′ekt′) *vt.* [ME. *affecten* < L. *affectare,* to strive after < *affectus,* pp. of *afficere,* to influence, attack < *ad-,* to + *facere,* DO¹] **1.** to have an effect on; influence; produce a change in [bright light *affects* the eyes] **2.** to move or stir the emotions of [his death *affected* us deeply] —*n.* **1.** [Obs.] a disposition or tendency **2.** [Ger. *affekt* < L. *affectus,* state of mind or body: see the *vt.*] *Psychol. a)* an emotion or feeling attached to an idea, object, etc. *b)* in general, emotion or emotional response **af•fect′a•ble** *adj.*

   ef•fect (e fekt′, i-; often ē-, ə-) *n.* [ME. < OFr. (& L.) < L. *effectus,* orig., pp. of *efficere,* to bring to pass, accomplish < *ex-,* out + *facere,* DO¹] **1.** anything brought about by a cause or agent; result **2.** the power or ability to bring about results; efficacy [a law of little *effect*] **3.** influence or action on something [the drug had a cathartic *effect*] **4.** general meaning; purport [he spoke to this *effect*] **5.** *a)* the impression produced on the mind of the observer or hearer, as by artistic design or manner of speaking, acting, etc. [to do something just for *effect*] *b)* something, as a design, aspect of nature, etc., that produces a particular impression [striking cloud *effects*] *c)* a scientific phenomenon [the Doppler *effect*] **6.** the condition or fact of being operative or in force [the law goes into *effect* today] **7.** [*pl.*] belongings; property [household *effects*] —*vt.* to bring about; produce as a result; cause; accomplish [to *effect* a compromise]

1. You should take your _____ problems to a counselor when they begin to affect your work.

2. If you have a problem with your employee health insurance, you should contact the _____ department.

> **per•son•al** (pʉr′sə nəl) *adj.* [OFr. < L. *personalis*] **1.** of or peculiar to a certain person; private; individual **2.** done in person or by oneself without the use of another person or outside agency [a *personal* interview] **3.** involving persons or human beings [*personal* relationships] **4.** of the person, body, or physical appearance [*personal* hygiene] **5.** *a)* having to do with the character, personality, intimate affairs, conduct, etc. of a certain person [a *personal* remark] *b)* tending to make personal, esp. derogatory, remarks [to get *personal* in an argument] –*n.* a personal item or notice in a newspaper

> **per•son•nel** (pʉr′sə nəl′) *n.* [Fr. (lit., PERSONAL), prob. infl. by Ger. *personal*, earlier *personale* < ML; orig. neut. of L. *personalis*] **1.** persons employed in any work, enterprise, service, establishment, etc.: distinguished in military usage from MATERIEL **2.** a personnel department or office –*adj.* of or relating to the division within a business or other enterprise whose functions include hiring and training employees, and administering their benefits

Comprehension Skills Review: Valid and Invalid Inferences

Mark each inference V if it is valid and I if it is invalid. To be a valid inference, the information must be implied in the reading. If you mark V, please write the sentence from the reading that you used to make the inference on the lines provided.

_____   1. Senator Birch Bayh is an expert on lie-detector tests.

_____

_____

_____   2. Lie-detector tests are wrong about a third of the time.

_____

_____

_____   3. Polygraph operators have to pass licensing exams.

_____

_____

_____ 4. Lie-detector tests measure emotions, not necessarily lies.

_____

_____

_____ 5. Polygraph operators belong to a professional association that sets standards.

_____

_____

_____ 6. Lie-detector tests can cause emotional damage.

_____

_____

_____ 7. More than 100,000 lie-detector tests are given each year.

_____

_____

_____ 8. Employers know that lie-detector tests are an invasion of privacy.

_____

_____

_____ 9. Lie-detector tests are regulated by the federal government.

_____

_____

_____ 10. Most employees don't want to take lie-detector tests.

_____

_____

12   Lie-Detector Tests Should Not Be Prohibited

Vocabulary Preview

abolish (ə bäl′ish): to do away with completely; put an end to; esp., to make (a law, etc.) null and void

Example: Many people would like to abolish the death penalty.

deter (dē tur′, di-): to keep or discourage (a person, group, or nation) from doing something by instilling fear, anxiety, doubt, etc.

Example: Supporters of the death penalty believe that it will deter crime.

psychotic (sī kät′ik): seriously mentally ill

Example: Some drugs can cause psychotic symptoms such as hearing voices.

potentially (pō ten′shə lē, pə-): possibly; able to become

Example: Some houseplants are potentially deadly if they are eaten.

sadistic (sə dis′tik): getting pleasure from inflicting physical or psychological pain on another or others

Example: Some child abusers are sadistic; other have poor self-control.

cat, āte, fäther; pen, ēvil; if, kīte; nō, ôr, fōōd, book; boil, house; up, turn; chief, shell; thick, *the*; zh, treasure; ŋ, sing; ə for *a* in *about*; ′ as in *able* (ā′b'l)

Preread

Preview the following reading selection by reading the title and the first paragraph. Answer the questions without looking back at the reading.

1. What is the subject?

2. What is the thesis (the main point the author is making about the subject)?

3. Now take a moment to compare your beliefs about lie-detector tests with the author's. On a scale of 1 (no way) to 5 (definitely), how open is your mind to the author's thesis?

Read

Read the selection without underlining. Focus on understanding the author's arguments.

◆ *Lie-Detector Tests Should Not Be Prohibited*

From Rudolph F. Verderber

My opponent has stated that the use of lie-detector tests by employers should be abolished. I strongly disagree; I believe employers have to use these tests.

Before examining the two reasons she presented, I'd like to take a look at why more than 20 percent of the nation's largest businesses feel a need to use these tests and why the number is growing each year. Employers use lie-detector tests to help curb employee theft. According to the National Retail Merchants Association, employees steal as much as $40 billion of goods each year. Moreover, the figure increases markedly each year. The average merchant doesn't recognize that he loses more to employees than to outsiders—50 to 70 percent of theft losses go to employees, not to shoplifters. This use of lie-detector tests is a necessity to curb this internal theft.

Now, I do not believe that my opponent ever tried to show that there is not a problem that lie-detector testing solves; nor did she try to show that lie-detector testing doesn't help to deter internal theft. Notice that the two reasons she presented are both about abuses. Let's take a closer look at those two reasons.

First my opponent said that the accuracy of results is open to questions; in contrast, I would argue that these tests are remarkably accurate. She mentioned that Senator Bayh reported a 70-percent level of accuracy. Yet the literature on these tests as reported by Ty Kelley, vice president of government affairs of the National Association of Chain Drug Stores, argues that the level is around 90 percent, not 70 percent.

She went on to give two examples of people who were intimidated and/or became emotional and upset when subjected to the test. And on this basis she calls for them to be abolished. I would agree that some people do become emotional, but this is hardly reason for stopping their use. Unless she can show a real problem among many people taking the test, I think we'll have to go along with the need for the tests.

If these tests are so inaccurate, why are one-fifth of the nation's largest companies using them? According to an article in *Business Week,* "Business Buys the Lie Detector," more and more businesses each year see a necessity for using the tests because they deter crime. These tests are now being used by nearly every type of company—banks, businesses, drugstores, as well as retail department stores.

Her second reason for why the tests should be abolished is that they are an invasion of privacy. I believe, with Mr. Kelley, whom I quoted earlier, that there must be some sort of balance maintained between an individual's right to privacy and an employer's right to protect his property. In Illinois, for instance, a state judge ruled that examiners could ask prying questions—there has yet to be any official ruling that the use is "an invasion of privacy."

My opponent used the example of asking questions about sexual habits and change of underwear. In that regard, I agree with her. I think that a person is probably pretty sick who is asking these kinds of questions—and I think these abuses should be checked. But asking questions to screen out thieves, junkies, liars, alcoholics, and psychotics is necessary. For instance, an Atlanta nursing home uses polygraph tests to screen out potentially sadistic and disturbed nurses and orderlies. Is this an invasion of privacy? I don't think so.

It is obvious to me that some type of lie-detector test is needed. Too much theft has gone on, and something must be done to curtail this. I say that lie-detector tests are the answer. First, they are accurate. Companies have been using them for a long time, and more and more companies are starting to use them. And second, it is only an invasion of privacy when the wrong types of questions are asked. I agree that these abuses should be curbed, but not by doing away with the tests. Employers cannot do away with these tests and control theft; the benefits far outweigh the risks.

700 words

Analyze What You Read

STEP
3

Identify the Thesis and Arguments

A. In the margin of the reading, write *thesis* next to the two places the author presents her point of view.

B. There are three major arguments:

1. Employers need the tests to curb employee theft.

2. Lie-detector tests are accurate.

3. A balance should be maintained between an individual's right to privacy and an employer's right to protect his property.

Go back to the reading selection and find each argument. Write *Arg. 1, Arg. 2,* or *Arg. 3* in the margin next to where each argument appears.

Identify Supporting Details

Following are details that support each argument.

A. Go back to the reading and underline each supporting detail.

B. In the blank before each detail below, write the number of the argument (1, 2, or 3) that the detail supports.

_____ a. The opponent did not show that many people are harmed by misleading lie-detector test results.

_____ b. More than 20 percent of the nation's largest businesses use lie-detector tests.

_____ c. Ty Kelley says that lie-detector tests are around 90 percent accurate.

_____ d. Employees steal up to $40 billion of goods each year.

_____ e. Use of inappropriate questions can and should be stopped.

_____ f. 50 to 70 percent of theft losses are to employees, not shoplifters.

_____ g. The opponent did not deny that lie-detector tests help employers identify employees who steal.

_____ h. There has been no official ruling that lie-detector tests are an invasion of privacy.

_____ i. Lie-detector tests deter internal theft.

C. Write the most common type of support: facts, examples, testimony, or reasons.

Evaluate Supporting Details

The two authors writing on this issue have presented evidence for several arguments, but can you tell who is right? In the blank preceding each question on the next page, write the answer to each question. If you can't tell what the answer is, write a question mark (?). If you wrote a question mark, use the blank lines under the question to write what evidence you would need to be able to answer the questions.

_____ 1. What percentage of accuracy do lie-detector tests have?

Evidence needed: _____

_____

_____

_____

_____ 2. Are many people harmed by misleading results of lie-detector tests?

Evidence needed: _____

_____

_____

_____

_____ 3. What percentage of theft is caused by employees?

Evidence needed: _____

_____

_____

_____

_____ 4. Do lie-detector tests deter theft?

Evidence needed: _____

_____

_____

_____

_____ 5. How likely is it that the abuses will be stopped?

Evidence needed: _____

_____

_____

_____

_____ 6. How competent are the lie-detector test operators?

Evidence needed: _____

_____

_____

_____

_____ 7. Are there other ways to reduce employee theft that are as effective as lie-detector tests?

Evidence needed: _____

_____

_____

_____

Make Graphic Organizers

Fill in the blanks in the idea map.

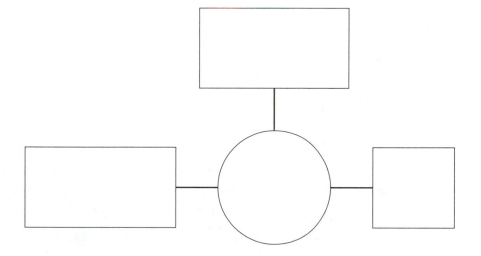

Remember What's Important

Review your marginal notes identifying the thesis and the major arguments. Review the underlining that identified the supporting details. Review the idea map. Test yourself until you are sure you will remember the material. Test yourself as needed on the Vocabulary Preview words.

Make Use of What You Read

When you are ready, complete the Comprehension Check on p. 365 and the Vocabulary Check on p. 367. Do not look back at the reading or the graphic organizer. Remember that essays must follow the graphic organizer.

STEP 6

Evaluate Your Active Critical Thinking Skills

After your tests have been graded, record your scores on the Progress Chart, p. 416, and answer the questions on the Evaluation Checklist on p. 417.

Vocabulary Skills Review

For explanation see p. 140

Analogies

Write the word from the following list that best completes each analogy.

| polygraph | technological | intimidate | curtail | misconstrue |

| abolish | deter | psychotic | potentially | sadistic |

1. abolish : create : : _____ : understand

2. psychotic : insane : : _____ : frighten

3. potentially : possibly : : _____ : lie detector

4. sadistic : kind : : _____ : lengthen

5. deter : encourage : : _____ : preindustrial

Word Memory

We have discussed four ways to memorize new words: (1) make the word meaningful by using it in context, (2) make associations between a familiar word and the new word, (3) use word parts, and (4) use flash cards.

1. *Use the word in context.* Write sentences that make clear the meanings of the following words:

   a. curtail _____

   _____

   b. potentially _____

   _____

   c. sadistic _____

   _____

   d. abolish _____

   _____

   e. vigorous _____

   _____

For explanation
see p. 15

2. *Make word associations.* In the space next to each of the following words, write a familiar word that can help you remember the next one.

   a. psychotic   _____

   b. intimidate   _____

   c. polygraph   _____

For explanation
see pp. 5–7

3. *Use word parts.* Write the correct word from the following list in each blank. Make sure the words match their definitions. Use the dictionary if you need help.

Word part	Example
psych = mind	psychology
de = from	deduct
timid = fear	timid
tech = art	technique
graph = write	autograph
mis = wrong	misspell

Word	Definition
1. __ __ __ __nological	having to do with the practical or industrial <u>arts</u>
2. __ __ __construe	understand something <u>wrong</u>
3. in __ __ __ __ __ ate	to make <u>fearful</u>
4. __ __ ter	to stop or discourage <u>from</u> doing something
5. poly __ __ __ __ __	an instrument that <u>writes</u> changes in pulse rate, blood pressure, etc.
6. __ __ __ __ __ otic	having an illness of the <u>mind</u>

For explanation
see pp. 15–16

4. *Make flash cards.* Find ten words from this or previous readings in this book that you are having trouble remembering. On the front of the card, write the word and its pronunciation. On the back, write the definition in your own words and use the word in a sentence. Test yourself by looking at the front of the card and trying to restate the definition and a sentence. The average person needs seven self-testing sessions to master a new word.

Comprehension Skills Review: Summarizing

Summarizing and most other types of writing are easy if you have a graphic organizer. It's hard if you don't. For this reading selection you have two graphic organizers. The first one is the underlining and notes in the margin of the reading. The second one is the idea map. Here is how to summarize using both of them.

1. To summarize using the underlining and marginal notes, do the following: First, write the thesis in a complete sentence. Then write each argument and its support in complete sentences. Use transition words. For example, you might say, "The first reason is . . . The second reason is . . . And finally, . . ." Use paragraph form. Do not just make a list.

2. To summarize using the idea map, do the following: First, write the thesis in a complete sentence. Next, make each heading in the map into a complete sentence followed by its support. Use paragraph form, not outline form. Use transition words to lead the reader from one idea to another.

Here is an example of a summary of Reading 11:

Lie-detector tests should be prohibited, both for screening job applicants and for trying to uncover employee theft. The first reason is that the accuracy of the tests is not very high. Senator Birch Bayh says that tests are only about 70 percent accurate. One victim of inaccurate testing was Linda Boycose. In her job as a bookkeeper she reported $1.50 missing one day. She was given a lie-detector test and accused of stealing the money. She quit her job and suffered great emotional upset; eventually a jury awarded her $100,000. Another example is a supermarket clerk who was fired after giving an emotional response to the question, "Have you ever given discount groceries to your mother?" Her mother had been dead for five years. Much of the inaccuracy may be related to the competence of the examiner. Jerry Wall, a Los Angeles tester, says that out of about 3,000 U.S. testers, only fifty are competent. The second reason for prohibiting use of lie-detector tests is that they are an invasion of privacy. Examiners often ask about extremely private matters unrelated to stealing. Excesses are so great that the federal government has been conducting hearings on misuse, and employers are afraid of being sued.

Now, write a summary of Reading Selection 12 on a separate piece of paper.

Comparing Views on Lie-Detector Testing

Use the following activities to evaluate your understanding of the issue of whether lie-detector testing by employers should be prohibited. Write your answers on a separate sheet of paper.

1. Read the summary of each selection.

2. Evaluate the support for each reading. Is it true? Is it reasonable?

3. Compare the readings. Do you believe that one author's arguments are stronger than the other's? Why?

4. Go back to the self-questioning survey on p. 178. Would you change any of your responses after reading the selections? Summarize your opinion on the issue, noting how your opinion has been affected by your reading.

UNIT III

Using the ACT Method for Study

An important difference between good students and poor students is the way they study. Poor students read the material passively, without really thinking about it. They may underline or highlight almost everything, because everything looks important to them. They go over it, sometimes several times, hoping that the ideas will stick in their memory. Sometimes this works better than other times, but one thing is certain; this is not a method that can be counted on to earn high grades.

Good students use a study system. A good study system does two things. First, it helps you figure out what will be on the test, so you know what to memorize. Second, it gives you a successful way to memorize. We believe that the most effective study system of all is ACT.

Preread

As you remember from Unit II, prereading increases your comprehension. First, it gives you an overview of all the major ideas, so that you have the mental categories set up. In psychology, these categories are called *advance organizers*. Second, when you think about what you know and don't know about the subject and generate questions, you activate your background knowledge and increase your curiosity. This sets the stage for active rather than passive reading. Active readers interact with what they are reading, using what they already know, questioning, and getting answers.

Prereading Textbooks

Early in the semester or quarter, take ten or fifteen minutes to preview each textbook. First, look at the front matter. This includes title, author, date of publication, table of contents, preface, introduction, foreword, and so on. Second, look at the back matter: index, glossary, appendixes. Then flip through the book, noting the organization of the chapters. Are there chapter objectives or outlines? Are new words defined in the margins? Are there many illustrations? Are there chapter summaries or review questions at the end? This type of preview lets you know what is in the book and how it is organized. It also lets you know whether there are any study aids.

Prereading Chapters

When a chapter is assigned, take a few minutes to preview it. Read the chapter objectives or outline, if any. Read the title and all the headings and subheadings. If there are no headings, read the first sentence of each paragraph. Look at the illustrations and try to figure out the main idea of each one. Read the chapter summary and review questions, if they are included. This preview will give you an overview of all the main ideas, and it will increase your comprehension, memory, and speed.

Next, take a moment to activate your mind, the same way you did in Unit II. Think about what you know and don't know about the topic and what you might find out from your reading. Make up a few questions.

Read

If the chapter is long, break it into logical sections. Use the headings as guides to the sections. Take the first section and read *with your pencil down.* Do not underline or highlight at this point. Just try to understand what you are reading and find answers to your questions. If there is anything you don't understand, there are several things you can do. First, mark what you don't understand. Then look for an explanation. You can ask your instructor in class or during office hours. You can ask other students. Another thing you can do is find books, tapes, or computer programs that cover the same subject using different explanations and/or different examples. Sometimes, especially in math, the problem isn't really that you don't understand a point or a problem. It's that you just need more practice. So, for example, if you have problems with percentages, find something that you can use to get the practice you need. The same goes for grammar or any other subject that requires practice. One way or another, do what you need to make sure you understand the material.

Analyze What You Read—Create a Study Guide

First, find out whatever you can about the test. You can ask the instructor which chapters and lectures will be covered, how much time you will have, and the number and type of questions. There are four different types of test questions: objective, essay, application, and problem-solving. The study guide you create will depend on the type of test. You can also ask other students who have had the class about the tests. If you can obtain copies of old tests, so much the better.

Second, you must predict the questions. This may sound hard to do, but it really isn't. Put yourself in the instructor's place. What you (the instructor) really want to do is find out who learned the material and who didn't so that you can assign grades. You hope the students do well on the test because that means you did a good job teaching them. Therefore, most instructors will test the students on the most important material and skip what is less important.

Review both the text and the lecture notes. Pay attention to the topics your instructor stressed in class. Let's say the test will cover five chapters and will have fifty objective items (true-false, multiple choice, matching, and completion/short answer). The test will probably cover the fifty most obvious items. If you pick the seventy most obvious items to memorize, you will probably get an A. If the test will have five essay questions, and you pick the ten most obvious questions to prepare in advance, you should score very well.

Study Guide for Objective Tests

1. *Underline.* Let's say you have just finished reading the first section of a chapter as described in Step 2. Look it over, thinking about what is likely to be on the test and which of those things you might have trouble remembering. Underline or highlight *only those things.* Do not underline too much. The purpose of underlining is quick review for tests. If you underline too much, you will defeat your purpose.

2. *Make marginal notes.* In the margin, next to each idea you have underlined, write a note that you can use to test your memory. Don't write a summary. Write something you can use as a question. Another way of thinking about it is to consider the marginal note as the subject and the underlining as the main idea. Look at this example:

3 types of insomnia

It is convenient to distinguish <u>three main types of insomnia</u>. People with **onset insomnia** have trouble falling asleep. Those with **termination insomnia** awaken early and cannot get back to sleep. Those with **maintenance insomnia** awaken frequently during the night, though they get back to sleep each time. (From James Kalat, *Introduction to Psychology,* 4th ed., Brooks/Cole, 1996, p. 195.)

Notice that the marginal note doesn't give a definition. It only lets you test your memory.

3. *Flash cards.* Instead of, or in addition to marking in your book, you can use flash cards. On the front of the flash card, write what you would have put in the margin (the subject). On the back, write what you would have underlined (the main idea). Here is an example:

Front	Back
3 types of insomnia	1. Onset insomnia 2. Termination insomnia 3. Maintenance insomnia

Flash cards can easily be carried in a pocket or purse. One secret of successful study is to use small bits of time instead of waiting until you have a few hours free. For example, while you are eating lunch alone, standing in line, or riding the bus, you can be memorizing your flash cards. Look at the topic on the front, and test yourself to see if you remember what's on the back. If you get your memorization done in advance, you won't have much to worry about just before the exam.

Study Guide for Essay Tests

Essay questions are broader and more general than most objective questions. Therefore, you will have to look for important ideas rather than details when you predict the questions.

After you have predicted the questions, you have to put the answers in a form that can be memorized. This means making up pictures, or *graphic organizers*. A graphic organizer can be an outline, a study map, a chart, a time line, or whatever other visual form you can think of. They are just like the ones you already used in Unit II. You can put them on flash cards or paper, depending on the amount of room you need. Put the subject on the front and the graphic organizer on the back. If your graphic organizers are small enough to carry with you, you can use them like flash cards to take advantage of small bits of time you would otherwise waste.

Study Guide for Problem-Solving or Application Tests

Problem-solving tests often occur in mathematics and science courses. Application tests occur when you have to *use* what you've learned, as in foreign languages or music. In either case, try to predict the types of problems or performance that will be tested. Then make a plan to make sure you get enough practice to reach the level of mastery you need. For example, if you know the test will cover decimals, schedule enough time to practice decimals until you feel confident. If the test requires swimming the backstroke, schedule the number of practice sessions you will need.

Some tests require more than one type of preparation. For example, a Spanish test might require memorization of flash cards for vocabulary and grammar. It might also require application; it could test your reading or listening comprehension or your speaking ability in Spanish. Many instructors have both objective and essay questions on tests. In addition, some objective questions can test application or problem-solving ability. Here are some examples:

True or false: The product of 2 and 2 is 4. (True)

Multiple choice:
Which of the following is a complete sentence? (The answer is a.)

   a. Hurry up!

   b. Having a good day.

   c. Jimmy and his brother.

   d. All of the above.

Learning style

During your years in school, you probably liked some subjects better than others. The ones you liked were probably easier for you. Part of the reason is your learning style. For example, some people understand the logic of mathematics and science. Others enjoy the creativity of literature or art. Some people find it easy to memorize facts, but they hate to write essays. Others enjoy expressing themselves in words, but they hate to memorize. Some learn best from reading; they understand things better when they see them. Others learn best from lectures and discussions; they learn better from hearing.

Just as you have a learning style, each of your instructors also has a teaching style. Some prepare well-organized lectures and assignments. Others come to class without notes and teach through informal discussion. Some give tests that focus on memorizing facts. Others give tests that require you to analyze information and draw conclusions.

You will probably have little trouble when your learning style matches your instructor's teaching style. You are more likely to have problems when there is a mismatch. One of the best things you can do in that case is join a study group with people whose learning styles are more like the instructor's. For example, let's say you are studying for a history exam that will require analysis, and you have trouble with analysis. Try to find other students who can help you predict questions. Then you can make your graphic organizers and memorize.

Remember What's Important

In this step you memorize what is on your study guides for essay and objective tests, or you practice what is on your study guides for problem-solving and application tests.

Remembering

Some students try to memorize by reading the material they have underlined over and over, hoping something will stick. A better way to memorize is by self-testing. Test yourself the first time immediately after Step 3. If you cannot remember the material at this point, you probably won't remember it for a test.

If your study guide consists of underlining and marginal notes, cover the page and use the marginal notes to test your memory of what you have underlined. Pay attention to any points you miss. Keep self-testing until you remember everything.

If you are using flash cards, test yourself on the subject written on the front of the card. Put the cards away as you memorize them, so you don't keep retesting on those you already know. Try to have no more than ten to twenty cards to work on at one time. The night before the exam you should have just a few that still need reviewing. Review them before going to bed, get a good night's sleep, and review them again just before the test.

If you have broken the chapter into sections for Steps 2, 3, and 4, repeat the steps for each section until you reach the end of the chapter.

When you have finished a chapter, retest yourself on the marginal notes or flash cards for the whole chapter. Concentrate on what is most difficult, and keep testing until you reach mastery. If you are using graphic organizers, self-test the same way you would with flash cards. If you need to, you can draw each graphic organizer from memory and make sure it matches the original. If there are any study questions at the end of the chapter, answer them. Check your answers by looking back at the chapter. Review again about one week later and then as often as needed until the test. The more difficult the chapter, the more frequent the review should be. That way you won't have to cram for the test.

Practicing

If your study guide contains a plan or schedule for practicing for application or problem-solving tests, follow the study guide. Keep practicing until you reach mastery.

Make Use of What You Read—Take the Test

The following suggestions are good for taking all types of tests:

1. Arrive at the test on time. Bring pencils, blue books, a calculator, or whatever you need.

2. Look the test over and then look at the clock. Make a schedule that will give you the most points. For example, if you have to answer fifty multiple-choice questions in fifty minutes, make sure that after twenty-five minutes have gone by, you are somewhere near the twenty-fifth question. If there is an essay worth fifty points and fifty objective questions worth one point each, make sure you spend approximately half your time on the essay. Allow enough time to review the test before you turn it in.

3. Answer the easy questions first. Mark those you don't know and come back to them later. Unless there is a penalty for guessing, don't leave anything blank. If there is a penalty, find out what it is and figure out mathematically when you should guess. For example, let's say there are five multiple choices and 25 percent is deducted for each wrong answer (as on the SAT test). If you have absolutely no idea which choice is right, you have a 20 percent (one-fifth) chance of being right by making a wild guess. However, 25 percent (one-fourth of a point) is deducted if you're wrong. In that case, don't guess. If, however, you can eliminate one of the choices that you are sure is wrong, then you have a 25 percent chance of being right by guessing among the remaining four. Your reward for being right is equal to your penalty for being wrong. If you can eliminate two choices, then your odds increase to 33 percent (one-third). In that case, you should definitely guess.

Essay Tests

In addition to the skills already described, there are some special skills you need for essay tests.

1. *Follow the directions.* The topics you memorized by using your graphic organizers will be turned into test questions by your instructor. You will have to direct your answers in such a way that they answer what is asked. The following words are often used in the directions for essay tests. Review them carefully and be sure you know what they mean so you can do exactly what they say when you take a test.

List = make a list

Compare = show similarities

Contrast = show differences

Discuss = give an overview

Outline = make an outline

Enumerate = list with numbers

Trace = describe in order

Summarize = write the major ideas in a few words

Diagram = draw an illustration

Criticize = say what's wrong with it

Evaluate = give good and bad points

2. *Organize.* Before writing an essay, draw the outline, map, or other graphic organizer from your study guide. Write the essay from your graphic organizer; and use an introduction, conclusion, and signal words (*first, most important, finally*). If your essay is disorganized, the instructor will think you don't know the answer. If you really don't know the answer, write anything that comes to mind in the hopes that you will pick up a few points.

Application and Problem-Solving Tests

Follow the general directions given earlier. As with essay tests, if you don't know an answer or have not mastered a skill, and if credit is given for partial mastery, do whatever you can in the hopes of picking up a few points.

Evaluate Your ACT Skills—Analyze Test Results

When you get your test back, first make sure you understand your mistakes. Then analyze your test-taking skills. Answering the following questions will help you do better next time.

- Did you find out enough about the test? For example, did you study the right chapters, did you prepare for the right number and types of questions (essay, objective, problem-solving)? If not, ask more questions next time.

- Did you predict the right questions? If there were any questions you didn't expect, go back to the book and find out why you didn't anticipate them.

- Did you use good test-taking skills? Did you arrive on time with the right materials? Did you organize your time so you were able to answer all the questions and check them over before turning in the test?

- Did you remember the material you studied? If not, make better use of marginal notes, flash cards, and graphic organizers for self-testing.

- If there were essay questions, did you follow directions and organize your answers before beginning to write?

- If there were problem-solving or application questions, did you practice enough?

At first, you might not feel comfortable using the ACT system because it is new to you, but keep trying. By the end of this unit, you will find that your time and effort have been well spent.

13   Reading Textbook Illustrations

Vocabulary Preview

generalization (jen′ər əl i zā′shən): a broad inference drawn from specific instances

> *Example:* It is a generalization to say that women are more sensitive than men.

variable (ver′ē ə bəl): something that can change or vary

> *Example:* In a study that measures the effects of different types of instruction on reading achievement, the variables are (1) type of instruction and (2) reading achievement.

mean (mēn): an average

> *Example:* The highest annual average snowfall in the United States occurs in Stampede Pass, Washington, with a mean of 432.5 inches.

sustainable (sus tān′ə bəl): can be kept in existence; can be maintained or prolonged

> *Example:* The cheetah, the world's fastest land animal, can reach speeds of 70 mph, sustainable for only short distances.

residual (ri zid′joo əl): remaining

> *Example:* After the Vietnam War ended, many veterans had residual psychological effects, such as sleep disturbances.

cat, āte, fäther; pen, ēvil; if, kīte; nō, ôr, fōōd, book; boil, house; up, turn; chief, shell; thick, *the*; zh, treasure; ŋ, sing; ə for *a* in *about*; ′ as in *able* (ā′b′l)

Preread

Preview the following selection by reading all the headings, as well as everything in boldface and italics, and examining all the illustrations. For now, ignore the notes in the margin, which are for a later step. Answer the following questions without looking back at the reading.

1. What is the subject?

   _____

2. What is the main idea?

   _____

3. Now take a moment to think about textbook illustrations. Think about what you know about them, what you don't know, and what you might

find out from reading this selection. Make up three questions that might be answered by reading the selection.

a. _____

_____

b. _____

c. _____

Read

Read the selection without underlining.

◆ *Reading Textbook Illustrations*

Janet Maker

Sometimes a picture is worth a thousand words. Illustrations are added to textbooks to help readers understand what is written. If you can effectively "read" textbook illustrations, you will increase your comprehension and speed.

Since the ideas presented in illustrations are usually the most important ones, we recommend that you read the illustrations as part of your prereading step. This will introduce you to the main ideas before you read. Go over them again when you read the chapter, relating them to what you are reading. To get as much information from illustrations as possible, use the following steps.

Steps in Reading Textbook Illustrations

1. Identify the subject. Read the caption and look at the illustration. Who or what is it about?

2. Identify the main idea. Sometimes the main idea as well as the subject is stated in the caption. If not, you can infer the main idea by asking yourself, "What is the main thing the illustration is telling me about the subject?"

3. Pay attention to the details. Look at the keys, scales, symbols, and whatever other markings there are. Try to understand exactly what the illustration is telling you.

4. Think about what can be inferred. Are there any conclusions or generalizations that you can draw?

Margin notes:

Reason to read illus.

When to read illus.

4 steps in reading illus.

Types of Textbook Illustrations

The most common types include pictures, graphs, maps, diagrams, tables, and charts.

6 types of illus.

1. **Pictures** can be photographs, drawings, or cartoons. They are added to textbooks to give the reader a feeling for the subject. Look at Figure 1 and read the caption. Then answer the following questions.

   3 types of pictures
   Purpose of picture

   a. What is the subject?_____

   _____

   b. What is the main idea? _____

   _____

   c. What specific details do you notice? _____

   _____

   d. What inferences can you make about nuclear weapons? _____

   _____

   Sample Answers:

   a. The subject is Nagasaki after the A-bomb attack.

   b. The main idea is that the A-bomb has flattened everything in a huge area.

Figure 1 **Nagasaki after the A-bomb attack.**
Williams & Knight, *Healthy for Life,* Brooks/Cole, 1994, p. 16.29.

c. Specific details include the absence of anything sticking up in the central area and the size of the area.

d. Inferences can be drawn about the awesome powers of nuclear destruction. We can think about the risk of nuclear war and the nuclear risk as a deterrent to war, among other things.

What graphs show

3 types of graphs

2. **Graphs** show the relationship between two or more variables. Graphs are usually in the form of bars, pies, or lines. In Figure 2, the variables in the bar graph on the left are (1) mean income and (2) number of women. The variables in the pie graph on the right are (1) reasons women were not awarded child support and (2) the percent of cases for each reason. Look first at the bar graph and read the caption.

a. What is the subject?_____

_____

b. Now look at all the figures on the bar graph. What is the main idea?

_____

_____

Figure 2   Levels of Child Support and Alimony.
From Joan Ferrante, *Sociology, A Global Perspective,* 2nd ed., Wadsworth, 1995, p. 410.

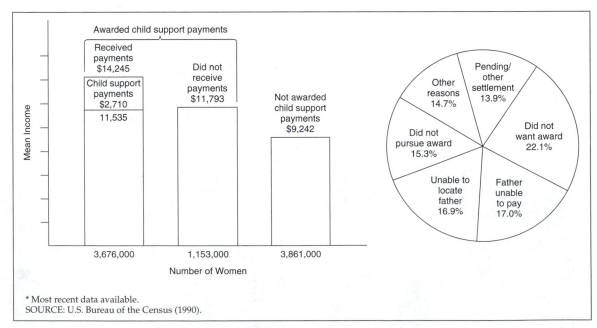

* Most recent data available.
SOURCE: U.S. Bureau of the Census (1990).

Left: Mean income of female-headed households with children under age 21 in 1987*
Right: Reasons women were not awarded child support as of spring 1988*

c. Details:

(1) Did most families receive child support? _____

(2) Which of the three groups is the poorest? _____

_____

(3) Of the group that received child support, what was the average

payment for the year? _____

d. What can you infer about child support? _____

_____

Sample Answers:

a. The subject is the mean income of female-headed households with children under age 21 in 1987.

b. The main idea is that most women received no child support payments. The poorest (and largest) of the three groups of women were not even awarded any child support.

c. (1) no

(2) the group not awarded child support payments

(3) $2710

d. You can infer that most women don't get any child support, and those who do don't get much.

Now look at the pie graph and read the caption.

e. What is the subject?_____

_____

f. What is the biggest reason women were not awarded child support?

_____

g. What do you think was the reason some women did not ask for

child support? _____

_____

_____

Sample Answers:

e. The subject is reasons why women were not awarded child support as of spring 1988.

f. Did not want award (22%)

g. One logical inference would be that asking for child support makes the process of divorce longer and more complicated. If the women thought that they weren't going to get anything anyway, they probably wouldn't bother to ask for it. Most likely, the fathers in these cases were unable to pay.

Figure 3 shows a line graph. Look at the graph and the caption and answer the following questions.

h. What are the two variables? _____

_____

i. What is the subject?_____

_____

j. What is the main idea? _____

_____

k. Details:

(1) How many metric tons were caught in about 1972?

_____

(2) What is the maximum sustainable yield?

_____

(3) How many metric tons were caught in 1980?

_____

l. What inferences can you make about the effects of this situation?

_____

Figure 3 **The Peruvian anchovy catch, showing the combined effects of overfishing and El Niño.** From Tom Garrison, *Essentials of Oceanography.* Wadsworth, 1995, p. 287.

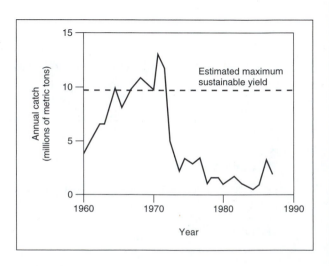

Sample Answers:

h. The two variables on the line graph are annual catch and year.

i. The subject is the effects of overfishing and El Niño on the Peruvian anchovy catch.

j. The main idea is that when the catch is greater than the maximum sustainable yield, there is a dramatic drop in the catch in future years, especially in years of El Ninõ.

k. (1) approximately 13 million

(2) approximately 10 million

(3) approximately 2 million

l. You might infer that overfishing, especially when combined with El Niño, can undermine a fishing industry.

3. **Maps** can show many different things, such as population, geography, history, politics, and streets. When reading a map, make sure you understand the caption, keys, and symbols. Look at Figure 4 and answer the following questions.

Types of maps

Captions, keys, and symbols

a. What is the subject?_____

_____

b. What is the main idea? _____

_____

c. Details:

(1) Look at the scale. Estimate the width of Africa at its widest point.

_____

(2) Look at the lines of latitude and longitude. What countries have colonies on the equator? _____

_____

(3) Look at the keys. What countries have colonies that export diamonds? _____

d. What can you infer about how Africa changed after World War I?

_____

_____

_____

_____

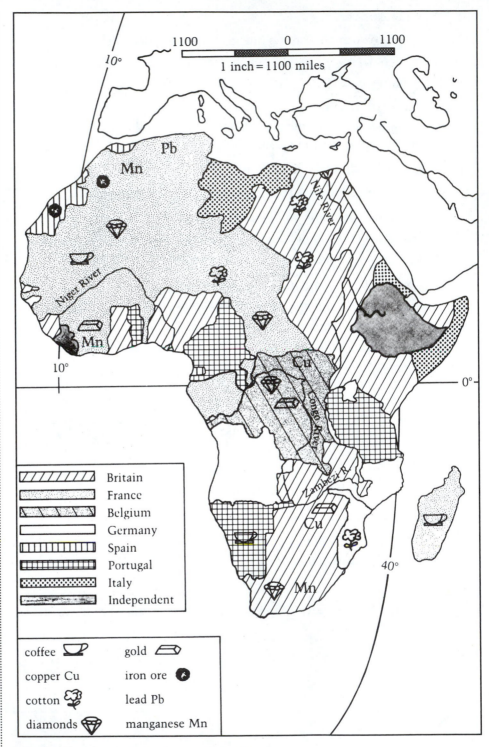

Figure 4 Colonial Africa before World War I.

Sample Answers:

a. The subject is colonial Africa before World War I.

b. The main idea is that Africa was carved up into colonies of European countries that were exploiting her natural resources.

c. (1) 4575 miles (your estimate should have been between 4000 and 5000)

(2) France, Portugal, Belgium, and Britain

(3) France, Belgium, and Britain

d. Since Africa is no longer controlled by colonial powers, there must have been a shift in power, possibly violent in some places. There are most likely some residual effects of colonial times, such as traces of European languages, laws, money, and racial tension.

4. **Diagrams** are drawings that explain something by showing its parts. Look at Figure 5 and answer the following questions.

Def. of diagrams

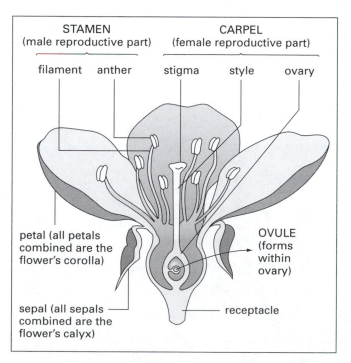

Figure 5 **Structure of a flower—a cherry blossom (*Prunus*).**
As is true of the flowers of many plants, it has a single carpel (a female reproductive part) and stamens (male reproductive parts). Flowers of other plants have two or more carpels, often united as a single structure. Single or fused carpels consist of an ovary and a stigma. Often the ovary extends upward as a slender column (style). From Cecie Starr, *Biology Concepts and Applications,* 3d ed., Wadsworth, 1997, p. 406.

a. What is the subject?_____

_____

b. What is the main idea? _____

_____

c. Details:

(1) What are the male parts?_____

(2) How many carpels does it have? _____

d. What can you infer about how this plant reproduces? _____

_____

Sample Answers:

a. The subject is the structure of a cherry blossom.

b. The main idea is that the cherry blossom has male and female reproductive parts.

c. (1) stamens (anthers and filaments)

   (2) one

d. You can infer that this plant can fertilize itself.

Def. of
tables

5. **Tables** show the arrangement of facts, usually in rows and columns. The multiplication table is an example. Look at Figure 6 and answer the following questions.

a. What is the subject?_____

_____

b. What is the main idea? _____

_____

c. Details:

(1) What was the date of the biggest spill?_____

(2) Where was the second biggest spill? _____

(3) How many millions of gallons did the *Exxon Valdez* spill? _____

d. What can you infer about oil spills?_____

_____

_____

_____

_____

The *Exxon Valdez* disaster of March 1989 was the worst in U.S. history: But when ranked with other massive oil spills involving both shipping and well disasters, it falls to the bottom of the top 21.

Date	Incident and Location	Size of Spill (millions of gallons)
3 June 1979	Well spill in Bay of Campeche off coast of Mexico	140
19–28 Jan. 1991	Discharged into Persian Gulf during Gulf War	126
4 Feb. 1983	Well spill at Nowruz, Iran, that dumped oil into Persian Gulf	80
6 Aug. 1978	Fire aboard *Castillo de Vellver,* off Cape Town, South Africa	78.5
16 March 1978	Tanker *Amoco Cadiz* ran aground off coast of France	68.7
19 July 1979	Collision of two ships off Trinidad and Tobago, *Atlantic Empress* and *Aegean Captain*	48.8
Aug. 1980	Leak at well No. D103, Libya	42
2 Aug. 1979	Wreck of *Atlantic Empress,* Barbados	41.5
23 Feb. 1980	Wreck of *Irenes Serenade,* Greece	36.6
20 Aug. 1981	Leak at Kuwait National Petrol Tank, Kuwait	31.2
15 Nov. 1979	Wreck of *Independence,* Istanbul, Turkey	26.9
25 May 1978	Leak at No. 126 well/pipe, Iran	28
Jan. 1993	Wreck, *Braer,* Northern Scotland	25
6 July 1979	Leak at British Petroleum storage tank, Nigeria	23.9
15 Aug. 1985	Wreck of *Nova,* Kharg Island, Persian Gulf	21.4
11 Dec. 1978	Leak at BP-Shell fuel depot, Zimbabwe	20
7 Jan. 1983	Wreck of *Assimi,* off Oman	15.8
12 June 1978	Tohoku Oil Co., Japan	15
31 Dec. 1978	Wreck of *Andros Patria,* Spain	14.6
10 Dec. 1983	Wreck of *Peracles,* Qatar	14
March 1989	Wreck of *Exxon Valdez,* Alaska	12.7

Figure 6 **The 21 Worst Oil Spills in History.**
Source: Oil Spill Intelligence Report; National Public Radio; *Los Angeles Times,* 28 Jan., 1991.

Sample Answers:

a. The subject is the 21 worst oil spills in history.

b. The main idea is that since 1978 there have been at least 21 disastrous oil spills.

c. (1) June 3, 1979

   (2) the Persian Gulf

   (3) 12.7

d. You can infer that during the period covered by the table, disastrous oil spills occurred rather frequently. You also notice that none of the major disasters occurred before 1978. Something must have changed about that time; possibly the use of supertankers began then.

6. **Charts** are information sheets. They include tables, diagrams, graphs, and maps. One type of chart that we see a lot lately is the **flowchart.** Flowcharts are sketches that show the steps in a process. Look at Figure 7 and answer the following questions.

Figure 7   Computer virus flowchart.

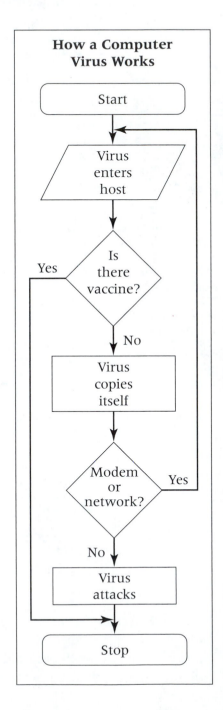

a. What is the subject?_____

b. What is the main idea? _____

_____

c. Details: There are four shapes in this flowchart: oval, parallelogram, diamond, and rectangle.

   (1) Which shape indicates the beginning or end of the process?

   _____

   (2) Which shape indicates input to the process or output from the process? _____

   (3) Which shape indicates a decision? (Look for the questions.)

   _____

   (4) Which shape indicates a step in the process?_____

d. What can you infer about the problem of a computer virus?_____

_____

Sample Answers:

a. The subject is how a computer virus works.

b. The main idea is that the computer virus works by infecting one computer and spreading to other computers via a modem or network.

c. (1) oval

   (2) parallelogram

   (3) diamond

   (4) rectangle

d. You can infer that a computer virus will keep spreading when there is no vaccine.

Another type of chart often seen in textbooks is the **time line.** A time line shows us the important events in the history of something. Look at Figure 8.

Def. of time line

e. What is the subject?_____

_____

f. What is the main idea? _____

_____

_____

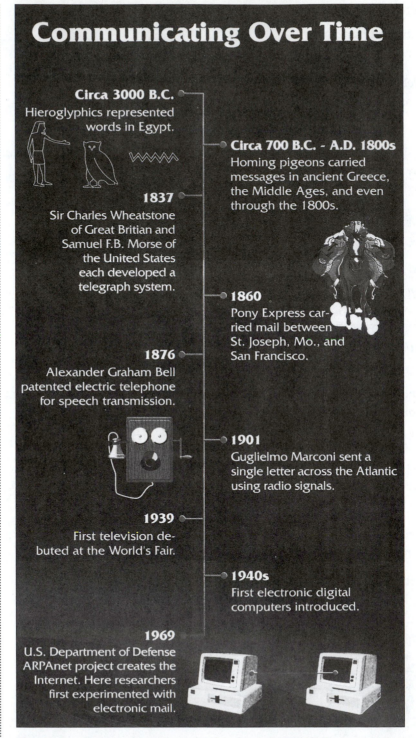

Figure 8 Changes in communication from Egyptian times to our own.

g. Details:

    (1) What happened in 3000 B.C.? _____

    (2) When was the Internet created?_____

    (3) Who sent the first radio signal across the Atlantic?

    _____

h. What can you infer about communications between 3000 B.C.

    and 1969? _____

    _____

Sample Answers:

e. The subject is the changes in communications between 3000 B.C. and 1969.

f. The main idea seems to be that the rate of change has sped up. There wasn't much change between 3000 B.C. and the early 1800s. There have been huge changes since then.

g. (1) use of hieroglyphics

    (2) 1969

    (3) Marconi

h. One thing we can infer is that the rate will continue to speed up.

1500 words

Analyze What You Read—Create a Study Guide

Objective Questions

1. Go back to the article and think about what would likely be on a test. Then think about whether or not you will remember it. *Underline only if (1) you think it will be on a test and (2) you don't think you will remember it.*

2. Since this is your first article for study reading, we have written the marginal self-test notes for you. You can use the notes as a guide to what should be underlined. Remember that the notes are like the subject and the underlining is like the main idea. If you prefer, you may write the self-test note on the front of a flash card and write what you would have underlined (change it into your own words) on the back.

Essay/Application Questions

Predict Essay Questions: There are two topics in this article important enough for essay questions. Write them here.

1. _____

2. _____

Make Graphic Organizers:

1. Prepare for an essay question on the four steps in reading textbook illustrations by filling in the following graphic organizer.

Front	Back

2. Prepare for an essay question on the types of textbook illustrations by drawing a sample of each one.

Type of Illustration	Drawing
Picture	
Bar graph	
Pie graph	
Line graph	

Map	
Diagram	
Table	
Flowchart	
Time line	

For explanation see p. 196

Skill Development: Start with the main idea. Then use the underlining, the marginal notes, and the graphic organizer to write a summary of the article. Use a separate sheet of paper.

Remember What's Important

STEP 4

Use the marginal self-test notes or the flash cards and the graphic organizers to memorize the material.

To use the marginal self-test notes, cover the page with your hand, look at the note, and see if you can give the answer. Remove your hand and check your answer. If it is not correct, do it again until it is correct.

To use flash cards, look at the topic on the front and try to give the answer. Check the answer on the back. If it is not correct, keep self-testing until you can remember it.

Use the first graphic organizer the same way as a flash card.

Use the second graphic organizer by covering up the right side and trying to remember the drawing for each type of illustration.

If it is easier or more fun for you to have someone else test you, that's fine. Have the person give you the topic and you give the answer. Remember to keep testing until you think you can remember everything for the Comprehension Check. Test yourself on the Vocabulary Preview words as needed.

Make Use of What You Read

When you are ready, complete the Comprehension Check on p. 369 and the Vocabulary Check on p. 371. Do not look back at the reading selection or the study guide.

Evaluate Your Active Critical Thinking Skills

After your tests have been graded, record your scores on the Progress Chart, p. 416, and answer the questions on the Evaluation Checklist on p. 417.

14   The Life Cycle of Romantic Relationships

Vocabulary Preview

consolidation (kən säl′ə dā′shən): making or becoming strong and stable

Example: When the ancient Romans conquered a new area of Europe or Africa, they sent out governors to <u>consolidate</u> that part of the empire.

deterioration (dē tir′ē ə rā′shən): making or becoming worse

Example: You have to spend time and money to maintain a house; otherwise it will show signs of <u>deterioration</u>.

stable (stā′bəl): firm; lasting

Example: Nowadays it's harder than it used to be to find a <u>stable</u>, well-paying job.

initial (i nish′əl): beginning; first

Example: Because <u>initial</u> impressions are important, you should dress carefully for a job interview.

status (stat′əs): position; rank

Example: People commonly strive for money and <u>status</u>.

cat, āte, fäther; pen, ēvil; if, kīte; nō, ôr, fo͞od, book; boil, house; up, turn; chief, shell; thick, *the*; zh, treasure; ŋ, sing; ə for *a* in *about*; ′ as in *able* (ā′b′l)

Preread

STEP 1

Preview the following selection by reading everything in italics. Examine the illustration. For now, ignore the notes in the margin, which are for a later step. Answer the following questions without looking back at the reading.

1. What is the subject of the reading?

   _____

2. What is the main idea of the reading?

   _____

3. Look at Figure 1.

   a. What is the subject of Figure 1?

   _____

   b. What is the main idea of Figure 1?

   _____

4. Now take a moment to think about romantic relationships. Think about what you know about them, what you don't know, and what you might

find out from reading this selection. Make up three questions that might be answered by reading the selection.

a. _____

_____

b. _____

_____

c. _____

_____

Read

STEP 2

Read the selection without underlining.

◆ *The Life Cycle of Romantic Relationships*

James W. Kalat

5 stages

Romantic relationships have a beginning, a middle, and sometimes an end. George Levenger believes that relationships go through five stages. First is attraction. Second is buildup. Third is continuation and consolidation. Fourth is deterioration. Last is the ending. Of course, not all relationships last long enough to go through all five stages.

Factors in initial attraction

First is the beginning, or *initial attraction.* Usually we have relationships with people we meet at school, at work, or near where we live. We are often attracted to people who are like us in age, social standing, financial status, family background, and physical appearance.

Buildup stage: description & stability

In the *buildup stage,* partners learn new things about each other. They tell each other very personal and even embarrassing information. Even at this point, the relationship may not be stable. In a study done at the beginning of the school year, 250 college students were asked to name their "closest, deepest" relationship. Almost half (47 percent) said that their closest, deepest relationship was with a romantic partner. We can take for granted that many of these partnerships were already in the buildup stage. But almost half of these couples broke up by the end of the college year.

Continuation stage

By the *continuation stage,* the relationship is more stable. It can be considered "middle aged." In this stage, the partners have worked out a complicated system of shared work and understandings. The first and second stages are over. The excitement of constantly discovering new things about each other has ended. Their emotions are not as aroused as they were. This

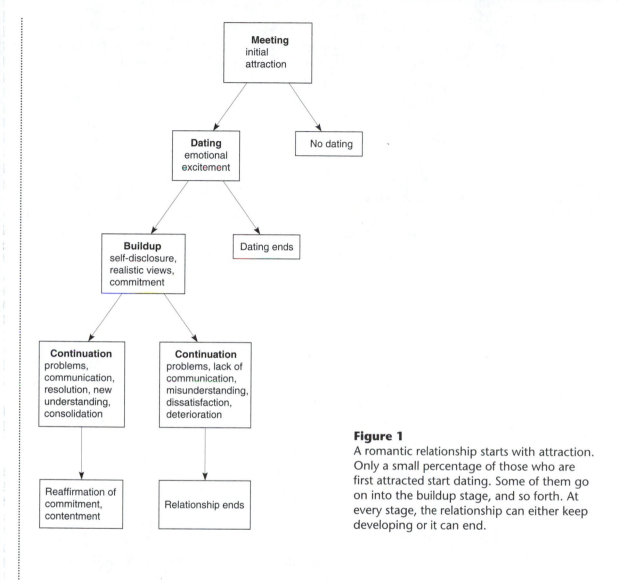

Figure 1
A romantic relationship starts with attraction. Only a small percentage of those who are first attracted start dating. Some of them go on into the buildup stage, and so forth. At every stage, the relationship can either keep developing or it can end.

does not mean that they have stopped loving each other. It is not always clear how much deep feeling remains in this type of mature relationship until there is a death or a separation of some other sort.

Although the partners in a successful mature relationship may not always be passionately involved with one another, they enjoy their closeness and the ease with which they can talk. John Gottman points out the difference between a successful and an unsuccessful marriage. In a successful marriage, the partners listen to each other carefully. They confirm each other's opinions. In an unsuccessful marriage, the partners nag, criticize, and complain but do not really listen.

Diff. between successful & unsuccessful marriage

Deterioration
stage
Exchange
theory

As time goes on, some relationships begin the *deterioration stage*. Why does this happen? One possible reason is found in exchange theory. This means that one of the partners has changed for better or for worse. Now the exchange between them is no longer fair to both. In a survey of 2,000 married couples, those who thought they were not getting their fair share out of the relationship were more likely to have an affair. (Or maybe it was the other way around. They may first have had an affair and then explained it by saying they had a bad marriage.)

4 ways to deal
with problems

How do partners in a relationship deal with problems? A study of college students found that they might react in one of four ways. First is *voice*. These couples talked about the problems and tried to work them out. Second is *loyalty*. These couples waited without saying anything in hopes that things would improve. Third is *neglect*. These couples allowed the relationship to deteriorate more. Fourth is *exit*. These couples left the relationship.

Ending stage

Men vs. women

Some relationships *end*. One partner may decide to end the connection before the other partner even realizes that there is any problem. Rarely do both partners agree to end the relationship at the same time. College men are usually less aware of problems than are college women. Therefore, the men are less likely to expect a breakup. When the breakup comes, the men seem more upset than the women. Maybe women think about relationships more. If they do, then they are more likely to prepare for what is ahead of them.

650 words

Analyze What You Read—Create a Study Guide

STEP
3

Objective Questions

1. Go back to the reading and underline what you think would likely be on a test.

2. We have written the marginal self-test notes for you, and you can use them as a guide to what should be underlined. If you prefer, you may use flash cards instead. Write the self-test note (the subject) on the front and what you have underlined (the main idea) on the back.

Essay/Application Questions

Predict Questions: One major topic would be likely to appear on an essay or application test. Write it here.

Make Graphic Organizers: Fill in the blanks on the following idea map.

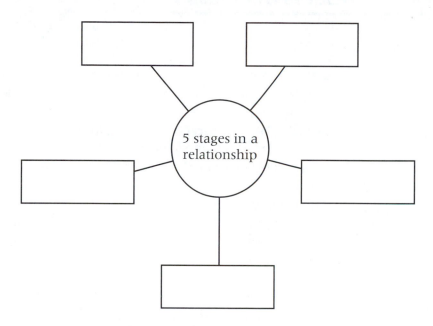

For explanation see p. 196

Skill Development: Use the underlining, the marginal notes, and the idea map as graphic organizers to write a summary of this reading. Use a separate sheet of paper.

Remember What's Important

Test yourself or have someone test you on the self-test notes or flash cards and on the graphic organizer. Keep testing until you know the material. Test yourself on the Vocabulary Preview words as needed.

Make Use of What You Read

When you are ready, complete the Comprehension Check on p. 373 and the Vocabulary Check on p. 375. Do not look back at the reading selection or the study guide.

Evaluate Your Active Critical Thinking Skills

After your tests have been graded, record your scores on the Progress Chart, p. 416, and answer the questions on the Evaluation Checklist on p. 417.

15   What Is Art Music?

Vocabulary Preview

stimulate (stim′yōō lāt′): to rouse or excite to activity or increased activity
Example: Alcohol can <u>stimulate</u> outgoing behavior in people who are usually quite shy.

sonata (sə nät′ə): a musical composition for one or two instruments, usually consisting of several movements
Example: Beethoven wrote his "Les Adieux" piano <u>sonata</u> as a way of saying goodbye to a friend.

cultivated (kul′tə vā′tid): developed
Example: Most people are not born appreciating caviar (fish eggs), escargot (snails), and calamari (squid); these tastes have to be <u>cultivated</u>.

gourmet (goor mā′): one who likes and is an excellent judge of fine foods and drinks
Example: In order to be a great chef, you first have to be a <u>gourmet</u>.

competent (käm′pə tənt): capable; fit
Example: If you have a broken water pipe, you want a <u>competent</u> plumber.

cat, āte, fäther; pen, ēvil; if, kīte; nō, ôr, fōod, book; boil, house; up, turn; chief, shell; thick, _the_; zh, treasure; ŋ, sing; ə for _a_ in _about_; ′ as in _able_ (ā′b′l)

Preread

STEP 1

Preview the following selection by reading the title, the headings, and the first sentence of each paragraph. Examine the illustration. For now, ignore the lines in the margin, which are for a later step. Answer the following questions without looking back at the reading.

1. What is the subject of the reading?

_____

2. What is the main idea of the reading?

_____

_____

3. Look at the cartoon.

  a. What is the subject of the cartoon?

_____

b. What is the main idea of the cartoon?

_____

_____

4. Now take a moment to think about art music. Think about what you know about it, what you don't know, and what you might find out from reading this selection. Make up three questions that might be answered by reading the selection.

a. _____

b. _____

c. _____

STEP 2

Read

Read the selection without underlining.

◆ *What Is Art Music?*

Charles R. Hoffer

The word *music* includes a great many different kinds of pieces that have been written for many different reasons. You already know many of the uses of music. In a movie, music in the background helps determine your mood. In a church or temple, music makes the ceremonies more effective. Some pieces of music promote unity in a group or in a country. The song "We Shall Overcome" is an example. It was sung by those working for civil rights in the 1960s. Some people use music or clothing or certain hair styles to help them feel a connection with a certain group. Teenagers who learn certain pieces of music because other teenagers like them are examples of this use of music. People use music as an outlet for deep feelings. Spirituals are examples of such music. At other times, people enjoy music just for fun. They might, for instance, sing "Ninety-Nine Bottles of Beer on the Wall" when riding a school bus. Many Americans use music as a background to activities such as studying, jogging, or driving a car. In some parts of the world, people use music along with physical work like paddling a canoe or gathering crops. All these uses of music have one thing in common. Music goes along with something else. It is not being listened to for itself.

1. _____
_____

One kind of music is different from those mentioned above. It exists *only* for the mental satisfaction it gives. This music is meant for careful

2. _____
_____

PEANUTS reprinted by permission of United Feature Syndicate, Inc.

listening. Those who are not musicians usually call it "classical music." Musicians call it "art music." People listen to art music because they enjoy hearing interesting combinations of sounds. They have no other reason for listening; art music exists only for itself. This is an idea that Schroeder cannot seem to get Lucy to understand in the "Peanuts" cartoon.

Many people are like Lucy. They cannot see that music can be important in and of itself. It is true that most things are made so people can use them. But art music and other *fine arts* are different. Painting, sculpture, poetry, literature, ballet, and music exist only for the interest people find in them. They have great importance for the mind, but they have no practical use.

3. _____
   _____

Why do people make things that stimulate only the mind? No one really knows, but there are some theories. Animals do not seem to possess the higher forms of thinking that would give them satisfaction from an art form. Nobody has yet discovered animal sonnets, animal sonatas, or animal sculptures.

The words *exist* and *live* represent a basic difference between humans and animals. People want to do more than exist. They want more than to survive in a cave or dig roots for food. They seek a richer, more satisfying life than that.

The arts are not human beings' only way of living instead of just existing. Recreation—playing tennis or cards, for example—is another attempt to enjoy life. There is, however, a difference between playing tennis and studying the arts. The arts call for a special kind of thinking. The arts make the person stand back and carefully consider the characteristics of an object. This type of thinking is different from recreation.

4. _____
_____

Why does the word *fine* get joined to the word *arts?* Start thinking back to when you were in elementary school. You decorated a paper plate, or you carved a figure on a potato in order to make a block print. Do you think these were works of art? Probably not. Why not? Weren't they the creations of a human being? Of course they were. But they weren't very good. Most other people could have done as well. The arts and craft project you made did not require much skill, loving care, or talent. You probably would not say that it was more than ordinary. In other words, it could not be considered "fine" or valuable. If nearly everyone can do something, it may be art, but it is not fine art. Symphonies and marble statues, skillfully created, are valuable. They can be considered "fine arts" because most people don't have the talent or energy to create them.

5. _____
_____

Why Learn About Art Music?

In a music appreciation class, you learn about melody, rhythm, and form. This information applies to almost all types of music. In a way, music is music. What you learn about one type helps you to understand other types.

6. _____
_____
_____

A piece of art music has to stand on its own. Listening to it requires far more care and thought than listening to other music. It requires more knowledge and listening skill to understand it and to enjoy it fully. Getting pleasure from art music is a "cultivated taste" like a fine gourmet dinner or a beautiful ancient Greek vase. Art music rarely reaches out to "grab" the listener who has little knowledge of it. It requires some education and getting used to. This is the second reason for studying art music.

There is a third reason. Because art music is created only to be listened to, it provides greater listening satisfaction and interest than music created for some other purpose. Because the composer does more things with the sounds, art music is more interesting and exciting to the listener.

"I Know What I Like"

7. _____
 _____
 _____
 _____

It's a fact that people usually like what they know. They keep away from what they don't know. If there is truth in the words "I know what I like," there is also truth in the phrase "I like what I know." This is partly because people don't hear unfamiliar types of music accurately or fully. They simply miss a lot the unfamiliar music has to offer. Another reason people prefer what they know is that they feel more comfortable and competent with it. An unfamiliar type of music may make you uncomfortable because you can't make much sense of it.

8. _____
 _____
 _____
 _____
 _____
 _____

The fact is that knowing something and liking it are two sides of the same coin. This is important for students of music. First, it means that you need to know something about a type of music before you decide whether or not you like it. In other words, be a student first. You can be a judge later when you have more information. Second, judge works of the same type. Don't try to compare a piano sonata with a song. Third, keep in mind the purpose of the music you are hearing. That knowledge will affect how you listen to it. Folk songs and concert music cannot be judged the same way.

1100 words

Analyze What You Read—Create a Study Guide

STEP 3

Objective Questions

1. Go back to the reading and underline what you think would likely be on a test.

2. Fill in the missing marginal self-test notes. To make this easier, all the self-test notes appear in random order below. Write each note on its correct lines in the reading. If you wish, you may write the self-test note on the front of a flash card, and paraphrase (write in your own words) the underlining (the answer) on the back.

Two reasons why many people don't like art music

Definition of art music

Three reasons to study art music

Seven uses of music

Reason for art

Difference between recreation and the arts

Definition of fine arts

Importance of the idea that knowing something and liking it are two sides of the same coin

Essay/Application Questions

Predict Essay Questions: Look at the headings as a guide to the three major points that the author makes about art music. Write them here.

1. _____

2. _____

3. _____

Make Graphic Organizers: Fill in the supporting details under each of the eight marginal notes that you made. You may look back at the reading.

   I. Uses of music

      A. _____

      B. _____

      C. _____

      D. _____

      E. _____

      F. _____

      G. _____

  II. Definition of art music _____

_____

 III. Reason for art _____

 IV. Difference between recreation and the arts _____

_____

   V. Definition of fine art _____

_____

 VI. Reasons to study art music

      A. _____

_____

      B. _____

      C. _____

VII. Reasons why many people don't like art music

    A. _____

    B. _____

VIII. Importance of the idea that knowing something and liking it are two sides of the same coin

    A. _____

    _____

    B. _____

    C. _____

| *For explanation see p. 196* |

Skill Development: Use the underlining, the marginal notes, and the graphic organizer to write a summary of the reading. Use a separate sheet of paper.

Remember What's Important

Test yourself or have someone test you on the marginal self-test notes or flash cards and on the graphic organizer. Keep testing until you know the material. Test yourself on the Vocabulary Preview words as needed.

Make Use of What You Read

When you are ready, complete the Comprehension Check on p. 377 and the Vocabulary Check on p. 379. Do not look back at the reading selection or the study guide.

Evaluate Your Active Critical Thinking Skills

After your tests have been graded, record your scores on the Progress Chart, p. 416, and answer the questions on the Evaluation Checklist on p. 417.

16   Stage Fright

Vocabulary Preview

reticence (ret′ə səns): the quality or state, or an instance, of being habitually silent or uncommunicative; not inclined to speak readily; reserved

Example: Shy students will show <u>reticence</u> about asking questions in class.

apprehension (ap′rē hen′shən): an anxious feeling of foreboding; dread

Example: I feel <u>apprehension</u> before going to the dentist.

cognitive (käg′nə tiv): having to do with knowing in the broadest sense, including perception, memory, and judgment

Example: A <u>cognitive</u> psychologist tries to get you to change your beliefs in order to change your life.

cope (kōp): to deal with problems, troubles, etc.

Example: We can be sure that life will give us plenty of difficulties to <u>cope</u> with.

hyperventilate (hī′pər vent′ə lāt): to breathe extremely rapidly or deeply, which may cause dizziness, fainting, etc. as a result of a rapid loss of carbon dioxide

Example: Some people <u>hyperventilate</u> when they are afraid.

lackadaisical (lak′ə dā′zi kəl): showing lack of interest or spirit; listless; languid

Example: A <u>lackadaisical</u> attitude about turning in assignments will hurt your grade point average.

impairment (im per′mənt): injury, weakness, damage

Example: Prolonged high fever can leave a person with permanent mental <u>impairment</u>.

devastating (dev′əs tāt′iŋ): overwhelming; destructive

Example: Criticism from a teacher can be <u>devastating</u> to a child.

dissipate (dis′ə pāt′): to drive completely away; make disappear

Example: The flu can <u>dissipate</u> your strength.

revision (ri vizh′ən): the act, process, or work of reading over carefully and correcting, improving, or updating where necessary

Example: Most manuscripts require <u>revision</u>.

adversity (ad vur′sə tē, əd-): an instance of misfortune; calamity

Example: Hard work is needed to overcome <u>adversity</u>.

visualize (vizh′oo əl īz′): to form a mental image of (something not present to the sight, an abstraction, etc.)

Example: Some people believe that it helps to <u>visualize</u> a goal—to picture yourself driving a Ferrari, for example.

implement (im′plə mənt): to carry into effect; fulfill; accomplish

Example: It's easy to make New Year's resolutions, but not so easy to implement them.

debilitating (dē bil′ə tāt′iŋ, di-): making weak or feeble; enervating

Example: Migraine headaches are debilitating.

perception (pər sep′shən): mental grasp of objects, qualities, etc. by means of the senses; awareness; comprehension

Example: Conflicts can occur when one person's perception of a situation is different from another person's.

cat, āte, fäther; pen, ēvil; if, kīte; nō, ôr, fōōd, book; boil, house; up, turn; chief, shell; thick, *the*; zh, treasure; ŋ, sing; ə for *a* in *about*; ' as in *able* (ā′b'l)

Preread

Preview the following selection by reading the title and the numbered, italicized sentences. For now, ignore the lines in the margin, which are for a later step. Answer the following questions without looking back at the reading.

1. What is the subject?

   _____

2. What is the main idea?

   _____

3. Take a moment to think about stage fright. Think about what you know, what you don't know, and what you might find out from reading the selection. Make up three questions that might be answered by reading the selection.

   a. _____

   _____

   b. _____

   c. _____

Read

Read the selection without underlining.

◆ *Stage Fright*

Rudolf F. Verderber

P eople are likely to feel nervous about giving speeches. Whether you label your feeling as nervousness or as stage fright, speech fright, shyness, reticence, speech apprehension, or some other term, the meaning of that feeling is essentially the same: a fear or anxiety about public speaking.

People's public-speaking nervousness is usually a function of either a trait or a state. A *trait* is a relatively ongoing characteristic of an individual; a *state* is the state of mind that a person experiences for a period of time.

1. _____
_____
_____

Nervousness is a trait when a person experiences a fear of any kind of communication. Those of us with trait nervousness are likely to experience similar fears in friendly conversations, group meetings, and public speaking, as well as in such mass-media situations as television, radio, or film. Research has shown that up to 20 percent of the population may experience trait communication nervousness.

2. _____
_____
_____

In contrast, public-speaking nervousness is a state when it is directed only to public speaking. For instance, many people who experience no apprehension at communicating on a one-to-one basis with peers, relatives, or authority figures may experience considerable fear of public speaking. State apprehension, especially public-speaking apprehension, is quite common. As much as 80 percent of the population admits to at least some public-speaking nervousness. If you have no major problems in interacting with people in other communication situations, your nervousness at the thought of giving a speech is likely to be less of a problem than you might think.

3. _____
_____
_____

Public-speaking nervousness may be cognitive (in the mind) or behavioral (physically displayed). Cognitively, speaker nervousness comes at the thought of speaking in public. People who say they are fearful of talking in public make negative predictions about the results of their speaking. People who experience fear may recognize the importance of having their ideas heard, but in their mind, any benefits that might come from giving a speech are far outweighed by the fear itself. Behaviorally, speaker nervousness is represented by such physical manifestations as stomach cramps, sweaty palms, dry mouth, and the use of such filler expressions as "um," "like," and "you know." At times, the behavior is an avoidance of speaking in public or speaking for the shortest time possible when required to speak.

4. _____
_____
_____

To help cope with this nervousness, keep in mind that fear is not an either-or matter—it is a matter of degree. Relatively few people experience such a small degree of nervousness about public speaking that they don't seem to notice it; likewise, an even smaller number are so afraid of speaking in public that they become tongue-tied, break out in hives, or hyperventilate at the thought. Most of us are somewhere between these two extremes.

5. _____
_____
_____

In other words, the fear of speaking in public is normal. The more important question is whether it is harmful. In all the years I have been teaching, I have had only one case of a person who began his speech normally, but after the first sentence literally ran back to his seat. Over the years, I have also had students who were obviously suffering discomfort at having to stand in front of the audience. Many of us wish that we could speak without these obvious reactions. But would we really be better off if we could be totally free from nervousness? Gerald Phillips, a speech scholar who has been studying public-speaking nervousness for more than twenty years, says no. Phillips has noted that "learning proceeds best when the organism is in a state of tension." In fact, it helps to be a little nervous to do your best: If you are lackadaisical about giving a speech, you probably will not do a good job.

6. _____
_____
_____

Because at least some tension is constructive, our goal is not to get rid of nervousness but to learn how to cope with our nervousness. Phillips cites results of studies that followed groups of students with speaker nervousness for one- and three-year intervals after instruction in dealing with their nervousness. Almost all the students had learned to cope with the nervousness, but they still experienced the same level of tension. Phillips goes on to say that "apparently they had learned to manage the tension; they no longer saw it as an impairment, and they went ahead with what they had to do."

So, we can conclude that nearly everyone who speaks in public, whether for the first or fiftieth time, experiences some nervousness. Now let's look at some factors to consider as you prepare your first speech.

7. _____
_____
_____

1. *Despite nervousness, you can make it through your speech.* Very few people are so bothered that they are unable to function. You may not enjoy the "flutters" you experience, but you can still deliver an effective speech.

The question is whether nervousness causes poor speech performance *or* poor speech performance causes nervousness, or are both statements accurate? Experience teaches us that some people who are nervous about speaking do find that the nervousness itself hurts their performance. But we have enough cases of famous performers who confessed nervousness but performed at high levels that we have to conclude that nervousness itself does not necessarily hurt performance. Helen Hayes, a classic actress, and Abraham Lincoln both confessed to great nervousness before facing an audience, yet in neither case was their performance hampered by the nervousness.

What my experience has shown is that many more people get nervous as a result of poor performance. So, the goal is to help students master the public-speaking skills that will enable them to perform competently regardless of how they may feel about it.

2. *Listeners are not as likely to recognize your fear as you might think.* The thought that audiences will notice an inexperienced speaker's fear often increases that fear. Thoughts that an audience will be quick to laugh at a speaker who is hesitant or that it is just waiting to see how shaky a person appears can have devastating effects. But the fact is that members of an audience, even speech instructors, greatly underrate the amount of stage fright they believe a person has.

3. *The better prepared you are, the better you will cope with nervousness.* Many people show extreme nervousness because either they are not well prepared or they think they are not well prepared. According to Gerald Phillips, a positive approach to coping with nervousness is "(1) learn how to try, (2) try, and (3) have some success." If you become well prepared for your speeches you will have more successful efforts. As you learn to recognize when you are truly prepared, you will find yourself paying less attention to your nervousness. A recent study reinforces previous research indicating "that students' self-perceived public speaking competency is indeed an important predictor of their public speaking anxiety."

4. *The more experience you get in speaking, the better you can cope with nervousness.* Beginners experience some fear because they do not have experience speaking in public. As you give speeches, and see improvement in those speeches, you will gain confidence and worry less about any nervousness you might experience. A recent study of the impact of basic courses on communication apprehension found that experience in a public-speaking course was able to reduce students' communication apprehension scores.

5. *Experienced speakers learn to channel their nervousness.* The nervousness you feel is, in controlled amounts, good for you. It takes a certain amount of nervousness to do your best. What you want is for your nervousness to dissipate once you begin your speech. Just as soccer players are likely to report that the nervousness disappears once they engage in play, so too should speakers find nervousness disappearing once they get a reaction to the first few sentences of their introduction.

Specific Behaviors

8. _____
   _____
   _____

The following are some specific behaviors that speakers can use to control nervousness. Coping with nervousness begins during the preparation process and extends to the time a speaker actually begins the speech.

1. *Pick a topic you are comfortable with.* The best way to control nervousness is to pick a topic you know something about, one that is important to you, and one that you know (as a result of your audience analysis) your audience is likely to respond to. Public speakers cannot allow themselves to be saddled with a topic they do not care about. An unsatisfactory topic lays the groundwork for a psychological mind-set that almost guarantees nervousness at the time of the speech. By the same token, having a topic you know about and that is important to you lays the groundwork for a satisfying speech experience.

2. *Take time to prepare fully.* If you back yourself into a corner and must find material, organize it, write an outline, and practice the speech all in an hour or two, you almost guarantee failure and destroy your confidence. On the other hand, if you do a little work each day for a week before the assignment, you will experience considerably less pressure and increased confidence.

Experience in preparation and the length and difficulty of the speech will affect your schedule. For instance, experienced speakers often begin research a month before the date they are to give the speech; they then reserve an entire week for rehearsal and revision.

Giving yourself enough time to prepare fully includes sufficient time for rehearsal. Practice your first speech at least two or three times. Your goal is to build habits that will control your behavior during the speech itself. If our national love affair with big-time athletics has taught us anything, it is that careful preparation enables athletes (or speakers) to meet and overcome adversity. Among relatively equal opponents, the winning team is the one that is mentally and physically prepared for the contest. When an athlete says "I'm going into this competition as well prepared as I can possibly be," he or she is more likely to do well. In this regard, speechmaking is like athletics. If you assure yourself that you have carefully prepared and practiced your speech, you will do the kind of job of which you can be proud.

3. *Try to schedule your speech at a time that is psychologically best for you.* When speeches are being scheduled, you may be able to choose the time. Are you better off "getting it over with"—that is, being the first person to speak that day? If so, volunteer to go first. But regardless of when you speak, do not spend time thinking about yourself or your speech. At the moment the class begins, you have done all you can do to be prepared. Focus your mind on the other speeches and become involved with what each speaker is saying. Then when your turn comes, you will be as relaxed as possible.

4. *Visualize successful speaking experiences.* Visualization involves developing a mental strategy and picturing yourself implementing that strategy. How many times have you said to yourself, "Well, if I had been in that situation I would have . . ."? Such statements are a form of visualization. Joe Ayres and Theodore S. Hopf, two scholars who have conducted extensive research on visualization, have found that if people can visualize themselves going through an entire process, they have a much better chance of succeeding when they are in the situation. With visualization, not only do people seem to be able to lower general apprehension, but they also report fewer negative thoughts when they actually speak. Successful visualization begins during practice periods. For instance, if during a practice you not only say "So, you can see how the shape of the wing gives a plane lift," but you also see members of the audience nodding, you are visualizing successful response.

Finally, when your turn comes, walk to the speaker's stand confidently. Research indicates that your fear is most likely to be at its greatest right before you walk forward to give your speech and when you have your initial contact with the audience. As you walk to the speaker's stand, continue to visualize success: Remind yourself that you have good ideas, that you are well prepared, and that your audience wants to hear what you have to say. Even if you make mistakes, the audience will profit from your speech.

5. *Pause for a few seconds before you begin.* When you reach the stand, stop a few seconds before you start to speak. Take a deep breath while you make eye contact with the audience; that may help get your breathing in order. Try to move about a little during the first few sentences; sometimes a few gestures or a step one way or another is enough to break some of the tension.

Persistent Nervousness

9. _____
_____
_____

When is speaker nervousness a real problem? When it becomes debili-tating—when the fear is so great that a person is unable to go through giving a speech. Recent research has shown that a small number of students are adversely affected by their feelings about speaking. Unfor-tunately, many of those students respond by dropping the course. But that is not an answer to speech anxiety. In all areas of life, people have to give speeches—they have to get up before peers, people from other organiza-tions, customers, and others to explain their ideas. Although it is never too late to get help, a college speech course is the best time to start working on coping with speech nervousness. Even if your fears prove to be more perception than reality, its important to take the time to get help.

To start, see your professor outside class and talk with him or her about what you are experiencing. Your professor should be able to offer ideas for people you can see or programs you can attend. Research in communication apprehension shows that some people do need special programs. One of the most popular programs is systematic desensitization, which repeatedly exposes people to the thing they fear, associating it each time with something pleasant. Another program is cognitive restruc-turing, which helps people to identify the illogical beliefs they hold and provides individualized instruction in changing their beliefs. Over time, people can condition themselves to overcome their fears and take a more positive approach to their communication. Many communities offer such programs.

But keep in mind that there are very few speech students who have been so hurt by fear that they can't deliver a speech. The purpose of a speech course is to help you learn and develop the skills that will allow you to achieve even when you feel extremely anxious.

2400 words

Analyze What You Read—Create a Study Guide

STEP 3

Objective Questions

1. Go back to the reading and underline what you think would be on a test.

2. Fill in the missing marginal self-test notes. You should be able to use the marginal notes to test yourself on everything you underlined. To make this easier, all the self-test notes appear in random order. Write each note

on the correct lines in the reading selection. If you wish, you may write the self-test note on the front of a flash card and paraphrase the underlining on the back.

Goal

Trait vs. state

Cognitive vs. behavioral nervousness

Five specific behaviors

Percent of trait nervousness

Normality of stage fright

Coping with debilitating nervousness

Five factors to consider

Percent of state nervousness

Essay/Application Questions

Predict Essay Questions: Look at your marginal notes and pick three topics that would be broad enough for essay questions. Write them here.

1. _____

2. _____

3. _____

Make Graphic Organizers:

1. Fill in the following chart with a definition for each term. You may look back at the reading.

Trait nervousness	
State nervousness	
Cognitive nervousness	
Behavioral nervousness	

2. Fill in the rectangles on the idea map.

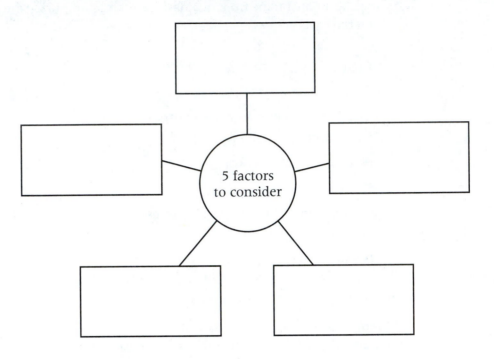

3. Fill in the rectangles on the idea map.

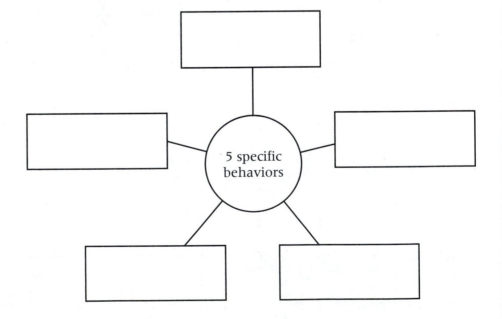

For explanation
see p. 196

Skill Development: Use the underlining, the marginal notes, and the graphic organizers to write a summary of the reading selection. Use a separate sheet of paper.

Remember What's Important

Test yourself or have someone test you on the marginal self-test notes or flash cards and the graphic organizers. Keep testing until you know the material. Test yourself on the Vocabulary Preview words as needed.

Make Use of What You Read

When you are ready, complete the Comprehension Check on p. 381 and the Vocabulary Check on p. 383. Do not look back at the reading selection or the study guide.

Evaluate Your Active Critical Thinking Skills

After your tests have been graded, record your scores on the Progress Chart, p. 416, and answer the questions on the Evaluation Checklist on p. 417.

17   Identity

Vocabulary Preview

social psychology (sō'shəl sī käl'ə jē): the study of the behavior of individuals in groups
Example: The willingness of some soldiers to commit murder and torture when commanded to do so is an issue studied in social psychology.

dictator (dik'tā tər): a ruler with absolute power
Example: Ugandan dictator Idi Amin nearly destroyed his country.

solitary confinement (sal'ə ter'ē kən fīn'mənt): being held in a cell away from other people
Example: Because most prisoners are afraid of solitary confinement, wardens can use it to make them behave.

exhibit (eg zib'it): to show
Example: If you are attacked and cannot get away, you should not exhibit fear; you are safer if you fight back.

socialization (sō'shəl ī zā'shən): the process of learning to fit into social groups
Example: Socialization is learned by living in families, going to school, and going to church.

cat, āte, fäther; pen, ēvil; if, kīte; nō, ôr, fo͞od, book; boil, house; up, turn; chief, shell; thick, *the*; zh, treasure; ŋ, sing; ə for *a* in *about*; ' as in *able* (ā'b'l)

Preread

STEP 1

Preview the following selection by reading the title, headings, and first sentence of each paragraph. Examine the illustrations. For now, ignore the lines in the margin, which are for a later step. Answer the following questions without looking back at the reading.

1. What is the subject of the reading?

_____

2. What is the main idea of the reading?

_____

3. Look at Figure 1.

a. What is the subject of Figure 1?

_____

b. What is the main idea of Figure 1?

_____

_____

4. Take a moment to think about your identity. Think about what you know about it, what you don't know, and what you might find out from reading the selection. Make up three questions that might be answered by reading the selection.

a. _____

b. _____

c. _____

STEP 2

Read

Read the selection without underlining.

◆ *Identity*

Earl Babbie

In the early 1970s, a group of psychologists at Stanford University in California carried out an experiment which turned out in ways that were not expected. The Stanford Prison Experiment was carried out under the direction of Dr. Philip Zimbardo. The experiment was designed to gain information about the social psychology of prison life.

1. _____
_____
_____
_____
_____

First Zimbardo asked Stanford students to volunteer to act out the part of prisoners or guards. He was careful to screen the volunteers and choose only those he judged "normal." Zimbardo felt he chose the students who were "the cream of the crop of this generation." By flipping a coin, it was decided which of the two dozen students would serve as prisoners and which would serve as guards.

The experiment began smoothly. The "prisoners" were picked up without notice at their homes. They were taken away in handcuffs to be booked. Later, they were assigned to their "cells" in the basement of a building on campus. The "guards" had the job of developing their own rules to keep law and order.

Early in the experiment, Zimbardo found that the guards were taking their jobs too seriously. They tended to become dictators to their prisoners. Some even showed cruelty. Not all the guards became cruel dictators, but

2. _____
_____
_____

Zimbardo noticed that none of the "good" guards ever tried to interfere with the cruelty of the "bad" guards.

The prisoners began to act like real prisoners, too. Some started causing trouble. They shouted names at the guards. Some went in the other direction, meekly following all the guards' orders. The prisoners had begun with a feeling of good-natured unity. However, the guards broke that down. At one point, the guards decided to put one prisoner in solitary confinement because he would not eat. Then they offered the other prisoners a choice: if they would give up their blankets for the night, the prisoner in "the hole," a small closet, would be brought back to his cell. Not one of the prisoners offered to give up his blanket.

Three prisoners had to be freed during the first four days. The experiment was too much for them. Later, the other prisoners begged to be let out of the experiment. Most were willing to give up the fifteen dollars a day they had already earned.

Zimbardo was shocked by the changes in the students. He was also amazed by his own reactions. He had made himself the prison superintendent. When he heard a rumor that a fraternity was planning to raid the prison to free the prisoners, he panicked. At first he called the local police to see if they would lock up his prisoners for safekeeping. "You want us to do what?" was the response he got. So Zimbardo secretly moved the prisoners to another room on the campus. There he kept them handcuffed to each other all night.

Now Zimbardo became aware how fully he and the students were playing their parts. He realized that the experiment had become dangerous. As a result, he ended the experiment early—after only six of the fourteen days. In addition, Zimbardo felt it important to offer counseling for the students. He needed to undo some of the learning that had taken place during the experiment.

More than anything else, the Stanford Prison Experiment showed how our behavior changes according to the situation we are in and the parts we are called upon to play. We can assume that each student had at some time seen something on television and in movies about prison life. But this knowledge did not really account for the students' behavior. There was something about being in a prison—even a make-believe one—that brought out the same kinds of behavior exhibited by real prisoners and real guards in real prisons.

The Stanford Prison Experiment suggests some deeper questions—questions of human identity. Who are you? Who am I? What is a human being?

Who Are You?

Let us explore the question "Who am I?" You have a sense that you *are*. But who or what is it that you are? The answers you discover when you examine this question may be of great personal interest to you. In 1954, Manford Kuhn and Thomas McPartland made up a questionnaire to determine the answer to this. Their very simple questionnaire asked college students to write down twenty answers to the question, "Who am I?" Over the years, thousands and thousands of students have completed the Twenty-Statement Test (TST), as it is called. Certain patterns have been discovered in their answers.

3. _____

_____

_____

Take a minute to consider how you would answer the test. You might even want to take a few more minutes and write down twenty answers to "Who Am I?"

If you are like most people, the first answers would describe the *statuses* you hold. You might first have answered "student." Or perhaps you said "man" or "woman." Some people answer by giving their race or their religion. Some give their age. They are naming some of their own characteristics.

Usually, those who reply to the questionnaire go a step further. They describe themselves in ways that might be more of an opinion: "I am a happy person." "I am overweight." "I am conservative." Although others might not agree with the characteristics we think suit us, these answers are also examples of statuses.

Statuses and Roles

Status is a basic idea in sociology. It refers to a *position* or *location* that a person holds within society or within a smaller social group. Mother, plumber, sophomore, safecracker are all types of statuses. Each member of a society has a part to play. More exactly, we should say that statuses have functions to serve. These functions are usually the roles that are connected with and expected of a status. If you have the status of mother, for instance, certain kinds of behavior are expected of you, behaviors that would not be expected of a plumber.

4. _____

_____

_____

To sum it up, a status is a position in society. Roles are the behaviors expected of each status. We hold statuses and act out roles. Often, statuses come in pairs. In other words, the roles expected of us are in relation to other statuses we hold. Each status is like a mask we hold up when we interact with others. (See Figure 1.) Thus, if you and I met, we might hold up the status/masks "student" and "professor."

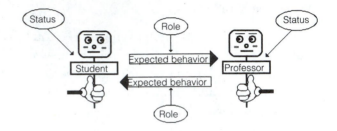

Figure 1
Statuses as masks.

There are no absolute rules for the behavior between professors and students. However, all of us who have held either or both statuses have some understanding of what is expected. At the least, we know that the expectations are very different from the interaction between a mother and her son, a prisoner and a guard, or a salesperson and a shopper. If you and I were to meet for the first time, we would try to discover the statuses we hold in relation to each other. Then we would behave according to those statuses.

In real life, of course, each of us occupies a number of statuses. We act out the parts of different statuses in different situations. In some situations, it might be correct for you to act out the role of son or daughter. At other times, "student" would be your correct role. At still other times, you act out the status of a driver, a shopper, a citizen, or a friend. Figure 2 shows a set of statuses that a particular person might occupy.

Notice the question mark in the center of Figure 2. It represents the person who is holding the masks, occupying the different social statuses. The question mark, in some sense, is *you,* so keep asking who you are as we go on.

Both of the two figures are very over-simplified. For example, each status you occupy has role relationships with many other statuses.

Figure 2
We each occupy several statuses.

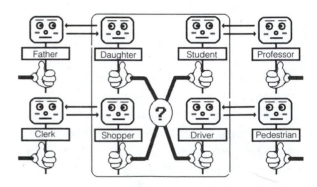

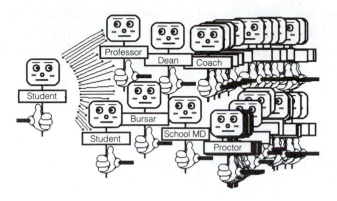

Figure 3
Each status relates to many other statuses.

Therefore, a college student is expected to behave a certain way with professors, with other students, with deans, with coaches, with those overseeing exams, and so forth. Figure 3 shows these roles and statuses and their interactions.

If we put everything together, we see that each individual occupies many, many statuses. Each status has role expectations that are relative to several other statuses. Take a minute to think about all the statuses you occupy and all the other statuses each of them relates to. You may be impressed by how much you have learned about being a person in an organized society. Figure 4 gives an over-simplified picture of the playing field for being a human being who happens to be a female attorney.

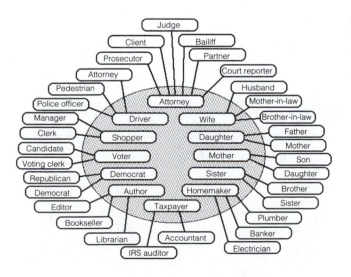

Figure 4
The playing field for being human.

5. _____
   _____
   _____

An important part of growing up and of socialization involves your learning the statuses you hold. It also involves learning the expectations of each role related to each status, and your relationship with other people holding other statuses. There is never an end to this learning. Once you figure out the rules of being a child, you find yourself playing the part of a teenager. Once you get that down pat, you find you have moved on to "responsible adult." Sooner or later, you may hear people say, "Act your age, you old coot!" No matter how you feel inside, the statuses you hold determine how others expect you to act. This is true no matter what your age.

1600 words

STEP
3

Analyze What You Read—Create a Study Guide

Objective Questions

1. Go back to the reading and underline what you think would be on a test.

2. Fill in the missing marginal self-test notes. To make this easier, all the self-test notes appear in random order below. Write each note on its correct lines in the reading. If you wish, you may write the self-test note on the front of a flash card and paraphrase the underlining on the back.

   Findings of the Stanford Prison Experiment

   TST

   Socialization

   Stanford Prison Experiment (who, what, where, when, why?)

   Definition of statuses and roles

Essay/Application Questions

Predict Essay Questions: Look at the headings as a guide. There are two topics big enough for essay questions. Write them here.

1. _____

2. _____

Make Graphic Organizers: Fill in the following chart. You may look back at the reading.

Stanford Prison Experiment

Status	Behaviors they assumed
Guards	
Prisoners	
Prison superintendent	

For explanation see p. 196

Skill Development: Use the underlining, the marginal notes, and the graphic organizer to write a summary of the reading. Use a separate sheet of paper.

Remember What's Important

Test yourself or have someone test you on the marginal self-test notes or flash cards and on the graphic organizer. Keep testing until you know the material. Test yourself on the Vocabulary Preview words as needed.

Make Use of What You Read

When you are ready, complete the Comprehension Check on p. 385 and the Vocabulary Check on p. 386. Do not look back at the reading selection or the study guide.

Evaluate Your Active Critical Thinking Skills

After your tests have been graded, record your scores on the Progress Chart, p. 416, and answer the questions on the Evaluation Checklist on p. 417.

18   AIDS: A Crisis of Our Time

Vocabulary Preview

implications (im'pli kā'shənz): things implied, from which inferences may be drawn

Example: The people's conservative vote has many <u>implications</u> for how they want the country run.

differentiate (dif'ər en'shē āt'): to perceive or express the difference in; distinguish between; discriminate

Example: Expert chefs can <u>differentiate</u> by taste all the ingredients in a particular dish.

vulnerable (vul'nər ə bəl): open to attack

Example: Not getting the proper rest and nutrition makes you <u>vulnerable</u> to colds and flu.

ultimately (ul'tə mit lē): finally; at last; in the end

Example: We can try to blame others, but <u>ultimately</u> we have to take responsibility for what happens to us.

intravenous (in'trə vē'nəs): in, or directly into, a vein or veins

Example: Nobody enjoys getting <u>intravenous</u> injections.

antibody (an'ti bäd'ē, -tə-): a specialized protein produced by certain lymphocytes, esp. in response to the presence of an antigen, to neutralize, thus creating immunity to, specific antigens; immunoglobulin

Example: A vaccination creates immunity to a disease by causing the formation of <u>antibodies</u>.

misconception (mis'kən sep'shən): incorrect interpretation; misunderstanding

Example: The old belief that the earth was flat was a <u>misconception</u>.

lulled (luld): brought into a specified condition by soothing and reassuring

Example: The con artist <u>lulled</u> his victims into a false sense of security.

discriminate (di skrim'i nāt'): to recognize the difference between; distinguish

Example: Expert wine tasters are able to <u>discriminate</u> the year a wine was produced.

asymptomatic (ā'simp tə ma'tik): without symptoms

Example: I didn't know I had an ulcer because I was <u>asymptomatic</u>.

lymph (limf): a clear, yellowish fluid resembling blood plasma, found in intercellular spaces and in the lymphatic vessels of vertebrates

Example: It is much harder to get rid of cancer after it has spread to the <u>lymph</u> glands.

anonymous (ə nän′ə məs): with no name known or acknowledged

Example: People who give to charity usually want to be known; an <u>anonymous</u> gift is rare.

contract (kən trakt′): to get, acquire, or incur

Example: You can <u>contract</u> hepatitis from a used needle that has not been sterilized.

gamut (gam′ət): the entire range or extent, as of emotions

Example: When you are in love, your feelings can run the <u>gamut</u> from intense joy to intense misery.

stigma (stig′mə): something that detracts from the character or reputation of a person, group, etc.; mark of disgrace or reproach

Example: In the United States, there is a <u>stigma</u> attached to being poor, old, or ugly.

perpetuate (pər pech′o͞o āt′): to cause to continue or be remembered

Example: Some women like to <u>perpetuate</u> the idea that women are helpless because they don't want to take care of themselves.

retard (ri tärd′): to hinder, delay, or slow the advance or progress of

Example: Many groups are trying to <u>retard</u> the destruction of the rain forest.

efficacy (ef′i kə sē): power to produce effects or intended results; effectiveness

Example: Because some bacteria have developed resistance, antibiotics have lost their <u>efficacy</u> against them.

abstinence (ab′stə nəns): the act of voluntarily doing without some or all food, drink, or other pleasures

Example: Members of Alcoholics Anonymous practice <u>abstinence</u> from liquor.

inhibitions (in′hi bish′ənz): ideas, feelings, or rules that hold us back or keep us from some action, feeling, etc.; check or repress

Example: We lose many of our <u>inhibitions</u> when we drink liquor.

cat, āte, fäther; pen, ēvil; if, kīte; nō, ôr, fo͞od, book; boil, house; up, turn; chief, shell; thick, *the*; zh, treasure; ŋ, sing; ə for *a* in *about*; ′ as in *able* (ā′b′l)

Preread

Preview the following selection by reading the title and the headings. For now, ignore the lines in the margin, which are for a later step. Answer the following questions without looking back at the reading.

1. What is the subject?

_____

2. What is the main idea?

_____

3. Take a moment to think about AIDS. Think about what you know, what you don't know, and what you might find out from reading the selection. Make up three questions that might be answered by reading the selection.

a. _____

b. _____

c. _____

Read

Read the selection without underlining.

◆ *AIDS: A Crisis of Our Time*

Gerald Corey and Marianne Schneider Corey

I f you have not already done so, you will inevitably come in contact with people who have tested positive for HIV, people who have AIDS, people who have had sexual contact with someone who has tested HIV-positive, and people who are close to individuals with HIV or AIDS.

1. _____
_____
_____

AIDS already affects a wide population and will continue to be a major health problem. You simply cannot afford to be unaware of the personal and societal implications of this epidemic. Unless you are educated about the problem, you are likely to engage in risky behaviors or live needlessly in fear. Accurate information is vital if you are to deal with the personal and societal implications of the AIDS epidemic.

You need to be able to differentiate between fact and fiction about the virus and about this disease. Because this is a relatively new disease, we continue to discover new information. Thus, the facts we provide here might be outdated by the time this book is published. You can contact the national HIV and AIDS hotline (1-800-342-AIDS) for free written material, as well as answers to your questions.

There is much ignorance and fear of AIDS, fueled by conflicting reports. Misinformation about the ways in which the disease is spread results in apprehension among many people. There is no reason to remain ignorant. Reading is a minimum step. You can also attend an AIDS work-shop or contact your local public health department or one of the HIV clinics that are being started all over the country.

As well as finding out about HIV and AIDS, we urge you to explore your own sexual practices, drug behaviors, and your attitudes, values, and fears pertaining to AIDS. Better understanding on all fronts will better equip you to make informed, wise choices.

Basic Facts about AIDS

What Is AIDS?

Acquired immunodeficiency syndrome (AIDS) is the last stage of a disease caused by the *human immunodeficiency virus* (HIV), which attacks and weakens the body's natural immune system. Without a working immune system, the body gets infections and cancers that it would normally be able to fight off. HIV was first isolated by French and American scientists in late 1983 and early 1984. People who have AIDS are vulnerable to serious illnesses that would not be a threat to anyone whose immune system was functioning normally. These illnesses are referred to as "opportunistic" infections or diseases. AIDS weakens the body against invasive agents so that other diseases can prey on the body.

2. _____
_____
_____

What Causes AIDS?

At this time, much is known about HIV, such as how it is transmitted, and also how it can be avoided. What is not known is how to destroy the virus. Although there is not yet a vaccine, treatment is improving with early detection and intervention. Infection with HIV does not always lead to AIDS. Research suggests that more than 50 percent of HIV-infected persons may develop AIDS; and almost everyone with the virus will ultimately become ill to some degree within five to ten years after infection. However, the complete natural history of the disease is still not known.

3. _____
_____
_____

How Is HIV Transmitted?

HIV can be transmitted by unprotected sexual intercourse (vaginal and anal) with a person infected with the virus or by sharing needles with an infected person during intravenous drug use. A woman infected with HIV who becomes pregnant or breastfeeds can pass the virus to the baby. Although some cases have developed through blood transfusions, this risk has been virtually eliminated by testing donated blood for HIV antibodies. "High concentration" agents of transmission of HIV include blood, semen, vaginal secretions, and breast milk. The virus can be spread by women or men through heterosexual or homosexual contact. It may also be possible to become infected with HIV through oral intercourse because the act often involves semen and vaginal secretions that may contain HIV. The virus can

4. _____
_____
_____

enter the body through the vagina, penis, rectum, or mouth or through breaks in the skin. The risk of infection with the virus is increased by having multiple sexual partners and by sharing needles among those using drugs. People are most able to infect someone in the first few months of being infected themselves. This is a major problem, since individuals can test HIV-negative during this time.

The virus has been found in "low concentration" in a number of body fluids and secretions, such as saliva, urine, and tears. However, you *do not* "catch" AIDS in the same way you catch a cold or the flu. It cannot be passed through a glass or eating utensils. The AIDS virus is not transmitted through everyday contact with people around you in the workplace, at school, and at social functions. You cannot get AIDS by being near someone who carries the virus. The virus is hard to get and easily avoided. It is a misconception that it is spread through casual contact or from a mosquito bite, a casual kiss, or a toilet seat.

Who Gets AIDS?

5. _____
_____
_____

Most of the AIDS public health effort has been focused on persons with high-risk behavior such as bisexual and gay men, intravenous drug users, and blood transfusion recipients. Some people have been lulled into feeling safe if they are not associated with a high-risk group, yet the epidemic is shifting and is spreading to women, youth, and minorities. AIDS has been called an "equal opportunity disease" because it is found among people of all ages, genders, races, and sexual orientations. Unlike people, AIDS does not discriminate, but it is *behavior* that puts people at risk, not the group to which they belong. Perhaps the largest growth in HIV infection is occurring among women. The World Health Organization estimates that 8 to 10 million women worldwide are infected with HIV. By the year 2000 the number of worldwide cases of HIV is expected to be 40 million. It is predicted that, at the same time, AIDS will have become the third most common cause of death in the United States. Presently, in this country the leading cause of death for individuals in the 25 to 44 age group is AIDS.

What Symptoms Are Associated with HIV Infection?

6. _____
_____
_____

HIV may live in the human body for years before symptoms appear. These people are asymptomatic. Although many individuals infected with the virus have no symptoms, some victims develop severe and prolonged fatigue, night sweats, fever, loss of appetite and weight, diarrhea, and swollen lymph glands in the neck. Anyone having one or more of these symptoms for more than two weeks should see a health care provider. Of course, other diseases besides AIDS can cause similar symptoms.

What Kind of Test Is There for AIDS?

An HIV antibody test looks for antibodies, not the virus. Couples can test negative but be positive during a six-month window period. This is why it is important to get a second test about six months after a person thinks he or she might have been exposed to the virus. A positive test result does not mean that the person will get AIDS, because many people who test positive either remain symptom-free or develop less serious illnesses. The antibody test cannot tell whether the individual will eventually develop signs of illness related to the viral infection or, if so, how serious the illness might be. Early intervention is the key. What a positive test result does indicate is that the person has been infected by the virus and can transmit it to others. It does not mean that you have AIDS. It means that you have been infected with the virus and your body has developed a reaction to it. If you suspect that you have been exposed to the virus, it is crucial that you get tested. With early medical attention, it is possible to delay the diseases that stem from AIDS. Testing is completely anonymous and confidential, but you should inquire if the test site provides these safeguards. It is generally free if you go to the health department in your county.

7. _____
_____
_____

What Are Common Reactions to Testing HIV-Positive?

People who believe or have discovered that they are carriers of HIV are typically highly anxious. Both those who have tested positive and those who have contracted AIDS need immediate help. Upon learning that they are HIV-positive, it is not uncommon to experience a gamut of emotional reactions from shock, to anger, to fear and anxiety, to grieving for the loss of sexual freedom, to alarm over the uncertain future. Some feel that they have been given a death sentence. They will need to find a support system to help them cope with the troubled times that lie ahead. In *AIDS: The Ultimate Challenge* (1993), Elizabeth Kübler-Ross applied the five stages of dying—denial, anger, bargaining, depression, and acceptance—to AIDS patients. As is the case with any loss, individuals tend to experience emotional reactions to the news that they have tested HIV-positive.

8. _____
_____
_____

It needs to be emphasized that HIV-positive individuals can live long and relatively symptom-free for many years. Many new medications are now available to treat the opportunistic infections that often kill people with AIDS. Today, much more is known about the disease than was the case when AIDS was first discovered.

Why Is a Stigma Attached to AIDS?

9. _____
   _____
   _____

Both those who have AIDS and those who discover that they have the virus within them struggle with the stigma attached to this disease. People who are HIV-positive live with the anxiety of wondering whether they will come down with this incurable disease. Most of them also struggle with the stigma attached to AIDS. They live in fear not only of developing a life-threatening disease but also of being discovered and thus being rejected by society in general and by significant persons in their lives. Of course, those who develop AIDS must also deal with this stigma. The stigma stems from the fact that during the early years when this disease was discovered, those who contracted AIDS belonged primarily to the sexually active gay male or bisexual male population or were present or past abusers of intravenous drugs. Among the mainstream population there is still a general negative reaction toward gay men, lesbians, and bisexuals. However, increasing numbers of the general population are being infected, in addition to these "risk groups."

For some, the stigma may be worse than the diagnosis itself. Very often people afflicted with AIDS stigmatize themselves and perpetuate beliefs such as "I feel guilty and ashamed." "I'm a horrible person, and therefore I deserve to suffer," "I'm to blame for getting this disease."

Many of the social fears felt by people with HIV or AIDS are realistic. Some family members actually disown the person with AIDS out of fear. This type of treatment naturally inspires anger, depression, and feelings of hopelessness in the person who has been rejected. He or she may express this anger by asking, over and over: "What did I do to deserve this? Why me?" This anger is sometimes directed at God for letting this happen, and then the person may feel guilty for having reacted this way. Anger is also directed toward others, especially those who are likely to have transmitted the virus.

How Is AIDS Treated?

10. _____
    _____
    _____

At this point, those who carry the virus are likely to have it for the rest of their lives. No drugs have been shown to cure AIDS, but an antiviral agent called azidothymidine (AZT), dideoxyinosine, and others, appear to retard the progress of the disease in some patients. Several experimental drugs have also shown potential efficacy in delaying the onset of AIDS. Although no treatment has yet been successful in restoring the immune system, doctors have been able to treat the various acute illnesses affecting those with AIDS.

How Can the Spread of HIV Be Prevented?

There are conflicting reports and evidence about the disease. The changing nature of information about AIDS and misinformation about the ways in which the disease is spread can block programs aimed at prevention.

11. _____
_____
_____

Because the AIDS crisis shows no signs of decreasing, education to stop the spread of the disease is the key to prevention. Individuals can do a lot to avoid contracting the disease. The following specific steps aimed at prevention have been taken from a number of sources:

12. _____
_____
_____

- All sexually active individuals need to know the basic facts about this disease and how to avoid the risk of infection.

- Talk to your partners about past and present sexual practices and drug use.

- Engage in sexual activities that do not involve vaginal, anal, or oral intercourse.

- Avoid having sex with multiple partners. The more partners you have, the more you increase your risk. Have intercourse only with one uninfected partner.

- Avoid sex with persons with AIDS, with those at risk for AIDS, or with those who have had a positive result on the HIV antibody test.

- Effective and consistent use of condoms and spermidical barriers will reduce the possibility of transmitting the virus, but they are not 100 percent effective in preventing HIV or other STDs. Use latex condoms correctly from start to finish with each act of intercourse.

- It is essential to talk with your partner about his or her sexual history, STD history, and safer sex history. It is important to negotiate safer sex with your partner.

- Making responsible choices is of the utmost importance in avoiding sexually transmitted diseases, including HIV infection. Sexual abstinence is certainly a safe course to follow. If you choose to practice abstinence as a way to prevent infection, this strategy will be effective only if you always abstain.

- If you intend to have unprotected sexual intercourse, you are *not* safe, and you need to recognize the risks of infection. Rather than thinking in terms of "safe sex," it is helpful to consider practices that are "unsafe," "relatively safe," and "safer." In this book, *What You Can*

Do to Avoid AIDS, Earvin "Magic" Johnson emphasizes that "the most responsible thing you can do is to act as though you yourself and anybody you want to have sex with could have HIV and to practice safer sex every time."

- "Safer" behavior includes choosing not to be sexually active; restricting sex to one mutually faithful, uninfected partner; and not injecting drugs. Safer sex practices are especially critical if you sense that your partner may not be totally honest about his or her past or present sexual practices.

- If you use intravenous drugs, don't share needles.

- Avoid using drugs and alcohol, which cloud your judgment. Many college students attend parties in which there is a great deal of peer pressure to "drink and have fun." Intoxication lessens inhibitions, which often leads to unprotected sex. It takes a good bit of courage to take a stand and not engage in irresponsible use of drugs and alcohol, especially when many of your friends may be drinking excessively.

- People who carry the AIDS virus are often not sick and often are unaware that they are infected. They can be HIV-positive and still look fine and feel well.

- Although AIDS has created a tremendous amount of fear for most people, it can be reassuring to know that it's *unprotected* sex that can lead to HIV infection, not any and all sexual experiences.

2600 words

Analyze What You Read—Create a Study Guide

STEP 3

Objective Questions

1. Go back to the reading and underline what you think would be on a test.

2. Fill in the missing marginal self-test notes. You should be able to use the marginal notes to test yourself on everything you underlined. This time we have not provided them; you will have to make them up yourself. If you need help, review Reading Selections 13–17. If you wish, you may write the self-test note on the front of a flash card and paraphrase the underlining on the back.

Essay/Application Questions

Predict Essay Questions: There is only one topic (with subtopics) for an essay question. Write the topic and its subtopics here.

_____

_____

_____

_____

Make Graphic Organizers:

1. Fill in the following chart. You may look back at the reading.

Why should everyone be informed about AIDS?	
What is AIDS?	
What causes AIDS?	
How is HIV transmitted?	
Who gets AIDS?	
What symptoms are associated with HIV infection?	

continued

What kind of test is there for AIDS?	
What are the common reactions to testing HIV-positive?	
Why is a stigma attached to AIDS?	
How it AIDS treated?	
How can the spread of HIV be prevented?	

For explanation
see p. 196 **Skill Development:** Use the underlining, the marginal notes, and the graphic organizer to write a summary of the reading selection. Use a separate sheet of paper.

Remember What's Important

Test yourself or have someone test you on the marginal self-test notes or flash cards and the graphic organizers. Keep testing until you know the material. Test yourself on the Vocabulary Preview words as needed.

Make Use of What You Read

When you are ready, complete the Comprehension Check on p. 387 and the Vocabulary Check on p. 389. Do not look back at the reading selection or the study guide.

Evaluate Your Active Critical Thinking Skills

After your tests have been graded, record your scores on the Progress Chart, p. 416, and answer the questions on the Evaluation Checklist on p. 417.

19   Anger, Aggression, and Assertiveness

Vocabulary Preview

suppressed (sə prest´): kept back; restrained

> *Example:* Some psychologists believe that <u>suppressed</u> feelings can cause mental illnesses.

cited (sīt´id): to mention by way of example, proof, etc.

> *Example:* In one study of college couples, the most commonly <u>cited</u> reason for breaking off the relationship was not conflict but boredom.

catharsis (kə thär´sis): a relieving of the emotions

> *Example:* Sigmund Freud pioneered the idea that <u>catharsis</u> can be healthier than holding back feelings.

retaliation (rē tal´ē ā´shən): returning like for like, especially injury for injury

> *Example:* Some religions, such as Christianity and Buddhism, don't believe in <u>retaliation</u> for people who do wrong.

civility (si vil´ə tē): politeness

> *Example:* We show respect for other people by always behaving with <u>civility</u>.

cat, āte, fäther; pen, ēvil; if, kīte; nō, ôr, fōōd, book; boil, house; up, turn; chief, shell; thick, *the*; zh, treasure; ŋ, sing; ə for *a* in *about*; ´ as in *able* (ā´b'l)

STEP 1

Preread

Preview the following selection by reading the title, headings, and first sentence of each paragraph. Ignore the lines in the margin. Answer the following questions without looking back at the reading.

1. What is the subject?

   _____

2. What is the main idea?

   _____

3. Take a moment to think about anger, aggression, and assertiveness. What do you know about it? What don't you know? What could you find out from reading this selection? Make up three questions that might be answered by reading the selection.

   a. _____

   b. _____

   c. _____

Read

STEP 2

Read the selection without underlining.

◆ *Anger, Aggression, and Assertiveness*

Brian K. Williams and Sharon M. Knight

How often do you get angry? In one study, people were asked to keep careful records of the times when they got angry. Most reported becoming at least a little angry several times a week. Some reported being angry several times a day. In more than half the cases, the person who was upset felt unfairly treated by a family member or a friend. Anger was especially common when a person felt the situation could have been avoided or was, in some way, not fair.

1. _____

_____

2. _____

_____

Clearly, anger is one of the most important and one of the strongest emotions we ever have to learn to deal with. It can be positive and help people reach their goals. Many great leaders have worked hard to achieve their goals because they thought something was unfair.

3. _____

_____

Although anger can sometimes be a positive emotion, it can also be very negative. It can destroy relationships. It can lead to violence such as abuse or even killing. If anger is suppressed, it can show itself in unexpected and destructive ways. Anger handled properly and appropriately can help show people how they can improve their behavior.

Expressions of Anger

Needless to say, it is not usually a good idea to express rage. For example, if something happens at work that makes you very angry, you are not in the right setting to give vent to your feelings. "Men and women who are employed full time cited work twice as often as all other locations combined for occasions of feeling angry but remaining silent . . . ," writes Carol Tavris in a book called *Anger: The Misunderstood Emotion*. "The most popular location for screaming arguments and physical violence is—as you might expect—the home."

4. _____

_____

Is an angry outburst a good way to handle rage? Some people believe in the idea of catharsis—reducing your anger by letting it "all hang out." This can work if you are convinced that the other person deserves retaliation and if you will not feel guilty or anxious. It is wise to understand that expressing anger while you feel angry often makes you feel angrier. Such a reaction can harm your relationships.

5. _____

_____

6. _____
   _____

Even talking it out is risky. In one study, several laid-off aerospace engineers and technicians were allowed to "blow off steam" about the employer who had fired them. It was found that instead of this being cathartic, the engineers and technicians showed even more anger afterwards. In other words, talking about anger to a third person does not always reduce it; it sometimes makes it stronger.

7. _____
   _____

Two very different ways of expressing anger are with aggression and with assertiveness. We need to distinguish between the two.

8. _____
   _____

- Aggression: Sometimes the word *aggression* can have a positive meaning as in "an aggressive sales campaign." The more common meaning of *aggression,* however, is a hostile and violent act. Aggression in that sense means physical or verbal behavior meant to hurt someone. Aggression is not the same as anger. You may feel anger and express it in positive ways. One example would be expressing your anger by cleaning the house thoroughly. You can also act aggressively without feeling anger, the way soldiers do.

9. _____
   _____

- Assertiveness: *Assertiveness* is behavior in which you stand up for your rights. Instead of being angry or getting other people angry, you simply state your feelings honestly and calmly.

Handling Anger

How is it best to handle anger? It is not useful to sulk and think you are keeping the peace. Neither is it useful to show rage or cruelty in the name of honesty. Sometimes the best response is to do nothing at all. "Let it go, and half the time it will turn out to be an unimportant, momentary shudder," says Tavris. "The other half of the time, keeping quiet gives you time to cool down and decide whether the matter is worth discussing or not."

10. _____
    _____

So the first step is learning to nip your temper in the bud and disconnect yourself from an argument. Perhaps you can say, "This is becoming a fight."

11. _____
    _____

A second step is to learn to deal with anger with *civility.* Civility means knowing when to keep quiet about annoying but unimportant things; it means knowing when to discuss important matters clearly and assertively.

12. _____
    _____

Here is a good example of assertiveness. Suppose you are upset when someone in your family leaves dirty clothes on the floor. Do not blame the person by saying, "You *never* do anything about the dirty clothes." Instead, tell the other person how he or she makes you *feel.* "I get upset when you leave the laundry for me." This type of expression will get better results.

800 words

Analyze What You Read—Create a Study Guide

Objective Questions

1. Go back to the reading and underline what you think would be on a test.

2. Fill in the missing marginal self-test notes on the blank lines. We have not provided them; you will have to make them up yourself. If you wish, you may write the self-test note on the front of a flash card and paraphrase the underlining on the back.

Essay/Application Questions

Predict Essay Questions: Write what you think would be the most likely topic for an essay question here.

_____

Make Graphic Organizers: Use your marginal notes as guides to fill in the blanks in the following outline.

Anger, Aggression, and Assertiveness

I. _____

II. _____

III. _____

IV. _____

    A. _____

    B. _____

V. _____

VI. _____

VII. _____

    A. _____

    B. _____

VIII. _____

    A. _____

    B. _____

IX. _____

For explanation
see p. 196
Skill Development: Use the underlining, the marginal notes, and the graphic organizer to write a summary of the reading. Use a separate sheet of paper.

Remember What's Important

Test yourself or have someone test you on the marginal self-test notes or flash cards and on the graphic organizer. Keep testing until you know the material. Test yourself on the Vocabulary Preview words as needed.

Make Use of What You Read

When you are ready, complete the Comprehension Check on p. 391 and the Vocabulary Check on p. 393. Do not look back at the reading selection or the study guide.

Evaluate Your Active Critical Thinking Skills

After your tests have been graded, record your scores on the Progress Chart, p. 416, and answer the questions on the Evaluation Checklist on p. 417.

20 | Understanding Prejudice

Vocabulary Preview

component (kəm pō′nənt): a part, element, or ingredient
Example: Violence seems to be a component of all action-adventure films today.

affective (a fek′tiv): having to do with emotions; feelings
Example: Many women complain that men ignore the affective part of relationships.

selectivity (sə lek′tiv′ə tē): making choices in what you see, hear, etc.
Example: Children show selectivity in what they hear; they don't hear "clean up your room" but they can hear very well "do you want an ice cream cone?"

subjective (səb jek′tiv): resulting from the feelings of the person thinking; personal
Example: Different people may take part in the same event, yet their subjective experiences can be quite different.

bias (bī′əs): prejudice
Example: When selecting people to serve on a jury, a defense lawyer will eliminate people who are suspected of bias against the defendant.

attribution (a′trə byōō′shən): thinking of something as belonging to a certain person or thing
Example: People often make attribution errors about the careers of actors and actresses; their "overnight success" is usually really caused by years of dedication and hard work.

defensive (dē fen′siv): ready to protect oneself against attack
Example: When people are feeling defensive they become hard to talk to; they argue instead of listening.

proximity (präks im′ə tē): nearness
Example: Some people like to live in close proximity to their families.

repulsion (ri pul′shən): strong dislike
Example: Many people feel repulsion toward slimy bugs.

ethnocentrism (eth nō sen′trism): the emotional attitude that one's own race, nation, or culture is superior to all others
Example: An example of ethnocentrism was Hitler's Aryan "master race."

cat, āte, fäther; pen, ēvil; if, kīte; nō, ôr, fōod, book; boil, house; up, turn; chief, shell; thick, *the*; zh, treasure; ŋ, sing; ə for *a* in *about*; ′ as in *able* (ā′b′l)

Preread

STEP 1

Preview the following selection by reading the title, the headings, everything in boldface and italics, and the illustrations. Answer the following questions without looking back at the reading.

1. What is the subject?

   _____

2. What is the main idea?

   _____

3. What is the main idea of Figure 1?

   _____

4. In Figure 2, which example shows prejudice without discrimination?

   _____

   _____

5. In Figure 3, what is a stable external cause?

   _____

6. Take a moment to think about prejudice. Think about what you know about it, what you don't know, and what you might find out from reading this selection. Make up three questions that might be answered by reading the selection.

   a. _____

   b. _____

   c. _____

Read

STEP 2

Read the selection without underlining.

◆ *Understanding Prejudice*

Wayne Weiten

Prejudice is a major problem in society. It hurts people's images of themselves; it lessens people's ability to accomplish what is possible; it strains relationships between groups; it can even stir up wars. The first step to reducing prejudice is to understand where it comes from.

Prejudice and discrimination are closely related. Most people use one word to mean the other. However, social scientists prefer to define their words more carefully. *Prejudice* **is a negative attitude held toward members of a group.** Prejudice has three major parts. (See Figure 1.) One part is belief: "Most Indians are alcoholics." A second part is emotion: "I despise Jews." The third part is willingness to behave in a particular way: "I wouldn't hire a Mexican."

When we think about prejudice, most of us have in mind certain ethnic groups. But prejudice is not only that. Other targets of widespread prejudice have been women, homosexuals, the aged, the handicapped, and the mentally ill. Many people are prejudiced against one group or another; many have also been victims of others' prejudices.

Prejudice may lead to *discrimination*. Prejudice is an attitude: **discrimination means behaving differently, usually unfairly, toward the members of a group.** Prejudice and discrimination tend to go hand in hand. But attitudes and behavior do not necessarily go together. (See Figure 2.) This discussion will deal mostly with the attitude of prejudice. To begin, let us examine what happens in a person's awareness to make prejudice grow.

Figure 1   The three components of prejudice as an attitude.

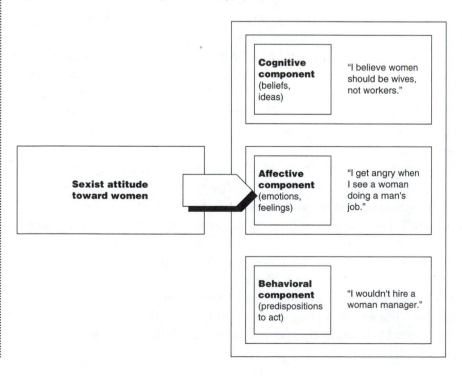

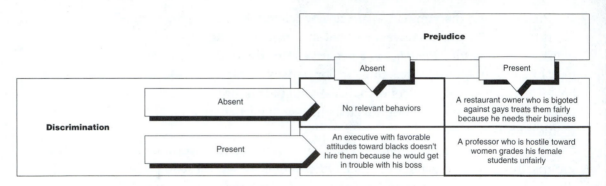

Figure 2 Relationship between prejudice and discrimination.

Stereotyping and Selectivity in Person Perception

Stereotypes play a large part in prejudice. However, not all stereotypes are negative. The stereotype that "what is beautiful is good" is positive for attractive people. Even stereotypes about ethnic groups are not always negative. It is not insulting to say that Americans are ambitious or that Japanese are hard working. Of course, both these statements are greatly exaggerated.

Unfortunately, many people do believe in negative stereotypes of various ethnic groups. Studies suggest that negative racial stereotypes have lessened over the last fifty years, yet they are not a thing of the past. Racism today, according to many who study the problem, is simply not as open. Many people no longer show their prejudices openly, but they continue to hold negative attitudes toward racial minorities. Such people say they believe in racial equality. However, when it comes to specific programs which may help overcome inequality, they quickly say that discrimination is no longer a problem.

Recent research has shown that some stereotypes are held even by people who have little prejudice. Such prejudicial stereotypes often are put into action automatically. Let us consider, for instance, a man who feels uncomfortable sitting next to a gay male on a bus. This same man does not believe in prejudice against homosexuals; yet he is still uncomfortable.

Stereotypes seem to last a long time. This is true, in part, because of *selectivity*. Selectivity makes it likely that people will see what they expect to see when they actually come into contact with groups they view with prejudice. For example, Duncan had white subjects watch and judge inter-action on a TV monitor that was supposed to be live. (Actually, it was a videotape.) The subjects watched people get into an argument (in which) one gave the other a slight shove. Sometimes the shover was white and sometimes black. What were the results? When the actor giving the shove was black, 73 percent of the subjects saw the shove as violent behavior. When the actor was white, only 13 percent saw it as violent. What we notice is extremely subjective. That is, we seem to overlook what happens because of our own personal feelings. Because of stereotypes, even "violence" may lie in the eye of the beholder.

Memory biases are also tilted toward agreeing with a person's prejudices. If a man believes that "women are not cut out for leadership roles," he may spend a great deal of time talking happily about his female boss's mistakes, but quickly forgetting her achievements. Actual interaction cannot make stereotypes vanish. Gender stereotypes are very common even though men and women interact all the time.

Biases in Attributions

Stereotypes and prejudices are also made more lasting by the attribution process. Weiner has shown that people often make *biased attributions to explain success and failure.* For example, men and women do not get equal credit for their successes. Some attribute a woman's success to good luck, great effort, or having an easy task. (This would not be true of a task that is considered feminine.) In comparison, a man's success is more likely to be attributed to his outstanding ability. (See Figure 3.) These biased patterns of attribution help support the stereotype that men are more competent than women.

Figure 3 Bias in the attributions used to explain success and failure by men and women.

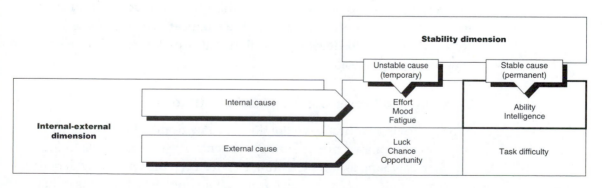

Patterns of bias have also been seen in explanations of ethnic minorities' successes and failures. Often, when minorities are successful at something that does not fit the stereotype, their success is attributed to outside factors or to unusual causes.

The *fundamental attribution error* is a bias that explains events by pointing to the personal characteristics of the person as the cause. People are likely to make this error when they judge targets of prejudice. When people look at neighborhoods full of crime and poverty, they blame the personal qualities of the people who live there. They ignore explanations like job discrimination and poor police service. They find it easy to say, "They should be able to pull themselves up by their own bootstraps." This dismisses factors outside the personal qualities of the people, factors which make it difficult for minorities to move out of their situation.

Defensive attribution unjustly blames victims of misfortune for their own problems. It can contribute to prejudice. In recent years, some have felt that homosexuals brought the AIDS crisis on themselves; therefore, they deserve their fate. Blaming AIDS on the personal character of gays may help make heterosexuals feel that AIDS cannot strike them.

Nearness and Similarity Effects in Attraction

Interpersonal attraction may encourage prejudice and discrimination in at least two ways. First, the effects of *proximity*, or nearness, may cause prejudice to continue. Segregated patterns of housing and schooling limit the chance for contact with others of different races. People tend to become friends with those who live near them and go to school with them. They are not likely to become friends with minorities who cannot live in their neighborhoods, go to their schools, or join their country clubs. Under the right circumstances, more contact between groups can reduce prejudice.

Second, the effects of *dissimilarity* may be great. If people look down on those who are not like themselves, this causes prejudice against many groups such as minorities, the aged, the handicapped, and homosexuals. Rosenbaum calls this feeling of disliking those different from ourselves the "repulsion hypothesis."

Forming and Preserving Prejudicial Attitudes

If prejudice is an attitude, where does it come from? Many prejudices appear to be handed down from our parents. Prejudices can be found in children as young as four. Handing down a prejudice probably depends to some extent on *observational learning.* If a young boy hears his father make fun of homosexuals, his father's attitude is likely to affect him. Now, suppose this young boy goes to school and makes comments that belittle homosexuals. If his peers agree with his comments, his prejudice will be strengthened.

One recent study found that college students' opinions on race were influenced by hearing others voice racist or antiracist feelings. From this, it follows that social standards that accept expressions of prejudice encourage those attitudes.

Dividing the World into Ingroups and Outgroups

When people join together in groups, they sometimes divide their world into "us versus them," or *ingroups versus outgroups.* These divisions promote **ethnocentrism—a tendency to view one's own group as superior to others and as the standard for judging the worth of others' ways.**

As you might guess, people tend to judge members of the outgroup less well than members of the ingroup. The more strongly one identifies with an ingroup, the more prejudiced one tends to be toward outgroups. People tend to think in very simple terms about outgroups. They tend to see differences among the members of their own ingroup, but they are convinced that everyone in the outgroup is exactly alike. At an elementary level, this idea is captured by the statement "They all look alike." As a matter of fact, studies have found that blacks and whites do have more difficulty distinguishing the faces of outgroup members. The false idea of everyone in the outgroup being alike makes it easier to hold stereotypes about its members.

This discussion has shown that a great many things help us both create and hold onto personal prejudices. Most of the factors reflect normal social behavior. In other words, it is understandable that more people—whether they are privileged or underprivileged, minority members or majority members—hold some prejudices. Knowing the causes of prejudice may allow you to identify your own prejudices as well as where they originated. More awareness of your personal prejudices may help you become more accepting of the endless differences in human behavior.

1500 words

Analyze What You Read—Create a Study Guide

Objective Questions

1. Go back to the reading and underline what you think might be on a test.

2. Make marginal self-test notes to remember what you have underlined. No blanks were left for the notes this time, so it is up to you to decide where they go. If you need help, review the marginal notes in Readings 13–19. If you wish, you may write each self-test note on the front of a flash card and paraphrase the underlining on the back.

Essay/Application Questions

Predict Essay Questions: What is the most likely essay question?

_____

Make Graphic Organizers: Fill in the following chart.

Term	Definition	Example
Prejudice		
Discrimination		
Cognitive component of prejudice		
Affective component of prejudice		
Behavioral component of prejudice		
Stereotypes		
Selectivity		
Memory biases		

Term	Definition	Example
Biased attributions for success and failure		
Fundamental attribution error		
Defensive attribution		
Effects of proximity		
Effects of dissimilarity		
Repulsion hypothesis		
Observational learning		
Ingroups versus outgroups		
Ethnocentrism		

For explanation see p. 196

Skill Development: Use the underlining, the marginal notes or flash cards, and the graphic organizer to write a summary of the reading. Use a separate sheet of paper.

Remember What's Important

Test yourself or have someone test you on the marginal self-test notes or flash cards and on the graphic organizer. Keep testing until you know the material. Test yourself on the Vocabulary Preview words as needed.

Make Use of What You Read

When you are ready, complete the Comprehension Check on p. 395 and the Vocabulary Check on p. 397. Do not look back at the reading selection or the study guide.

Evaluate Your Active Critical Thinking Skills

After your tests have been graded, record your scores on the Progress Chart, p. 416, and answer the questions on the Evaluation Checklist on p. 417.

21   The All-American Male

Vocabulary Preview

conform (kən fôrm′): to be or become the same or similar
Example: Teenagers are under great pressure to <u>conform</u> to whatever their peers are doing.

objective (əb jek′tiv): without bias or prejudice; detached
Example: I am an <u>objective</u> observer.

rational (rash′ən əl): showing reason; not foolish or silly; sensible
Example: If you want to convince someone, you need a <u>rational</u> argument.

nurturing (nŭr′chər iŋ): raising or promoting the development of; training, educating, fostering, etc.
Example: Puppies require a lot of <u>nurturing</u>.

distorted (di stôrt′id): twisted; perverted
Example: Mirrors in amusement park fun houses show <u>distorted</u> images.

disclose (dis klōz′): to reveal; make known
Example: I cannot <u>disclose</u> the amount I paid.

façade (fə säd′): a superficial or false outward appearance
Example: She tried to keep up the <u>façade</u> of everything being fine, even though her life was falling apart.

impoverished (im päv′ər isht): made poor; reduced to poverty
Example: Women with children are often <u>impoverished</u> after a divorce.

compassion (kəm pash′ən): sorrow for the sufferings or trouble of another or others, accompanied by an urge to help; deep sympathy; pity
Example: Many Americans lack <u>compassion</u> for the homeless.

submissive (sub mis′iv): having or showing a tendency to give in without resistance; yielding
Example: In traditional Islamic culture, the women are supposed to be <u>submissive</u>, first to their fathers, then to their husbands.

deviate (dē′vē āt′): to turn aside (*from* a course, direction, standard, doctrine, etc.); diverge; digress
Example: When flying an airplane, you should not <u>deviate</u> from your flight plan.

obsession (əb sesh′ən): the fact or state of being preoccupied with an idea, desire, emotion, etc.
Example: Some politicians have an <u>obsession</u> with power.

intuitive (in tōō′i tiv, -tyōō-): having to do with intuition; known or learned without the conscious use of reasoning; immediately understood
Example: Popular culture considers women more <u>intuitive</u> than men.

affront (ə frunt′): insult; offense

    Example: In some cultures an <u>affront</u> requires revenge.

bravado (brə vä′dō): pretended courage or defiant confidence where there is really little or none

    Example: Sometimes you have to act with <u>bravado</u> and not let anyone know you're scared.

psyche (sī′kē): the mind or soul

    Example: Child abuse can have permanent effects on the child's <u>psyche</u>.

lethal (lē′thəl): causing or capable of causing death; fatal or deadly

    Example: Some states execute criminals by <u>lethal</u> injection.

contend (kən tend′): to hold to be a fact; assert

    Example: The witnesses <u>contend</u> that they saw him rob the store.

vigilant (vij′ə lənt): staying watchful and alert to danger or trouble

    Example: A watchman has to be <u>vigilant</u>.

susceptible (sə sep′tə bəl): easily influenced by or affected with

    Example: Most people are <u>susceptible</u> to flattery.

cat, āte, fäther; pen, ēvil; if, kīte; nō, ôr, fo͞od, book; boil, house; up, turn; chief, shell; thick, *the*; zh, treasure; ŋ, sing; ə for *a* in *about*; ′ as in *able* (ā′b′l)

Preread

STEP 1

Preview the following selection by reading the title, the boldface and italic headings, and the first sentence of each paragraph that doesn't have a heading. Answer the following questions without looking back at the reading.

1. What is the subject?

    _____

2. What is the main idea?

    _____

3. Take a moment to think about the male role. Think about what you know, what you don't know, and what you might find out from reading the selection. Make up three questions that might be answered by reading the selection.

    a. _____

    b. _____

    c. _____

STEP 2

Read

Read the selection without underlining.

◆ *The All-American Male*

Gerald Corey and Marianne Schneider Corey

What is the stereotype of the all-American male, and what aspects of themselves do many men feel they must hide to conform to it? In general, the stereotypical male is cool, detached, objective, rational, worldly, competitive, and strong. A man who attempts to fit the stereotype will suppress most of his feelings, for he sees the subjective world of feelings as being essentially feminine. A number of writers have identified the characteristics of a man living by the stereotype and the feelings he may attempt to suppress or deny. Keep in mind that the following discussion is about the *stereotypical* view of males, and certainly many men do not fit this narrow characterization. It would be a mistake to conclude that this picture is an accurate portrayal of the way most men are. But these characteristics outline the limited view of the male role that many men have accepted, to a greater or lesser degree.

- *Emotional unavailability.* A man tends to show his affection by being a "good provider." Frequently, he is not emotionally available to his female partner. Because of this, she may complain that she feels shut out by him. He also has a difficult time dealing with her feelings. If she cries, he becomes uncomfortable and quickly wants to "fix her" so she will stop crying.

- *Independence.* Rather than admitting that he needs anything from anyone, he may lead a life of exaggerated independence. He feels that he should be able to do by himself whatever needs to be done, and he finds it hard to reach out to others by asking for emotional support or nurturing.

- *Aggressiveness.* He feels that he must be continually active, aggressive, assertive, and striving. He views the opposites of these traits as signs of weakness, and he fears being seen as soft.

- *Denial of fears.* He won't recognize his fears, much less express them. He has the distorted notion that to be afraid means that he lacks courage, so he hides his fears from himself and from others. He lacks the courage to risk being seen as frightened.

- *Protection of his inner self.* With other men, he keeps himself hidden because they are competitors and in this sense potential enemies. With a women, he doesn't disclose himself because he is afraid they will think him unmanly if they see his inner core. A woman may complain that a man hides his feelings from her, yet it is probably more accurate to say that he is hiding his feelings from himself. Because he would find the range of feelings to be terrifying, he has unconsciously sealed off most of his feelings.

- *Invulnerability.* He cannot make himself vulnerable, as is evidenced by his general unwillingness to disclose much of his inner experience. He won't let himself feel and express sadness, nor will he cry. He interprets any expression of emotional vulnerability as a sign of weakness. To protect himself, he becomes emotionally insulated and puts on a mask of toughness, competence, and decisiveness.

- *Lack of bodily self-awareness.* Common physical stress signals that men identify include headaches, nausea, heartburn, muscle aches, backaches, and high blood pressure. However, a man often ignores these stress symptoms, denies their potential consequences, and avoids addressing their causes. He doesn't recognize bodily cues that may signal danger. For example, heart disease rates and cardiovascular disease death rates are twice as high in men as in women. He drives himself unmercifully and views his body as some kind of machine that won't break down or wear out. He may not pay attention to his exhaustion until he collapses from it.

- *Remoteness with other men.* Although he may have plenty of acquaintances, he doesn't have very many male friends he confides in. It is not uncommon for men to state that they don't have a single male friend with whom they can be intimate. He can talk to other men about things but finds it hard to be personal.

- *Drive to succeed.* He has been socialized to believe that success at work is the measure of his value as a man. He hides from failure and thinks he must at all times put on the façade of the successful man. He feels he's expected to succeed and produce, to be "the best" and to get ahead and stay ahead. He measures his worth by the money he makes. Based on his feelings of inferiority and insecurity, he is drive to prove his superiority. He has to win at all times, regardless of the costs, which means that someone else has to lose.

■ *Denial of "feminine" qualities.* Because he plays a rigid male role, he doesn't see how he can be a man and at the same time possess (or reveal) traits usually attributed to women. Therefore, he is highly controlled, cool, detached, and shuts out much of what he could experience, which results in an impoverished life. He finds it difficult to express warmth and tenderness, especially public displays of tenderness or compassion. Because he won't allow the feminine experience to be a part of his life, he disowns any aspects within himself that he does not perceive to be manly.

■ *Avoidance of physical contact.* He has a difficult time touching freely or expressing affection and caring to other men. He thinks he should touch a woman only if it will lead to sex, and he fears touching other men because he doesn't want to be perceived as a homosexual.

■ *Rigid perceptions.* He sees men and women in rigid categories. Women should be weak, emotional, and submissive; men are expected to be tough, logical, and aggressive. He does not give himself much latitude to deviate from a narrow band of expression.

■ *Devotion to work.* He puts much of his energy into external signs of success. Thus, little is left over for his wife and children, or even for leisure pursuits. A man's obsession with defining himself mainly through work provides an acceptable outlet for pent-up energy. The result of getting lost in his work is forgetting to make contact with his inner spiritual self and intimate contact with others.

■ *Loss of the male spirit.* Because he is cut off from his inner self, he has lost a way to make intuitive sense of the world. Relying on society's definitions and rules about masculinity rather than his own leaves him feeling empty, and he experiences guilt, shame, anxiety, and depression.

In our work with men we find that many of them show a variety of these characteristics. In the safe environment that group therapy can provide, we also see a strong desire in these men to modify some of the ways in which they feel they must live. They are willing to take the risk of expressing and exploring feelings on a range of topics. For instance, they are willing to let the other group members know that they do not always feel strong and that they are scared at times. As trust builds within the therapeutic group, the men become increasingly willing to share deep personal pain and longings. They struggle a great deal, not only in showing to others their tender side, but also in accepting this dimension of themselves. It takes some time for them to get beyond their embarrassment at owning feelings such as love, compassion, rejection, sadness, fear, joy, and anger. As these men become more honest with women, they typically discover that women are more able to accept, respect, and love them. The very traits that men fear to reveal to women are the characteristics that draw others closer to them. This often results in removing some of the barriers that prevent intimacy between the sexes.

Men often hide their feelings of vulnerability and are ever watchful of others' reactions, looking for indications that they might be exposed to ridicule. This theme of men hiding their true nature is characteristic of many men, regardless of their racial, ethnic, and cultural background. Audrey Chapman, a therapist with a good deal of experience working with black men, claims that black men have a desire to connect with someone after years of frustration at not "getting it right." She says that black men are skilled at hiding feelings. They see crying as the ultimate affront to manhood, and they test the waters to determine the level of safety. Underneath their surface bravado is likely to be a scared and lonely person. Chapman emphasizes how important it is to learn to listen and be patient when these men do express what they are feeling or thinking. Chapman writes: "If I could stress only one issue with black women, it would be the necessity of understanding and accepting the fragility of our men's psyche. They desire and need bonding as much as we do, but they need a road map to get where they long to be."

The Price Men Pay for Remaining in Traditional Roles

What price must a man pay for denying most of his inner self and putting on a false front? First, he loses a sense of himself because of his concern with being the way he thinks he should be as a male. Writing on the "lethal aspects of the male role," Sidney Jourard contends that men typically find it difficult to love and be loved. They won't reveal themselves enough to be loved. They hide their loneliness, anxiety, and hunger for affection, making it difficult for anyone to love them as they really are. Part of the price these guarded males pay for their seclusion is that they must always be vigilant for fear that someone might discover what is beneath their armor.

Another price men pay for living by stereotypical standards is the susceptibility to stress-related disorders. Although men have recently been paying more attention to their physical health, evidence continues to show that they have higher rates of stress and ailments related to stress than do women. For example, this year 8 men out of every 100 will die from heart problems, compared to only 4 women out of 100. (An exception is women who are striving to compete in heretofore "male" arenas.) This point reaffirms a key idea: The truth is in your body. Stress takes a toll on the body, as evidenced by a wide range of psychosomatic disorders. When denial and stress are chronic, the body will not lie but will show signs of wear and tear. Unfortunately, many men do not respect these messages until the damage to their bodies is severe.

In *The New Male,* Herb Goldberg develops the idea that if men continue to cling to the traditional masculine blueprint they will end their lives as pathetic throwaways. He describes such men as alive at 20, machines at 30, and burned out by 40. During their twenties, most of their energies are directed toward "making it" while denying important needs and feelings. At 20 these men are typically urgently sexual, restless and passionate about converting their ideas into reality, eager to push themselves to their limits (if they recognize any), curious and adventurous, and optimistic about the possibilities for living. In his early twenties the traditional male is driven by societal pressures to prove his manliness, long before he is aware of who he is and what it is he really wants for himself. He locks himself in a cage of expectations. At 30 he has convinced himself that he is not a person but a machine that has to function so the job can get done. By his forties he may experience "male menopause" as his functioning begins to break down. Goldberg sees this decline as the result of years of repression and emotional denial, which make him a danger to both himself and others.

In their excellent book, *Man Alive: A Primer of Men's Issues,* Rabinowitz and Cochran write about the price men pay for hiding their fears and attempting to live by a rigid traditional model of masculinity. They state that adhering to a rigid model of what it means to be a man keeps men looking for the perfect job, house, and partner to make them happy. Yet in the process, they avoid knowing themselves and appreciating the richness of life. The principal costs to men of remaining tied to traditional gender roles are excessive pressure to succeed, an inability to express emotions, and sexual difficulties.

If you are a man, ask yourself to what degree you are tied into your socialization regarding expected male patterns. The chances are good that you have been an active agent in your own gender-role socialization. Now might be a good time to reevaluate the costs associated with your gender-role identity and to consider in what ways, if any, you may want to alter your picture of what it means to be a man.

2100 words

Analyze What You Read—Create a Study Guide

Objective Questions

1. Go back to the reading and underline what you think would be on a test.

2. Make marginal notes to test yourself on everything you underlined. If you wish, you may write the self-test note on the front of a flash card and paraphrase the underlining on the back.

Essay/Application Questions

Predict Essay Questions: Look at your marginal notes and pick three topics that would be broad enough for essay questions. Write them here.

1. _____

2. _____

3. _____

Make Graphic Organizers:

1. Go back to the reading selection and find all the points that are filled in on the following outline. Write the Roman numerals and capital letters from the outline in the margin next to where the point is located in the reading.

2. Look for all the points that are missing in the following outline, and write the capital letter in the margin next to where each point appears.

3. Write the missing points on the blank lines below.

The All-American Male

    I. Characteristics of the all-American male

        A. _____

        B. _____

        C. _____

        D. _____

        E. _____

        F. _____

        G. _____

        H. _____

I. _____

J. _____

K. _____

L. _____

M. _____

N. _____

II. Therapy

   A. Men become more honest

   B. More intimacy

III. The price men pay for remaining in traditional roles

   A. _____

   B. Jourard: _____

   C. _____

   D. Goldberg: _____

   E. Rabinowitz and Cochran: _____

For explanation see p. 196

Skill Development: Use the underlining, the marginal notes, and the graphic organizer to write a summary of the reading selection. Use a separate sheet of paper.

Remember What's Important

STEP 4

The first category of the graphic organizer has fourteen points. Since there are so many, we recommend using a mnemonic device like those described in "Improve Your Memory in 7 Easy Steps" in Unit II. The fourteen points (A–N in the outline) begin with the following letters: E, I, A, D, P, I, L, R, D, D, A, R, D, L. Make up a sentence in which each word begins with each of those letters and write it below.

_____

_____

Make sure you can associate each word with a characteristic from the outline. Test yourself or have someone test you on the marginal self-test notes or flash cards and on the three Roman numeral headings in the outline. Keep testing until you know the material. Test yourself on the Vocabulary Preview words as needed.

Make Use of What You Read

When you are ready, complete the Comprehension Check on p. 399 and the Vocabulary Check on p. 401. Do not look back at the reading selection or the study guide.

Evaluate Your Active Critical Thinking Skills

After your tests have been graded, record your scores on the Progress Chart, p. 416, and answer the questions on the Evaluation Checklist on p. 417.

22   Sexual Abuse and Harassment

Vocabulary Preview

incest (in´sest´): sexual relations between persons too closely related to marry legally

Example: In some states, people are allowed to marry their cousins; in other states such marriages are outlawed as <u>incest</u>.

syndrome (sin´drōm´): any set of characteristics regarded as identifying a certain type, condition, etc.

Example: The flu <u>syndrome</u> consists of fever, congestion, and muscle aches.

therapeutic (ther´ə pyo͞ot´ik): serving to cure or heal; curative

Example: Once considered a folk remedy, there is now scientific evidence supporting the <u>therapeutic</u> effects of chicken soup on a cold.

molestation (mō´les tā´shən; also mäl´əs-): improper advances, esp. of a sexual nature

Example: Because children cannot legally consent to sexual acts, any sexual contact with a minor is <u>molestation</u>, whether or not the child was willing.

perpetrator (pʉr´pə trāt´ər): one who performs or is guilty of (something evil, criminal, or offensive)

Example: A criminal is a <u>perpetrator</u> of a crime.

conservative (kən sʉr´və tiv): moderate; cautious; safe

Example: The crowd was huge; I'd say 100,000 is a <u>conservative</u> estimate.

coercion (kō ʉr´shən): the use of force or compulsion, as by threats, to do something

Example: Children often require <u>coercion</u> to do their chores.

metaphorically (met´ə-fôr´ik lē): involving a figure of speech containing an implied comparison, in which a word or phrase ordinarily and primarily used for one thing is applied to another

Example: When Shakespeare said, "all the world's a stage," he was speaking <u>metaphorically</u>.

recurring (ri kʉr´iŋ): happening or occurring again, esp. after some lapse of time; to appear at intervals

Example: Love is a constantly <u>recurring</u> theme in popular music.

dysfunctional (dis fuŋk´shən əl): of or characterized by abnormal or impaired psychosocial functioning

Example: If a parent becomes a substance abuser, his or her family will become <u>dysfunctional</u>.

self-esteem (self e stēm′): belief in oneself; self-respect

Example: Low self-esteem will often cause people to accept jobs that are beneath their level of ability.

vacillate (vas′ə lāt′): to waver in mind; show indecision

Example: Most overweight people vacillate between wanting to overeat and wanting to lose weight.

resolution (rez′ə lōō′shən): a solving, as of a puzzle, or answering, as of a question; solution

Example: Divorce courts are moving toward conflict resolution instead of using a legal system in which one side wins and the other side loses.

dynamics (dī nam′iks): *a)* the various forces, physical, moral, economic, etc., operating in any field *b)* the way such forces shift or change in relation to one another *c)* the study of such forces

Example: Each family has its own special dynamics.

trauma (trô′mə; also trä′-, trou′-): *Psychiatry:* a painful emotional experience, or shock, often producing a lasting psychic effect and, sometimes, a neurosis

Example: Being bitten by a dog as a child caused such a trauma that she has been afraid of dogs ever since.

equate (ē kwāt′, i-): *a)* to make equal or equivalent; equalize *b)* to treat, regard, or express as equal, equivalent, identical, or closely related

Example: Some people equate wealth with happiness.

explicit (eks plis′it, ik splis′-): clearly stated and leaving nothing implied; distinctly expressed

Example: Sexually explicit ads should be kept off television.

demeaning (dē mēn′iŋ, di-): lowering in status or character; degrading; humbling

Example: Some people cannot work for a boss because they feel that taking orders is demeaning.

innuendo (in′yōō en′dō′): an indirect remark, gesture, or reference, usually implying something derogatory; insinuation

Example: Gossip columnists often rely on innuendo so they can be interesting to read, and, at the same time, avoid being sued for saying things that cannot be proved.

reprisals (ri prī′zəlz): injuries done in return for injuries received; retaliation or acts of retaliation

Example: It's hard to admit guilt when you fear reprisals.

cat, āte, fäther; pen, ēvil; if, kīte; nō, ôr, fōōd, book; boil, house; up, turn; chief, shell; thick, *the*; zh, treasure; ŋ, sing; ə for *a* in *about*; ′ as in *able* (ā′b'l)

Preread

Preview the following selection by reading the title and the first paragraph.

1. What is the subject?

   _____

2. What is the main idea?

   _____

   _____

3. Take a moment to think about sexual abuse and harassment. Think about what your know, what you don't know, and what you might find out from reading the selection. Make up three questions that might be answered by reading the selection.

   a. _____

   b. _____

   c. _____

Read

Read the selection without underlining

◆ *Sexual Abuse and Harassment*

Gerald Corey and Marianne Schneider Corey

Three topics that involve some form of abuse of sexuality are incest, rape, and sexual harassment. In each of these cases, power is misused or a trusting relationship is betrayed for the purpose of gaining control over the individual. Individuals are robbed of choice. Their only choice is how to react to being violated. Incest, date and acquaintance rape, and sexual harassment all involve abusive power, control, destructiveness, and violence. As such, these practices are never justifiable. In all of these forms of sexual abuse, victims tend to be reluctant to disclose that they have been wronged. In fact, many victims suffer from guilt and believe that they were responsible for what occurred. This guilt is increased by segments of society that contribute to the "blaming the victim" syndrome. The victims should not be given further insult by being blamed for cooperating or contributing to the violence that was forced upon them. Victims often carry psychological scars from these experiences that interfere with their ability to accept and express the full range of their sexuality.

Incest: A Betrayal of Trust

In our therapeutic groups we continue to meet women who suffer tremendous guilt related to early incestuous experiences. To a lesser extent we come across men who have been subjected to incest or some form of molestation. Because incest is a betrayal of trust and a misuse of power and control, it is never acceptable. The perpetrator is always responsible. This subject is being given much-deserved attention by both helping professionals and the general public. It appears that incest is far more widespread than ever before thought. It occurs on all social, economic, educational, and professional levels. At least one out of ten children is molested by a trusted family member. This number of victims is conservative, since many incidents are never reported. Many women do not remember their incestuous experiences until something triggers a certain memory in their adult years.

Our personal-growth groups are for relatively well-functioning people. However, we find a startling number of women who report incidents of incest and sexual experimentation. The perpetrators were fathers, uncles, stepfathers, grandfathers, and brothers. Black defines incest as "inappropriate sexual behavior, usually perpetrated by an adult family member with a minor child, brought about by coercion, deception, or psychological manipulation. It includes inappropriate touching, oral sex, and/or intercourse." The definition used by Vanderbilt is "any sexual abuse of a child by a relative or other person in a position of trust and authority over the child. It is the violation of the child where he or she lives—literally and metaphorically." Vanderbilt indicates that incest is a felony offense in all 50 states. However, its definition varies from state to state, as does the punishment. Father/daughter incest is the most common type of adult/child incest. Sexual relations also occur between mother and daughter, mother and son, and father and son. Although females are more often incest victims, males also suffer the effects of incestual experiences.

In *Betrayal of Innocence,* Forward and Buck describe recurring themes that emerge from the incest experiences of almost every victim: There is a desire by the victim to be loved by the perpetrator. The victim tends to put up little resistance. An atmosphere of secrecy surrounds the incest. Feelings include repulsion, fear, and guilt. Victims experience pain and confusion. They fear being punished or removed from the home. They feel isolated and have no one to turn to in a time of need. Most often the victim feels responsible for what occurred.

Children who have been sexually abused by someone in their family feel betrayed. They typically develop a mistrust of others who are in a position to take advantage of them. Often the sexual abuse is only one aspect of a dysfunctional family. There may also be physical abuse, neglect, alcoholism, and other problems. These children are often unaware of how psychologically abusive their family atmosphere really is for all members of the family.

Veronica Tracy conducted a research study to determine the impact of childhood sexual abuse on women's sexuality. Her study compared a group of women who were sexually abused with a group of women who had not experienced sexual abuse. She found that the women with a reported history of sexual abuse in childhood tended to have lower self-esteem and a greater number of sexual problems. They experienced less sexual satisfaction with a partner and less interest in engaging in sex. They had more sexual fantasies that involved force, and more guilt feelings about their sexual fantasies. Many of the women who were sexually abused reported that they were not able to reach orgasm with a partner, but only by themselves. Her research revealed that women who were sexual abuse survivors often blocked out their negative experiences. They only remembered the sexual abuse as they became sexually active. As the women began to feel safer with a partner, their sexual activity often triggered memories of the abuse. This tended to interfere with their ability to maintain satisfying intimate relationships.

The process of recovery from the psychological wounds of incest varies from individual to individual, depending on a number of complex factors. Many incest victims cut off their feelings as a survival tactic. Part of the recovery process involves regaining the ability to feel, getting in touch with buried memories, and speaking truths. They will likely have to deal with questions such as: "What is wrong with me? Why did this happen in my life? Why didn't I stop it? What will my future be like?" Victims may vacillate between denying the incestuous experiences and accepting what occurred. As they work through their memories surrounding the events, they eventually accept the fact that they were involved in incest. They typically feel sadness and grief, and then rage. If recovery is successful, they are finally able to forgive themselves and find a resolution to being stuck.

According to Forward and Buck, one of the greatest gifts that therapy can bestow is a full and realistic reversal of blame and responsibility from the victim to the victimizers. In her therapeutic practice with victims of incest, Susan Forward attempts to achieve three major goals:

- Assist the client in externalizing the guilt, rage, shame, hurt, fear, and confusion that are stored up within her.

- Help the victim place the responsibility for the events primarily with the aggressor and secondarily with the silent partner.

- Help the client realize that although incest has damaged her dignity and self-esteem, she does not have to remain psychologically victimized for the rest of her life.

We have worked with some adult men who were incest victims during childhood and adolescence. Regardless of gender or cultural background, the dynamics of incest are similar. Thus the therapeutic work is much the same for both women and men. However, the incestual traumas experienced by men have a different focus because of the roles men have traditionally held. Men are socialized to be in control and to demonstrate "masculinity." To be stripped of control and power is devastating to anyone, but that devastation takes a different toll on men. They have been socialized to reflect the supposedly masculine qualities of being strong and in charge at all times.

If you have been sexually abused in any way, regardless of whether you are a woman or a man, we encourage you to seek counseling. It is not uncommon for people to block out experiences such as sexual abuse, only to have memories and feelings surface later. Counseling can provide you with an opportunity to deal with unresolved feelings and problems that may linger because of earlier experiences. Support groups for incest survivors also can be most beneficial.

Date and Acquaintance Rape

In our contacts with college students it has become clear to us that date rape is common on the campus. *Acquaintance rape* takes place when a woman is forced to have unwanted sex with someone she knows. This might involve friends, coworkers, neighbors, or relatives. *Date rape* occurs in those situations where a woman is forced to have unwanted intercourse with a person in the context of dating.

Some writers consider acquaintance rape and date rape as examples of communication gone wrong. One myth about sexuality is that men are by nature sexually aggressive. Thus, men may feel that they are expected to be this way. As a consequence, they may misinterpret a woman's "no" as a "maybe" or a sign of initial resistance that can be broken down. Dating partners may not say what they really mean, or they may not mean what they say. This phenomenon is reinforced by the linkage of sex with domination and submission. In our society, masculinity is equated with power, dominance, and sexual aggressiveness. Femininity is associated with pleasing men, sexual passivity, and lack of assertiveness.

Weiten and Lloyd indicate that inadequate communication between dating partners is often a key factor contributing to date rape, and they offer these suggestions to people in dating relationships:

- Recognize that date rape is an act of sexual aggression.

- Beware of using excessive alcohol or drugs, which can lower your resistance and distort your judgment.

- Clarify your values and attitudes about sex before you are in situations where you have to make a decision about sexual behavior.

- Communicate your feelings, thoughts, and expectations about sex in a clear and open manner.

- Listen carefully to each other and respect each other's values, decisions, and boundaries.

- Exercise control over your environment.

- Know the warning signs associated with pre-rape behavior.

- Be prepared to act aggressively if assertive refusals don't stop the unwanted sexual advances.

Both date rape and acquaintance rape can be considered as a betrayal of trust. Much like in incest, when a woman is forced to have sex against her will, her dignity as a person is violated. Not believing that she is in danger, she may make herself vulnerable to a man, and then experience hurt. She might have explicit trust in a man she knows. Then she discovers that he is intent on getting what he wants, regardless of the cost to her. The emotional scars that are a part of date rape are similar to the wounds inflicted by incest. As in the case with incest victims, women who are raped by people they know often take responsibility. They blame themselves for what occurred. They are often embarrassed about or afraid of reporting the incident.

Currently, many college campuses offer education directed at prevention of date rape. One focus of this education is on the importance of being consistent and clear about what you want or don't want with your dating partner. Another focus is on providing information about factors contributing to date rape. Many prevention programs are designed for women to increase their awareness of high-risk situations and behaviors and to teach them how to protect themselves. Basow emphasizes the reality that because men rape, only they can stop rape. It is the man's responsibility to avoid forcing a woman to have sex with him, and he must learn that her "no" really does mean "no." Basow reports that campus programs aimed at men are just beginning, especially programs for men in fraternity groups.

Sexual Harassment

Sexual harassment is repeated and unwanted sexually oriented behavior. It can take the form of comments, gestures, or physical contacts. This phenomenon is of concern on the college campus, in the workplace, and in the military. Women experience sexual harassment more frequently than do men. Sexual harassment is abuse of the power difference between two people. Those who have more power tend to engage in sexual harassment more frequently than those with less power. Some of the many forms of sexual harassment include:

- comments about one's body or clothes

- physical or verbal conduct of a sexual nature

- jokes about sex or gender-specific traits

- repeated and unwanted staring, comments, or propositions of a sexual nature

- demeaning references to one's gender

- unwanted touching or attention of a sexual nature

- conversations tinted with sexually suggestive innuendoes or double meanings

- questions about one's sexual behavior

Men sometimes make the assumption that women like sexual attention. In fact, they resent being related to in strictly sexual terms. Sexual harassment diminishes choice, and surely it is not flattering. Harassment reduces people to objects to be demeaned. The person doing the harassing may not see this behavior as being a problem and may even joke about it. Yet it is never a laughing matter. Those on the receiving end of harassment often report feeling responsible. However, as in the case of incest and date rape, the victim should never be blamed.

As is true in cases of incest and date or acquaintance rape, many incidences of sexual harassment go unreported. Often the individuals involved fear the consequences, such as getting fired, being denied a promotion, risking a low grade in a course, and encountering barriers to pursuing their careers. Fear of reprisals is a foremost barrier to reporting. Riger suggests that gender bias in policies and procedures discourages women from making complaints.

If you are on the receiving end of unwanted behavior, you are not powerless. Sexual harassment is never appropriate. You have every right to break the pattern. Make it clear to the person doing the harassing that his or her behavior is unacceptable to you and that you want it stopped. If this does not work, or if you feel it would be too much of a risk to confront this individual, you can talk to someone else. If the offensive behavior does not stop, keep a detailed record of what is taking place. This will be useful in showing a pattern of unwanted behavior when you issue a complaint.

Most work settings and colleges have policies and procedures for dealing with sexual harassment complaints. You do not have to deal with this matter alone if your rights are violated. Realize that the college community does not take abusing power lightly. Procedures are designed to correct abuses. When you report a problematic situation, know that your college most likely has staff members who will assist you in resolving this situation. As is true for keeping the secret of incest, it will not help if you keep the harassment a secret. By telling someone else, you are breaking the pattern of silence that burdens sexual harassment victims.

2400 words

Analyze What You Read—Create a Study Guide

STEP 3

Objective Questions

1. Go back to the reading and underline what you think would be on a test.

2. Make marginal notes to test yourself on everything you underlined. If you wish, you may write the self-test note on the front of a flash card and paraphrase the underlining on the back.

Essay/Application Questions

Predict Essay Questions: Look at your marginal notes and pick the three topics that you think would be the most likely essay questions. Write them here.

1. _____

2. _____

3. _____

Make Graphic Organizers: Go back to the reading selection and fill in the blanks in the following outline.

Sexual Abuse and Harassment

   I. Abuse of sexuality

      A. Forms: _____

      B. What they have in common: _____

         _____

      C. Reactions of victims: _____

         _____

  II. Incest

      A. Responsibility: _____

      B. Frequency: _____

      C. Definition: _____

         _____

      D. Criminal status: _____

         _____

      E. Recurring themes: _____

         _____

         _____

         _____

         _____

      F. Effects of incest on children: _____

         _____

         _____

         _____

G. Veronica Tracy study: _____

_____

_____

_____

H. Recovery process: _____

_____

_____

   1. Forward and Buck: _____

_____

   2. Susan Forward:

      a. _____

      b. _____

_____

      c. _____

I. Men vs. women as victims: _____

_____

J. Value of counseling and support groups: _____

_____

III. Date and acquaintance rape

  A. Frequency of date rape on campus: _____

  B. Definitions of acquaintance and date rape: _____

_____

_____

  C. Communication issues: _____

_____

_____

  D. Suggestions: _____

_____

_____

_____

_____

_____

E. Effects on victims: _____

_____

_____

F. Campus educational programs: _____

_____

_____

IV. Sexual harassment

A. Definition: _____

_____

_____

B. Forms of harassment: _____

_____

_____

_____

_____

C. Attitudes of harassers and victims: _____

_____

_____

_____

D. Reporting: _____

E. Recommended actions: _____

_____

F. Importance of reporting harassment: _____

_____

For explanation
see p. 196

Skill Development: Use the underlining, the marginal notes, and the graphic organizer to write a summary of the reading selection. Use a separate sheet of paper.

Remember What's Important

STEP 4

Test yourself or have someone test you on the marginal self-test notes or flash cards and the outline. Keep testing until you know the material. Test yourself on the Vocabulary Preview words as needed.

Make Use of What You Read

When you are ready, complete the Comprehension Check on p. 403 and the Vocabulary Check on p. 405. Do not look back at the reading selection or the study guide.

Evaluate Your Active Critical Thinking Skills

After your tests have been graded, record your scores on the Progress Chart, p. 416, and answer the questions on the Evaluation Checklist on p. 417.

23 Ethical Considerations in Psychology Experiments

Vocabulary Preview

subject (sub′jekt): the person or animal used in an experiment

Example: Most experiments with auto crashes use dummies instead of live subjects.

guideline (gīd′līn): a principle or standard for a course of action

Example: Many employers now post guidelines to help their employees avoid sexual harassment.

censure (sen′shər): to blame publicly; to express disapproval of

Example: Professional societies, such as the American Bar Association for attorneys, can censure members who behave in unprofessional ways.

expel (ek spel′): to deprive of rights or membership

Example: Students can be expelled for dangerous behavior on campus.

simulation (sim′yo͞o lā′shən): an artificial experience

Example: Computers provide simulations of experiences that would be too dangerous for inexperienced people to try live, such as flying an airplane or doing brain surgery.

cat, āte, fäther; pen, ēvil; if, kīte; nō, ôr, fo͞od, book; boil, house; up, tʉrn; chief, shell; thick, *th*e; zh, treasure; ŋ, sing; ə for *a* in *about*; ′ as in *able* (ā′b′l)

STEP 1

Preread

Preview the following selection by reading the title, the headings, and the first sentence of each paragraph. Answer the following questions without looking back at the reading.

1. What is the subject?

____

____

2. What is the main idea?

____

____

3. Take a moment to think about ethical considerations in experiments. Think about what you know about the subject, what you don't know, and what

you might find out from reading the selection. Make up three questions that might be answered by reading the selection.

a. _____

b. _____

c. _____

Read

Read the selection without underlining.

◆ *Ethical Considerations*
in Psychology Experiments

James W. Kalat

In any experiment, psychologists try to change one variable to see how it affects behavior. You might not like the idea that someone would try to change your behavior. If not, keep in mind that every time you talk to people, you are trying to change their behavior at least a little. Most experiments produce effects that are no more lasting than the effects of a conversation. Still, some experiments do raise ethical questions. Psychologists are concerned about ethics, both in experiments with humans and with animals.

Ethical Concerns in Experiments with Humans

In order for experiments to be ethical, people who are part of a study should know exactly what will happen to them before they agree to participate. No one should leave an experiment saying, "If I had known what was going to happen, I never would have agreed to be part of the study." To be ethical, psychologists must make sure people are giving *informed consent*. When experimenters start signing up volunteers, they must begin by telling them what to expect. Will they receive electrical shocks? Will they have to drink sugar water? That way, anyone who does not want to participate can simply withdraw.

In colleges a Human Subjects Committee decides whether or not to approve each experiment. The members of the committee judge whether the experiment is ethical. Suppose, for example, that a psychologist wanted to give students large doses of cocaine. Even if students were eager to give their informed consent, the committee would not approve the experiment.

The committee also judges experiments in which some of the procedures are concealed from the subjects. For instance, the experimenters plan to put some subjects through a certain experience and then tell them to pick up a live snake. The object of the experiment is to see whether the subjects who had the experience would be more or less likely to obey orders to pick up the snake. The experimenter might not want to mention the snake before the subjects give their consent. In fact, the whole experiment might depend on the snake being a surprise. It's easy to see how this might cause ethical problems for the Human Subjects Committee.

Another group that sets ethical standards is the American Psychological Association (APA). The APA puts out a booklet describing how human volunteers must be treated. If any member of the APA does not follow these guidelines, that psychologist can be censured or expelled.

Ethical Experiments on Animals

Some kinds of research call for human subjects. For example, experiments on the effects of violence on television require people. Animals cannot be used for such a study. Actually animals are used on only 7 to 8 percent of the studies in psychology. The purpose of most animal experiments is to learn more about biological processes. For instance, much of what is known about the brain and brain damage comes from animal experiments. Other examples include how the senses work and the effects of drugs on behavior. Research to find treatments for schizophrenia, Huntington's disease, and Parkinson's disease begin with animal studies.

Although animal experiments have helped humans, not everyone agrees with such research. Animals, after all, cannot give informed consent. Animal rights supporters vary in their views. Some believe it is all right to experiment on animals if they feel no pain and the experiment is likely to benefit humans. Others believe animals should have the same rights as humans. They believe that keeping animals (even pets) is slavery. They consider killing an animal to be murder.

Most scientists who do animal research believe that animals should not be mistreated. But they deny that animals have the same rights as people. They give the following arguments in favor of animal research.

■ They support "the right of the incurably ill to hope for cures or relief from suffering through research using animals." Without animals, research in areas like brain damage would be almost impossible.

■ Research on animals has produced a wealth of information. Drugs have been developed to lower anxiety. New ways have been found to treat pain and depression. We have learned about the effects of drugs on unborn babies. We have new information on the ways old age affects memory. Animal research has helped people overcome neuro-muscular problems.

- Experiments that are very painful to animals are rare. They do occur, but much less often than people think.

- Scientists can use plants, tissue cultures, and computer simulations for some experiments. However, none of these alternatives gives informa-tion about animal or human behavior or about the working of the brain.

The debate goes on. Organizations such as the Neuroscience Society publish guidelines for the proper use of animals in research. Just as colleges have Human Subjects Committees, there are also Laboratory Animal Care Committees. These groups make sure that laboratory animals are treated well. They keep animals' pain and discomfort to a minimum. They ask experimenters to look for other ways to do their research before they cause any pain to animals.

Because these committees are dealing with difficult problems, their decisions can always be questioned. It is impossible to know ahead of time whether what will be learned from the experiment will be worth the pain the animals feel. We can't predict what will be learned, and we can't measure the animals' pain. Good arguments can be made for and against animal research. There is no solution that will satisfy everyone.

800 words

Analyze What You Read—Create a Study Guide

Objective Questions

1. Go back to the reading and underline what you think would be on a test.
2. Make marginal self-test notes to remember what you have underlined. If you wish, you may write each self-test note on the front of a flash card and paraphrase the underlining on the back.

Essay/Application Questions

Predict Essay Questions: What are the two most likely topics for essay questions?

1. _____

2. _____

Make Graphic Organizers: Fill in the following outline.

Ethical Considerations in Psychology Experiments

I. Ethical considerations in experiments with humans

   A. _____

   B. Groups that regulate ethics

      1. _____

      2. _____

II. _____

   A. 7 to 8 percent use

   B. Mostly to study biological processes

   C. Different opinions among supporters of animal rights

      1. _____

        _____

      2. _____

   D. Arguments in favor of animal research

      1. _____

        _____

      2. _____

        _____

        _____

        _____

      3. _____

        _____

      4. _____

        _____

        _____

III. Groups that set guidelines

   A. _____

   B. _____

      1. Make sure animals are treated well.

      2. _____

3. _____

   _____

IV. No perfect solution

For explanation see p. 196

Skill Development: Use the underlining, the marginal notes or flash cards, and the graphic organizer to write a summary of the reading. Use a separate sheet of paper.

Remember What's Important

Test yourself or have someone test you on the marginal self-test notes or flash cards and on the graphic organizer. Keep testing until you know the material. Test yourself on the Vocabulary Preview words as needed.

Make Use of What You Read

When you are ready, complete the Comprehension Check on p. 407 and the Vocabulary Check on p. 409. Do not look back at the reading selection or the study guide.

Evaluate Your Active Critical Thinking Skills

After your tests have been graded, record your scores on the Progress Chart, p. 416, and answer the questions on the Evaluation Checklist on p. 417.

24   Textbooks Distort History

Vocabulary Preview

sanitize (san′ə tīz): to make clean and harmless
Example: Fairy tales have been <u>sanitized</u>; all the endings have been changed so that nobody gets eaten and everybody lives happily ever after.

spruce up (sproos up′): to make neat and attractive
Example: Men get all <u>spruced up</u> before important dates.

exuberant (eg zoo′bər ənt): characterized by good health and high spirits
Example: Young people tend to be more <u>exuberant</u> than old people.

trust-buster (trust′bus tər): one who breaks up monopolies
Example: When a group of companies band together to control the market, we need a <u>trust-buster</u>.

progressive (prə gres′iv): one who favors progress, reform
Example: A <u>progressive</u> is the opposite of a conservative.

bigot (bi′gət): one who holds blindly and narrow-mindedly to his own beliefs
Example: A <u>bigot</u> imagines that everybody different from himself must be wrong.

squalid (skwa′lid): wretched; dismal; poor and dirty
Example: Even the people who live in <u>squalid</u> apartments are better off than the homeless.

guerrilla (gə ril′ə): involving a small defensive force of irregular soldiers, making surprise raids
Example: In the American Revolutionary War, the Americans beat the British in part because the British had no skills at <u>guerrilla</u> warfare.

puff up (puf up): exaggerate
Example: Ads often <u>puff up</u> the products they sell, for example, saying a laundry detergent will get your clothes "whiter than white."

unsophisticated (un′sə fis′tə kā′tid): simple; lacking worldly experience
Example: <u>Unsophisticated</u> travelers often don't know how much to tip cab drivers, porters, bellmen, and concierges.

cat, āte, fäther; pen, ēvil; if, kīte; nō, ôr, fōōd, book; boil, house; up, tʉrn; chief, shell; thick, *the*; zh, treasure; ŋ, sing; ə for *a* in *about*; ′ as in *able* (ā′b′l)

Preread

Preview the following selection by reading the title, the headings, and the first sentence of each paragraph. Answer the following questions without looking back at the reading.

1. What is the subject?

   _____

2. What is the main idea?

   _____

3. Take a moment to think about history textbooks. Think about what you know about them, what you don't know, and what you might find out from reading this selection. Make up three questions that might be answered by reading the selection.

   a. _____

   b. _____

   c. _____

Read

Read the selection without underlining.

◆ *Textbooks Distort History*

Howard Kahane and Nancy Cavendish

Public school history textbooks in the United States are more accurate today than ever before. But they still don't provide students with a true picture of the history of their nation. One reason is that they list dull facts one after another, without providing students with a good grasp of why things happened that way. But another reason has to do with the need to make students into loyal, proud citizens.

United States History Is Sanitized

History texts "clean up" our past so as to maintain student pride in America. As much as possible, our leaders are pictured as better than human, all dressed up and minus their flaws. Take the way in which Theodore Roosevelt, affectionately referred to as *Teddy* (the teddy bear was named after him), is spruced up in public school texts. Typically, he is portrayed as energetic, hard-driving, exuberant, and brave. He is seen as a trust-buster, conservationist, reformer, and progressive. He was against big business. In all, a great man deserving of his place on Mount Rushmore. And perhaps he was. But no textbooks the authors of this text have ever seen, or even heard of, tell students about another side of good old Teddy. They don't describe him as a bloodthirsty bigot who, though unusually brave, enjoyed the slaughter he personally engaged in and witnessed during the Spanish-American War. He expressed pleasure after 30 men had been shot to death in the Civil War draft riots ("an admirable object lesson to the remainder"). He justified slaughtering Indians on the grounds that their lives were only "a few degrees less meaningless, squalid, and ferocious than that of the wild beasts." He said that "All the great masterful races have been fighting races. . . . No triumph of peace is quite so great as the supreme triumph of war." Not exactly a teddy bear, this Teddy Roosevelt. History texts also falsely pump up the part played by Roosevelt's "Rough Riders" in the famous charge up San Juan Hill in Cuba during the Spanish-American War.

America's Role in History Is Distorted

Although outright lying is frowned upon, the writers of public school textbooks use other devices to satisfy social and political demands. The most commonly used of these devices is the complete *omission* of embarrassing historical events. For example, most of the CIA "dirty tricks" over the years in several foreign countries get passed over. Similarly, although all textbooks spend dozens of pages on World War II, most omit reference to the terrible firestorm bombing of Tokyo. It killed more people than either of the atomic bombs we dropped on Japan. They also frequently fail to mention the deliberate policy of the American and British air forces to bomb German civilians, mostly women and children, as a way of breaking down German will to continue fighting.

Embarrassing events also sometimes are covered over by carefully controlled *emphasis*. An example is the war that occurred between American troops and Philippine guerrillas. The Filipinos wanted independence after the United States annexed the Philippine Islands at the end of the Spanish-American War. The war is mentioned quickly, so as to mask the extreme nastiness of the way in which the Filipinos were conquered. The war with Spain gets relatively lots of space in most texts. The war against Filipino patriots gets extremely little. In fact, many more deaths and much greater destruction resulted from the war to force the Philippine people to knuckle under than from the war against Spain.

Textbooks also distort history by playing up the American role in foreign affairs at the expense of others. The part played by the United States in Word Wars I and II always is puffed up in this way. In the Second World War, for example, the principal fighting, and dying, against the Germans was done by Soviet troops, not American or British. Student readers of any of the current history textbooks are bound to draw the opposite conclusion.

These devices are very hard for uninformed or unsophisticated readers to see through. We all want very much to believe in the greatness of our own society. We tend to see national warts only after a good deal of experience has forced us to do so.

Even though the role of the United States in World War II is puffed up and cleansed, it might be supposed that the suffering and dying of American fighting troops would be explained in a way that would let students understand the extent of their sacrifices and the terror they suffered. For instance, on June 6th, 1944 ("D-Day"), several thousand American troops lost their lives on the beaches of Normandy, in France. Understanding this would show how brave and self-sacrificing American troops have been. But this would require explaining what warfare really is like. Soldiers have to advance into concentrated machine gun fire that is certain to mow down most of those who find themselves in this terrible and terrifying circumstance. They fly on bombing missions with the knowledge that sooner or later most bombers in their unit are likely to be shot down. They suddenly find themselves covered with the splattered brains of a buddy who has just been hit by an unseen sniper. They experience the last moments of men drowning on submarines. Tank crews are burned alive. Soldiers are blasted into thousands of tiny pieces by enemy shelling. (Back in high school did you see any pictures of dead American soldiers in history textbooks? Did you see anything that realistically conveys the true horror of modern warfare?)

Perhaps we should point out that the worst distortion of American history occurs in grade school texts. As students move up in grade level, textbooks become less goody goody and quite a bit more accurate. The idea seems to be that tiny tots are not ready for plain truth and need to be gently introduced into the "facts of life" over time. What we have stressed here is that even in high school, students are provided a dolled-up version of reality, an account that fails to square with the true history of the United States.

1000 words

Analyze What You Read—Create a Study Guide

STEP 3

Objective Questions

1. Go back and underline what you think will be on a test.

2. Make marginal notes to test yourself on everything you underlined. If you wish, you may write the self-test note on the front of a flash card and paraphrase the underlining on the back.

Essay/Application Questions

Predict Essay Questions: Look at your marginal notes and pick the topic that you think would be the most likely essay question. Write it here.

_____

Make Graphic Organizers: Go back to the reading selection and fill in the blanks in the following chart.

Ways U.S. history books distort reality	Examples
1.	
2.	
3.	
4.	
5.	

For explanation see p. 196

Skill Development: Use the underlining, the marginal notes, and the graphic organizer to write a summary of the reading selection. Use a separate sheet of paper.

Remember What's Important

Test yourself or have someone test you on the marginal self-test notes or flash cards and the graphic organizer. Keep testing until you know the material. Test yourself on the Vocabulary Preview words as needed.

Make Use of What You Read

When you are ready, complete the Comprehension Check on p. 411 and the Vocabulary Check on p. 413. Do not look back at the reading selection or the study guide.

Evaluate Your Active Critical Thinking

After your tests have been graded, record your scores on the Progress Chart, p. 416, and answer the questions on the Evaluation Checklist on p. 417.

Additional Resources

Tests: Comprehension and Vocabulary Checks

1   Listening: To Tell Fact From Opinion

Comprehension Check

True–False

Mark T or F.

_____ 1. A theory is a form of fact.

_____ 2. A law is a form of opinion.

_____ 3. An observation is a form of fact.

_____ 4. A hypothesis is a form of opinion.

_____ 5. Scientists should deal only in facts.

Multiple Choice

Circle the letter preceding the best answer to each of the following questions.

6. Which of the following statements is a hypothesis?

   a. Number 76 will win the lottery.

   b. Chinese food is better than Mexican food.

   c. You should try to lose weight.

   d. Vitamin C can reduce heart attacks.

7. Which is an example of a theory?

   a. Dinosaurs became extinct when the earth was hit by a meteor.

   b. Doctors earn more than nurses.

   c. Shakespeare is the world's greatest poet.

   d. Gentlemen prefer blondes.

8. Being able to distinguish between fact and opinion can help us

   a. vote for the best candidate.

   b. buy the best products.

   c. make the safest investments.

   d. do all of the above.

Short Answer

Fill in the blanks.

9. Write a fact _____

_____

10. Write an opinion _____

_____

Essay

Explain and give examples of the differences between facts and opinions.
Write your essay on a separate sheet of paper.

Vocabulary Check

Write the best word from the following list in the blank in each of the
sentences below.

observation   hypotheses   speculative   sounder   theory

1. Over the centuries, there have been many _____ about how
   the world began. Because of advances in space exploration, some of them
   can finally be tested.

2. The writer for *Vogue* made the _____ that recently fashion
   models have been looking more muscular and less skinny.

3. One _____ about the causes of depression is that the body
   lacks certain chemicals.

4. Buying and selling stock is always _____ because nobody
   can predict the future.

5. Since Company A has a _____ financial statement than
   Company B, I think it is wiser to buy stock in Company A.

2   A League of Her Own

Comprehension Check

True–False

Mark T or F.

   T   1. Sheryl Swoopes is as good a basketball player as Michael Jordan.

   F   2. The author plays basketball.

   T   3. The author has her own TV show.

   F   4. Women basketball players are paid as much as the men.

Multiple Choice

Circle the letter preceding the best answer to each of the following questions.

5. The main difference the author mentions between women's and men's basketball is the
   - (a.) money.
   - b. fame.
   - c. level of competition.
   - d. spirit of love.

6. You can infer that the author prefers women who are
   - a. passive and submissive.
   - b. powerful and commanding.
   - (c.) competitive with other women.
   - d. competitive against men.

7. The author says that the WNBA
   - a. empowers women and girls.
   - b. allows women players to use their talent.
   - c. allows women to dream.
   - d. does all of the above.

8. The author says that WNBA fans are distinctive because

   a. they are radical feminists.

   b. they know more about basketball then the men do.

   c. they love basketball on a different level than men do.

   d. all of the above are true.

Short Answer

9. Why does the author think team sports are good for women and girls?

   _____

10. The author contrasts NBA MVP Michael Jordan and WNBA MVP Sheryl Swoopes. Why does she say Jordan was MVP and why does she say Swoopes was MVP?

   _____

   _____

Essay

Why does the author think women should have a league of their own? Write your essay on a separate sheet of paper.

Vocabulary Check

Write the best word from the following list in the blank in each of the sentences below.

hypnotic   stereotypical   distinctive   tragic   empowers

committed   slogan   commanding   efficient   validate

1. "Dumb blonde" jokes are based on a _____ idea.

2. A scar is a _____ mark that could be used for identification.

3. "Better dead than Red" was an old anticommunist _____.

4. It is more _____ to write with a word processor than with an old manual typewriter.

5. A six-foot-tall woman in a basketball uniform is a _____ presence.

6. You usually need a sales receipt to _____ your claim to a rebate.

7. Watching waves roll in and out can have a _____ effect.

8. People should not have children unless they are _____ to being responsible parents.

9. The right to vote _____ citizens to participate in government.

10. The love affair of Romeo and Juliet has a _____ outcome.

3   How to Write a Business Letter

Comprehension Check

True–False

Mark T or F.

_____   1. In a business letter, adjectives are more important than nouns and verbs.

_____   2. A business letter should be as short as possible.

_____   3. The author implies that you are more likely to get what you want if you use threats.

Multiple Choice

Circle the letter preceding the best answer to each of the following questions.

4. Knowing what you want to say

   a. is not as important as good spelling and grammar.

   b. comes automatically once you start writing a business letter.

   c. is not as important as being polite.

   d. is necessary before you begin to write.

5. The author does *not* advise being

   a. positive.

   b. cute.

   c. nice.

   d. natural.

6. The author thinks it is important to

   a. begin with a joke.

   b. keep your letter short.

   c. be cute.

   d. begin the letter with "Dear Sir."

7. The author implies that you
   a. will have to make more than one draft if you want to write a good letter.
   b. know how to write good letters but don't bother.
   c. already write good business letters.
   d. can't learn to write a good letter and should have someone else write it for you.

8. Which of the following sentences or phrases can you infer that the author would approve of including in a business letter?
   a. To whom it may concern:
   b. At this point in time, I would like very much to request an opportunity to discuss future employment.
   c. Some stupid jerk in your accounting department messed up my bill, as usual.
   d. I want to apply for a job.

Short Answer

Fill in the blanks.

9. What should you write in the first paragraph of every business letter?

   _____

10. What should you write in the last paragraph of every business letter?

   _____

   _____

Essay

List the major points that Forbes recommends for writing business letters. Write your essay on a separate sheet of paper.

Vocabulary Check

Write the best word from the following list in the blank in each of the
sentences below. Because this Vocabulary Preview is so long, we have
divided the exercise into two parts.

Part A

asinine   mundane   jargon   flippant

emphasis   invariably   inflated

1. Using an exclamation point at the end of a sentence adds

   _____ to an idea.

2. It's _____ to build a house next to a river that floods

   every year.

3. As prices become _____, the price of gold rises as well.

4. A legal secretary must be able to understand legal _____.

5. As a form of rebellion, teenagers often make _____ remarks

   to teachers and parents.

6. Most children prefer _____ lunches like peanut butter and

   jelly to interesting ones like pasta primavera.

7. _____, the day you are absent from class is the day the

   instructor announces an important test.

Part B

stultifying   clichés   pretense   gospel

annihilated   ego   illegible   receptive

8. No matter what happens in his or her personal life, a clown must make

   a _____ of being happy.

9. Photocopies of notes written in pencil are often _____.

10. Some people find soap operas exciting, whereas others find them

    _____.

11. Thousands of people were _____ by the flu epidemic that swept the Western world in 1918.

12. His inflated _____ prevented him from thinking of any-body but himself.

13. You are more likely to get your ideas across if your boss is in a _____ mood.

14. Advertising slogans such as "You're not getting older, you're getting better" often become _____.

15. A critical thinker does not accept anyone's opinion as _____.

4   How to Read Faster

Comprehension Check

True–False

Mark T or F.

_____T_____ 1. You can infer from the article that a good reader reads every-thing at the same steady pace.

_____F_____ 2. You can infer from the article that if you want a high level of comprehension you must read every word.

_____T_____ 3. You can infer from the article that 50 percent comprehension is enough for many purposes.

Multiple Choice

Circle the letter preceding the best answer to each of the following questions.

4. An effective technique for getting the main idea from light reading material is

   a. previewing.

   (b.) skimming.

   c. thorough reading.

   d. all of the above.

5. Cosby advises previewing

   a. comic books.

   (b.) everything.

   c. heavy reading.

   d. instead of reading.

6. Previewing as compared to reading

   a. takes as little as one-tenth of the time.

   b. yields as much as half the comprehension.

   c. allows you to skip what you don't need to read.

   (d.) does all of the above.

7. The author implies that before you can learn to skim, you must be able to

   a. identify minor details.

   b. have a superior vocabulary.

   c. take a speed-reading class.

   d. identify main ideas.

8. Which sentence is clustered properly?

   a. Concentrate on seeing three to four words at once rather than one word at a time.

   b. Concentrate on seeing three to four words at once rather than one word at a time.

   c. Concentrate on seeing three to four words at once rather than one word at a time.

   d. Concentrate on seeing three to four words at once rather than one word at a time.

Short Answer

Fill in the blanks.

9. Looking at *all* the words in groups is called _____.

10. Looking at a few key words in each line is called _____.

Essay

Explain Bill Cosby's techniques for reading faster. Write your essay on a separate sheet of paper.

Vocabulary Check

Write the best word from the following list in the blank in each of the sentences below.

doctorate   novel   correspondence   nonfiction   successive

1. Because they receive so many letters, many companies now answer _correspondence_ by computer.

2. In a _nonfiction_ book, information must be factual.

3. The only president to earn a _doctorate_ was Woodrow Wilson, the twenty-eighth president of the United States.

4. With each _successive_ heart attack, the patient became weaker.

5. *The Spy Who Came In from the Cold* was the first thriller _novel_ to make the best-seller list.

5 Propaganda

Comprehension Check

Multiple Choice

Circle the letter preceding the best answer to each of the following questions.

1. A propaganda technique that is discussed in the article is

   a. statistics.

   b. false cause.

   c. testimonial.

   d. straw man.

2. Card stacking is the

   a. use of unclear statements on purpose.

   b. use of words with unpleasant connotations.

   c. presentation of only one point of view.

   d. presentation of the best of one point of view and the worst of the other point of view.

3. Using average-looking people in commercials is an attempt to use the propaganda technique called

   a. glad names.

   b. testimony.

   c. band wagon.

   d. plain folks.

4. Linking something you like or respect with a person, program, or a product is called

   a. glad names.

   b. band wagon.

   c. transfer.

   d. plain folks.

5. The statement "Everyone is smoking Brand X" is an example of

   a. card stacking.

   b. band wagon.

    c. glad names.

    d. plain folks.

6. A technique that would probably be associated with current fads is

    a. testimonial.

    b. bad names.

    c. band wagon.

    d. card stacking.

7. Showing a cat drooling over a certain type of cat food is an example of

    a. glad names.

    b. band wagon.

    c. testimonial.

    d. plain folks.

Short Answer

Following are three statements of propaganda. Label each with the correct propaganda technique.

8. Smith and Wesson are the most intelligent film critics on the air.

_____

9. Don't take Dr. Jones for Chemistry. He's a real idiot.

_____

10. Prices of houses in Paradise Hole are skyrocketing. You'd better buy fast, before they go up further.

_____

Essay

List seven propaganda techniques and give an example of each. Write your essay on a separate sheet of paper.

Vocabulary Check

Write the best word from the following list in the blank in each of the sentences below.

connotations   sophisticated   endorse   deception   mediocre

1. A low-priced suit is generally of _____ quality.

2. A well-traveled person is generally _____.

3. The word *mother* has _____ that go far beyond the dictionary definition of "the female parent."

4. They were unable to _____ the candidate from their party because all of her beliefs were opposite theirs.

5. To avoid paying taxes, some people resort to falsehood and

   _____.

6   How to Read a Newspaper

Comprehension Check

Multiple Choice

Circle the letter preceding the best answer to each of the following questions.

1. Walter Cronkite believes that reading a newspaper is

   a. necessary every day.

   b. difficult.

   c. a duty of every citizen.

   d. unnecessary when the same stories are on TV.

2. Rule #1 of American journalism is

   a. news stories should contain the reporter's opinion as well as fact.

   b. news stories should include analysis and interpretation.

   c. adjectives and adverbs should be added to news stories for color.

   d. news columns are reserved only for news.

3. Sidebars usually contain

   a. hard news.

   b. background and analysis.

   c. an inverted pyramid.

   d. pictures.

Short Answer

4. What is the difference between the news presented on TV and in the newspaper?

   _____

   _____

   _____

5. How do you do a three-minute overview?

   _____

   _____

   _____

6. Where is the main story in a newspaper?

_____

_____

_____

7. What does Walter Cronkite mean when he says "News is information, period"?

_____

_____

_____

8. Explain the upside-down pyramid.

_____

_____

_____

9. How does Walter Cronkite suggest you form your opinions?

_____

_____

_____

10. Why does Walter Cronkite suggest that you pick a TV story and follow it in the newspaper?

_____

_____

_____

Essay

How does Walter Cronkite advise us to read the newspaper? Write your essay on a separate sheet of paper.

Vocabulary Check

Write the best word from the following list in the blank in each of the sentences below.

caption   entice   analysis   slanting   conscientious

inverted   pundits   motivates   colleagues   heft

1. Faculty members join committees to work on school issues with their

     _____ .

2. The propaganda technique of card stacking is a way of

     _____ the facts.

3. Every illustration in a textbook should have a _____ .

4. Store window displays are made as attractive as possible to

     _____ shoppers to come inside.

5. I like to read movie reviews before deciding what movies to see because

     I usually agree with the _____ .

6. In an _____ fountain, the water comes out the sides and

     goes down a hole near the center.

7. Walter Cronkite says that TV news programs don't offer

     _____ of the news.

8. The hope of a more satisfying and higher-paid career is one of the main

     things that _____ students to attend college.

9. Children often _____ their Christmas presents to help them

     guess what is inside.

10. Male emperor penguins are very _____ fathers; they spend

     months standing in total darkness without eating during the Antarctic

     winter—while holding their egg on their foot.

Your Financial Independence in Ten "Foolish" Steps

7

Comprehension Check

True–False

Mark T or F.

_____ 1. The author believes that money can buy happiness.

_____ 2. The author distrusts financial professionals.

_____ 3. The author recommends diversifying among stocks, bonds, and real estate.

_____ 4. By "high-rate debt" the author means interest rates higher than you can usually earn in the stock market.

Multiple Choice

Circle the letter preceding the best answer to each of the following questions.

5. The author recommends that you

   a. cut up all your credit cards.

   b. don't charge more than you can pay off each month.

   c. borrow on your credit cards to invest in the stock market.

   d. do all of the above.

6. The stock market historically averages a return of about

   a. 3.7 percent.

   b. 20 percent.

   c. 5.6 percent.

   d. 11 percent.

7. By "long-term savings" the author means money you won't need for at least

   a. 1 year.

   b. 5 years.

   c. 10 years.

   d. 20 years.

8. The author believes that

   a. it isn't hard to earn a better return than the financial professionals do.

   b. you can learn everything that you need by visiting the Motley Fool web site or reading their publications.

   c. money management can be fun.

   d. all of the above are true.

Short Answer

Fill in the blanks.

9. What did Fred Schwed mean when he asked "Where are the customers' yachts?"

_____

_____

_____

10. Give an example of a depreciating financial asset.

_____

_____

_____

Essay

Describe the ten "foolish" steps in your own words. Use a separate sheet of paper.

Vocabulary Check

Write the best word from the following list in the blank in each of the sentences below.

Part A

withers	pummel	finagling	obstructs	substantial
perpetual	adhere	hazardous	stipulates	grovel

1. You hope your boss won't make you _____ when you ask for a raise.

2. Our skin _____ when we get old.

3. Succeeding in college requires a _____ effort.

4. Credit card debt is _____ to your financial health.

5. You can die from food lodged in your throat if it _____ your air passage.

6. When you borrow money, even from family or friends, you should have a written contract that _____ the date that payment is due, the interest rate, and penalties for late payment.

7. Most kids are skilled at _____ money and privileges from their parents.

8. If you set up a good study schedule and _____ to it, you should do well in your classes.

9. Boxers and their sparring partners regularly _____ each other.

10. It seems like toddlers are in _____ motion the whole time they're awake.

Part B

daunting	retroactively	scrupulously	negotiable	waive
leverage	depreciating	diversify	cryptic	syndicated

11. "Don't put all your eggs in one basket" means that you should

_____ .

12. After her _____ comment, I was unsure if I had been complimented or insulted.

13. When they ask you for something, spouses and bosses have a lot more _____ than strangers do.

14. In times of inflation money is worth less, so cash would be a _____ asset.

15. If you let it go too long, cleaning out your closet can be a _____ task.

16. Operating rooms in hospitals must be kept _____ clean.

17. Most cartoons are _____ , which lowers the price for each publication that subscribes.

18. When new educational requirements were set for hairdressers, the current license holders were grandfathered, which means that they met the requirements _____ and did not have to go back to school.

19. I am willing to discuss some of the issues, but others I feel so strongly about that they're just not _____ .

20. Many Internet service providers will _____ the first month's charge for new subscribers.

8   Improve Your Memory in 7 Easy Steps

Comprehension Check

Multiple Choice

Circle the letter preceding the best answer to each of the following questions. Don't look back at the article.

1. Using an acronym is an example of
   a. chunking.
   b. external memory.
   c. mediation.
   d. associations.

2. Using *claws* to remember Clausen is an example of
   a. chunking.
   b. external memory.
   c. mediation.
   d. associations.

3. If you are trying to recall a name you have forgotten,
   a. associate it with a current name.
   b. chunk it with new information.
   c. picture the place in which you learned it.
   d. do any of these things and it will help.

4. Which of the following is an example of a "pegword"?
   a. damp
   b. homes
   c. bun
   d. claws

5. Probably a major reason for forgetting is that
   a. we are afraid to remember something.
   b. we are afraid we will forget something so we never bother to learn it.
   c. we don't use a good technique to remember information.
   d. we haven't really forgotten the data but we don't know it.

6. Memory experts

    a. have concealed information about mnemonics so that they could appear to have excellent memories.

    b. are still learning about memory.

    c. use mnemonics to remember everything they need to remember.

    d. are not respected by scientists.

7. The article implies that

    a. most people never use mnemonic techniques.

    b. using mnemonic techniques won't help you study for tests.

    c. mnemonic techniques are not the answer to all memory problems.

    d. all these things are implied in the article.

8. The article implies that mnemonic techniques are

    a. usually a process of rhyming what you need to learn with something familiar.

    b. a way to quickly learn complicated information.

    c. a good way to learn the material in your college textbooks.

    d. useful for recalling simple information.

Short Answer

9. Give an example of external memory.

_____

10. Give an example of reliving the moment.

_____

_____

Essay

Explain how you can improve your memory. Give examples. Write your essay on a separate sheet of paper.

Vocabulary Check

Write the best word from the following list in the blank in each of the sentences below.

acronym   mediation   retrieve   sensory   mnemonic

1. Attaching a list of items to another list that is easy to remember, such as pegwords, is called _____.

2. The familiar rhyme "i before e except after c" is a _____ device.

3. Roy G. Biv is an _____ for the colors in the rainbow: red, orange, yellow, green, blue, indigo, and violet.

4. When you are using the computer, you should store your information on an external storage device, such as a floppy disk or tape. Otherwise, a power failure could make it impossible to _____ it.

5. One way to help people with learning disabilities is to use more _____ channels. For example, if they can't remember what they see in a book, they could listen to tapes. Teachers know that having students write their spelling words helps, because writing uses the sense of touch as well as vision and sound.

TESTS

9   How to Become an Effective Test Taker

Comprehension Check

Multiple Choice

Circle the letter preceding the best answer to each of the following questions.

1. The most important thing in succeeding on tests is

   a. knowledge of the subject matter.

   b. reviewing the text and lecture notes.

   c. having good test-taking skills.

   d. following directions.

2. One tip that is specific for taking objective exams is

   a. anticipate answers and prepare an outline.

   b. study information that is emphasized and enumerated.

   c. review other tests.

   d. eliminate the options.

3. During the test, you should sit

   a. in the back.

   b. in front of the instructor.

   c. where you can see a clock.

   d. near the door.

4. You should answer easy questions first because

   a. you can get through the test faster that way.

   b. your unconscious mind may have solved the hard questions by the time you get through.

   c. later items may give you the information you need.

   d. all of the above are true.

5. The author recommends using acronyms, acrostics, and word games as

   a. mnemonic devices.

   b. a way of reducing stress.

   c. a way of improving your vocabulary.

   d. all of the above.

Short Answer

What are the three tips the author gives about objective tests?

6. _____

7. _____

8. _____

9. How does the author tell you to budget your time?

_____

_____

_____

10. What does the author mean by "eliminate options" on multiple-choice tests?

_____

Essay

What tips does the author give for test taking? Write your essay on a separate sheet of paper.

Vocabulary Check

Write the best word from the following list in the blank in each of the sentences below.

acquire   enumerate   italics   methodically   strategies

penalized   pertinent   acrostics   phenomenon   demanding

1. A tornado is an unusual natural _____.

2. People who own computers can often avoid a trip to the library when they are researching a topic. This is because _____ data can often be obtained online.

3. As we get older we tend to _____ more and more possessions.

4. Graduate school is assumed to be more intellectually _____ than undergraduate studies.

5. When a test question asks you to list several items, they want you to _____ them.

6. In a basketball game, a player who commits six fouls is _____ by having to sit out the rest of the game.

7. Even if your tax return is prepared by an accountant, you still need to check it _____, because you are responsible for errors.

8. _____ is a typeface that originated in Italy.

9. Study skills are really _____ for learning and remembering.

10. _____ are more difficult than most crossword puzzles, because there are fewer clues.

10 | Obtaining Information about Employment Opportunities

Comprehension Check

True–False

Mark T or F.

_____ 1. Career center services are usually expensive.

_____ 2. Many professional organizations maintain nonprofit employment services for their members.

_____ 3. Services of private employment agencies are similar to those offered by most career centers.

_____ 4. Most college students can get help writing application letters from their campus career center.

Multiple Choice

Circle the letter preceding the best answer to each of the following questions.

5. The best way to obtain information about unsolicited positions is through

   a. looking in job-related publications.

   b. looking at newspaper ads.

   c. using Internet sources such as *Jobtrak.*

   d. using your network of contacts.

6. To look for government jobs, you should contact

   a. the federal government.

   b. the state government.

   c. city, county, and regional governments.

   d. all of the above.

7. In an aggressive, vigorous job campaign, you should seek assistance from

   a. your career center.

   b. private or government employment agencies.

   c. the Internet.

   d. all sources.

Short Answer

Fill in the blanks by listing at least three services offered by most career centers.

8. _____

_____

9. _____

_____

10. _____

_____

Essay

Explain how to conduct an effective job campaign. Write your essay on a separate sheet of paper.

Vocabulary Check

Write the best word from the following list in the blank in each of the sentences below.

Part A

solicited	credentials	résumé	minimal	database
reference	initiate	access	scope	comprehensive

1. College students often ask their instructors for letters of _____ to help them get jobs.

2. "Spam" is e-mail advertising that you have not _____.

3. Your campus career center can help you prepare a good _____.

4. The Human Resources department keeps a _____ of employee information.

5. A _____ insurance policy covers a number of different risks, such as fire, flood, earthquake, and theft.

6. If the IRS finds something suspicious on a spot-check of your tax return, they may _____ a full investigation.

7. A password is sometimes needed before you can _____ a Web site.

8. When you take a drug, you hope it has _____ side effects.

9. It's against the law to practice medicine or law without the proper _____.

10. Because you can't actually see the scenes, a book offers more _____ for the imagination than a film on the same topic does.

Part B

distribute	significant	extensive	sector	personnel
advent	cyberspace	diversity	hypertext	vigorous

11. Internet chat rooms allow people who have never seen each other to develop close friendships in _____.

12. Advertising campaigns often target a specific _____ of the population, such as 18- to 23-year-old African Americans.

13. _____ work involves hiring, firing, and employee benefits.

14. Politicians often _____ political favors known as "pork."

15. If you click on a _____ link, you will go to a different Web page.

16. Young people are more _____ than most old people.

17. Usually people who have few interests are more boring than those with a _____ of interests.

18. Unmarried partners are often called "_____ others."

19. A career counseling center can offer _____ testing of your interests, abilities, and values in order to match you with appropriate career choices.

20. The _____ of cable connections to the Internet is bringing about much faster Web-surfing, and may someday end the "World Wide Wait."

11   Lie-Detector Tests Should Be Prohibited

Comprehension Check

True–False

Mark T or F.

_____ 1. The fact that some people can lie without emotion supports the author's argument that lie-detector tests are inaccurate.

_____ 2. The author explains why Birch Bayh is an authority on lie-detector tests.

_____ 3. The author implies that the rights of employees are more important than the needs of employers.

_____ 4. The author implies that employers who use lie-detector tests have to worry about being sued for invasion of privacy.

_____ 5. The author implies that lie-detector tests are widely used.

_____ 6. The author implies that lie-detector tests have been getting better in recent years.

Multiple Choice

Circle the letter preceding the best answer to each of the following questions.

7. The author implies that

    a. lie-detector tests have no value.

    b. the potential harm from lie-detector tests outweighs the benefits.

    c. the benefits outweigh the harm.

    d. employers have no other methods for screening employees.

8. The author implies that polygraph operators

    a. try to get accurate responses.

    b. try to get emotional responses.

    c. lie about the responses they get.

    d. are paid according to how many lies they can detect.

9. The author implies that the federal government

    a. is trying to make polygraph testing illegal.

    b. is looking into limiting the use of polygraph testing.

    c. is passing licensing laws for polygraph operators.

    d. strictly regulates the use of lie-detector tests.

10. The author implies that an innocent person

    a. need have no fear of taking a lie-detector test.

    b. should be afraid of taking a lie-detector test.

    c. has only about a 30 percent chance of being considered innocent.

    d. should refuse to take a lie-detector test.

Essay

Why does the author say that use of lie-detector tests by employers should be prohibited? Write your essay on a separate sheet of paper.

Vocabulary Check

Write the best word from the following list in the blank in each of the sentences below.

polygraph   **technological**   **intimidating**   **curtail**   **misconstrue**

1. Many night clubs use bouncers of _____ size to keep the customers from getting too rowdy.

2. In order to balance the budget, most households have to _____ their spending.

3. When men and women are friendly to one another, they must be careful not to _____ friendliness as romantic interest.

4. _____ change in the field of computers is so rapid that you can expect your computer to be outdated in about 18 months.

5. Use of the _____ is based on the idea that emotions cause changes in the body.

12 Lie-Detector Tests Should Not Be Prohibited

Comprehension Check

True–False

Mark T or F.

_____ 1. The author believes that lie-detector tests can be used to protect the public as well as employers.

_____ 2. The author implies that Ty Kelley knows at least as much about lie-detector tests as does Birch Bayh.

_____ 3. The author suggests a good solution to the problem of the tests' inaccuracies.

_____ 4. According to the author, the main reason employers use lie-detector tests is to screen potential employees for psychological deviance.

_____ 5. The author states that at least half of all business theft is caused by employees.

_____ 6. Employers who use lie-detector tests believe they deter crime.

Multiple Choice

Circle the letter preceding the best answer to each of the following questions.

7. The author implies that

  a. many employers consider the polygraph the best way to detect employee theft.

  b. lie-detector tests cause no harm.

  c. most employees are dishonest.

  d. all of the above are true.

8. The author believes that

  a. protecting employers is more important than protecting employees.

  b. people give up their right to privacy when they apply for a job.

  c. unnecessary invasion of privacy should be stopped.

  d. all of the above are true.

9. The percentage of businesses that use lie-detector tests is approximately

   a. 20 to 30 percent.

   b. 40 to 50 percent.

   c. 70 to 80 percent.

   d. 90 to 100 percent.

10. The author criticizes the opponent's support for the argument that tests are inaccurate because some emotional responses are not caused by lying by saying that

   a. the examples of the bookkeeper and the supermarket clerk were phony.

   b. there were only two examples, not enough to prove a significant problem.

   c. curbing theft is more important than protecting the feelings of employees.

   d. some people will get upset about anything.

Essay

Why does the author think use of lie-detector tests by employers should not be prohibited? Write your essay on a separate sheet of paper.

Vocabulary Check

Write the best word from the following list in the blank in each of the sentences below.

abolished   **deter**   **psychotic**   **potentially**   **sadism**

1. According to their motto, neither rain nor snow nor dark of night will _____ mail carriers from delivering the mail.

2. The word _____ comes from the Marquis de Sade, who wrote sexually deviant novels involving pain.

3. You can avoid _____ dangerous situations on the Internet by making sure you never give out your name, address, phone, photo, place of employment, or school.

4. The phrase "mad as a hatter" came from the eighteenth- and nineteenth-century practice of using mercury to cure felt for hats, which often caused hatmakers to become _____.

5. The 1954 Supreme Court decision, "Brown vs. Board of Education of Topeka" _____ legal racial segregation in public schools.

13   Reading Textbook Illustrations

Comprehension Check

Short Answer

Look at the graph and answer the questions below.

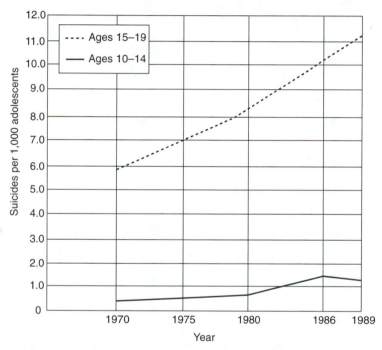

Figure 1   **Changes in suicide rates for U.S. adolescents, 1970 to 1989.**
Source: Adapted from U.S. Bureau of the Census, 1992, p. 90.

1. What are the two variables?

    _____

2. What is the subject?

    _____

3. What is the main idea?

    _____

    _____

4. How many of each 1,000 15- to 19-year-olds committed suicide in 1986?

_____

5. What can you infer about the causes of the suicide pattern seen on the graph?

_____

_____

_____

_____

Matching

In the blank, write the letter preceding the best definition of each type of illustration.

Type	Definition
_____ 6. picture	a. a chart that shows the history of something
_____ 7. graph	b. a photograph, drawing, or cartoon
_____ 8. diagram	c. an illustration of a relationship between variables
_____ 9. flowchart	d. a drawing that explains something
_____ 10. time line	e. a sketch that shows the steps in a process

Essay

List and briefly describe the types of illustrations commonly found in text-books. You may use drawings if you wish. Use a separate sheet of paper.

Vocabulary Check

Write the best word from the following list in the blank in each of the sentences below.

generalization   variable   mean   sustainable   residual

1. Mount Waialeale, on the Hawaiian island of Kauai, is the rainiest spot in the world, with a _____ annual rainfall of 460 inches.

2. In studies concerning whether smoking is related to lung cancer, one _____ is smoking and the other is lung cancer.

3. Adult survivors of child abuse often have _____ effects, such as a tendency to abuse their own children.

4. Living under conditions of high stress does not seem to be _____ for very long; eventually one's organs start to break down.

5. It is a _____ to say that Pit Bull dogs are dangerous.

14   The Life Cycle of Romantic Relationships

Comprehension Check

True–False

Mark T or F.

_____ 1. According to the reading, people are usually attracted to their opposites.

_____ 2. The buildup stage is the most stable one in a relationship.

_____ 3. College men are more likely to suggest a breakup than are college women.

Multiple Choice

Circle the letter preceding the best answer to each of the following questions.

4. According to the author, the partners in successful relationships

   a. have a good sex life.

   b. listen to each other.

   c. have similar interests and values.

   d. have financial security.

5. Which of the following reasons for ending a relationship is mentioned in the reading?

   a. The partners argue too much.

   b. One of the partners is bored with the other.

   c. One partner feels he or she is not getting a fair share.

   d. One partner meets someone else she or he is more attracted to.

6. The method of dealing with relationship problems called *loyalty* refers to

   a. talking about the problem.

   b. ignoring the problem and hoping it will go away.

   c. letting the relationship deteriorate.

   d. withdrawing from the relationship.

7. During what stage do the partners learn the most about each other?

   a. initial attraction

   b. buildup

   c. continuation

   d. deterioration

Short Answer

8. To whom are most people initially attracted?

   _____

   _____

   _____

9. Describe the continuation stage.

   _____

   _____

   _____

   _____

   _____

10. Explain exchange theory.

   _____

   _____

   _____

   _____

Essay

Describe the five stages of romantic relationships. Use a separate sheet of paper.

Vocabulary Check

Write the best word from the following list in the blank in each of the sentences below.

consolidated   **deterioration**   **stable**   **initial**   **status**

1. Movie stars have personal trainers and plastic surgeons to slow down the physical _____ that comes with age.

2. Expensive cars are _____ symbols.

3. Many people form their most _____ friendships during their high school and college years.

4. The thirteen original colonies were _____ to form a new country, the United States of America.

5. In bargaining, the buyer makes an _____ offer, and the seller usually counters with a higher price.

15   What Is Art Music?

Comprehension Check

True–False

Mark T or F.

_____ 1. Classical music is slightly different from art music.

_____ 2. According to the author, listening to art music requires a type of thinking very similar to that required for sports such as tennis.

_____ 3. According to the author, something is fine art only when it requires unusual talent or skill.

_____ 4. The reason many people don't like art music is that it causes them to feel uncomfortable and incompetent because they don't understand it.

Multiple Choice

Circle the letter preceding the best answer to each of the following questions.

5. The reason to study art music is that

    a. what you learn can be applied to all types of music.

    b. you need some knowledge in order to understand and appreciate it.

    c. it provides greater listening satisfaction than other types of music.

    d. all of the above are true.

6. According to the author, when you listen to music you should

    a. know something about a type of music before deciding you don't like it.

    b. compare only the same types of works, such as songs with songs or sonatas with sonatas.

    c. keep in mind the purpose of the music.

    d. do all of the above.

Short Answer

List some uses for music. Give an example of a specific piece of music for each use.

7. _____

_____

8. _____

_____

9. _____

_____

10. _____

_____

Essay

Explain what art music is and why you should study it. Use a separate sheet of paper.

Vocabulary Check

Write the best word from the following list in the blank in each of the sentences below.

stimulate   sonatas   cultivate   gourmet   competent

1. Gold and Fizdale are two pianists who recorded several

   _____ for four hands.

2. The Peter Principle says that people rise in organizations until they reach
   the level at which they are no longer _____.

3. A good teacher tries to _____ the students' interest in what
   they are studying.

4. It's hard to be a _____ and have healthy eating habits;
   many of the world's greatest dishes are loaded with fat and/or sugar.

5. Taking courses such as music appreciation and art history helps you

   _____ your taste in the arts.

16   Stage Fright

Comprehension Check

True–False

Mark T or F.

_____ 1. Nervousness usually hurts a speaker's performance.

_____ 2. For most people, taking a public speaking course will reduce stage fright.

_____ 3. Most people's stage fright is caused by a trait.

_____ 4. Sweaty palms are caused by cognitive nervousness.

Multiple Choice

Circle the letter preceding the best answer to each of the following questions.

5. The percentage of the population admitting to public speaking nervousness is approximately

   a. 20 percent.

   b. 50 percent.

   c. 80 percent.

   d. 100 percent.

6. In the author's experience, most people's nervousness

   a. hurts their performance.

   b. is caused by their poor performance.

   c. can be eliminated by proper instruction.

   d. is a trait rather than a state.

7. Coping with nervousness is most improved by

   a. positive thinking.

   b. other people having faith in you.

   c. self-confidence.

   d. good preparation.

8. The amount of time students usually need to pick a topic, find material, organize it, write an outline, and practice the speech is usually one or two

    a. hours.

    b. days.

    c. weeks.

    d. months.

Short Answer

Fill in the blanks.

9. What does it mean to prepare fully?

_____

_____

10. What is the difference between cognitive and behavioral nervousness?

_____

_____

_____

Essay

List the specific behaviors that speakers can use to control nervousness. Use a separate sheet of paper.

Vocabulary Check

Write the best word from the following list in the blank in each of the sentences below.

reticence   apprehension   cognitive   cope   hyperventilate

lackadaisical   impairment   devastating   dissipate   revision

adversity   visualize   implemented   debilitating   perception

1. Roller coasters fill me with _____.

2. Your idea of what happened is quite different from my _____ of the situation.

3. Her _____ on the subject made me suspicious that she was hiding something.

4. He suffers from such _____ allergies that some days he can't even get out of bed.

5. Sometimes people who _____ can lose so much carbon dioxide that they actually faint.

6. Polio can cause _____ of the central nervous system, resulting in paralysis.

7. The new tax laws will be _____ beginning next year.

8. Learning and remembering are _____ acts.

9. You should make at least one _____ of your first draft, correcting all the mistakes, before you turn it in.

10. On good days I feel in complete control, but on bad days I can't _____ at all.

11. The effects of Hurricane Robert were _____, leaving hundreds dead and thousands homeless.

12. Developing a passion for a hobby, such as gardening, can _____ boredom.

13. Unlucky people have more _____ in their lives than lucky ones, but everybody has some.

14. Some government employees have a _____ attitude toward their jobs, believing they can't be fired.

15. Young people find it hard to _____ themselves as senior citizens.

17   **Identity**

Comprehension Check

True–False

Mark T or F.

_____ 1. A role is a position or location in society.

_____ 2. A status is an expectation of behavior consistent with a role.

_____ 3. The Stanford Prison Experiment had the effect of making the prisoners unite against the guards.

_____ 4. We can infer from the Stanford Prison Experiment that the statuses and roles we learn can be both good and bad for us.

_____ 5. We can infer from the Stanford Prison Experiment that the way we see ourselves can be determined by the status we are given by others.

_____ 6. We can infer from responses to the Twenty-Statement Test that people's identities are determined by their statuses and roles.

Multiple Choice

Circle the letter preceding the best answer to each of the following questions.

7. As it is used in the reading, the Stanford Prison Experiment illustrates

   a. the basic meanness of human nature.

   b. how much our status affects our behavior.

   c. the importance of good mental health practices.

   d. the need for prison reform.

8. We can infer from the Stanford Prison Experiment that people are controlled by statuses given to them by

   a. their families.

   b. their religion.

   c. their socioeconomic status.

   d. all of the above.

TESTS

Short Answer

Write one of the statuses you fill and the roles associated with it.

9. Status _____

10. Roles _____

_____

Essay

Describe the Stanford Prison Experiment in terms of roles and statuses. Explain what this information adds to our knowledge of social psychology. Use a separate sheet of paper.

Vocabulary Check

Write the best word from the following list in the blank in each of the sentences below.

social psychology   dictators   solitary confinement

exhibit   socialization

1. Most people can bear _____ much better if they have books or television to keep their minds busy.

2. People who are hypnotized can _____ nearly super-human strength, something they do not have in their ordinary states of mind.

3. A child's _____ will be different from that of most other children if he is raised in a family of criminals.

4. There can be _____ from the left wing as well as from the right wing. Examples are Josef Stalin from the left and Adolf Hitler from the right.

5. It is said that the _____ of the criminal justice system makes it hard for police officers and judges to resist taking bribes and abusing their power.

18 | AIDS: A Crisis of Our Time

Comprehension Check

True–False

Mark T or F.

_____ 1. Everyone who tests HIV-positive will get AIDS.

_____ 2. AIDS is highly contagious, similar to a cold or the flu.

_____ 3. If your partner has tested HIV-negative, you can be sure he or she does not have HIV.

_____ 4. Correct and consistent use of latex condoms and spermicidal barriers will guarantee 100 percent protection against HIV and other STDs.

Multiple Choice

Circle the letter preceding the best answer to each of the following questions.

5. AIDS can be transmitted by

   a. using the same eating utensils that an infected person has used.

   b. a casual kiss.

   c. a mosquito bite.

   d. breast-feeding by an infected person.

6. It is possible to

   a. test negative but be HIV-positive.

   b. be HIV-positive but not be able to transmit the disease.

   c. destroy the HIV virus if it is caught early enough.

   d. neutralize the virus so that an infected person cannot infect others.

7. People infected with AIDS die of

   a. the AIDS virus.

   b. other diseases.

   c. HIV.

   d. pneumonia.

8. In the United States AIDS is the leading cause of death in what age group?

   a. 15–24

   b. 24–44

   c. 45–54

   d. 55–64

Short Answer

Fill in the blanks.

9. Describe the treatments for AIDS.

_____

_____

_____

_____

_____

_____

10. Why is a stigma attached to having AIDS?

_____

_____

Essay

Discuss AIDS: need to be informed; what it is; causes; transmission; who gets it; symptoms; testing; reactions to being HIV-positive; stigma; treatment; prevention. Use a separate sheet of paper.

Vocabulary Check

Write the best word from the following list in the blank in each of the sentences below.

Part A

implications	differentiate	vulnerable	ultimately	intravenous
antibodies	misconception	lulled	asymptomatic	lymph

1. A common _____ is that redheads have hot tempers, particularly if they're Irish.

2. During surgery, patients are given an _____ solution of anesthetic and nutrients.

3. _____ is a bodily fluid that transports nutrients and oxygen to the cells and collects waste products.

4. Having a disease that's _____ is not necessarily good; if you don't know you're sick you can't seek treatment, and meanwhile the disease could progress.

5. It is difficult to _____ between identical twins.

6. The soft, gentle sound of the waves _____ me to sleep.

7. As children get older, they become less influenced by their parents and more _____ to peer pressure.

8. HIV testing doesn't look for the HIV virus; instead, it looks for _____ to the virus.

9. The _____ of the new law were far reaching, affecting 3 out of every 10 Canadians.

10. We can ask people's advice, but _____ the decision about whom we marry is ours alone.

Part B

discriminate	anonymous	contract	gamut	stigma
perpetuate	retard	efficacy	abstinence	inhibitions

11. Some teenagers who wear glasses consider it such a _____ that they beg their parents to buy them contact lenses.

12. Some people send _____ letters to the IRS reporting their friends and neighbors for tax evasion.

13. Under hypnosis, some people lose their _____ and do things they would otherwise not do.

14. You can test the _____ of different window cleaners by cleaning half the window with each one.

15. People who want to lose weight should practice _____ from sugary and fatty foods.

16. When buying a house, most people _____ a large mortgage debt.

17. Unexplained sightings of UFOs _____ the belief that aliens are visiting us.

18. The hardware store carried a full _____ of nails, from the biggest to the smallest.

19. A musician can _____ all the notes in a chord.

20. A firebreak is a strip of land cleared or plowed to _____ the spread of fire.

19   Anger, Aggression, and Assertiveness

Comprehension Check

True–False

Mark T or F.

_____ 1. The author implies that civilized people rarely get angry.

_____ 2. Most angry outbursts occur at home.

_____ 3. Assertive behavior is angry and hostile.

_____ 4. Studies have shown that catharsis is usually the best way to deal with anger.

Multiple Choice

Circle the letter preceding the best answer to each of the following questions.

5. The author implies that you should usually

   a. try not to get angry.

   b. cool off before you decide what to do.

   c. express your feelings openly and honestly.

   d. be afraid of your own anger and the anger of others.

6. According to the author, talking about anger

   a. lets you get rid of it by "blowing off steam."

   b. can make it stronger.

   c. should be avoided because it leads to violence.

   d. is good only if you talk to the right person.

7. According to the author, most anger is directed at

   a. enemies.

   b. people at work.

   c. family and friends.

   d. all of the above equally.

Short Answer

Give an example of dealing with anger with

8. civility _____

_____

_____

9. assertiveness _____

_____

_____

10. aggression _____

_____

_____

Essay

Explain the difference between aggression and assertiveness in dealing with anger. Use a separate sheet of paper.

Vocabulary Check

Write the best word from the following list in the blank in each of the sentences below.

suppressing   **cited**   **catharsis**   **retaliation**   **civility**

1. Behaving with _____ can take a lot of self-control.

2. The most frequently _____ reason for divorce is "irreconcilable differences."

3. _____ your feelings is the opposite of expressing them.

4. If a loved one mistreats you, your relationship is more likely to last if you respond with forgiveness rather than _____.

5. A temper tantrum would be an example of _____.

20 Understanding Prejudice

Comprehension Check

Multiple Choice

Circle the letter preceding the best answer to each of the following questions.

1. Observational learning refers to

   a. the tendency to view one's own group as superior.

   b. behaving differently toward members of a group.

   c. picking up the attitudes of other people.

   d. all of the above.

2. Let's say you are a Republican. When you view the record of a Democratic president, you are likely to notice everything that had a bad result and ignore everything that had a good result. This is called

   a. the fundamental attribution error.

   b. a proximity effect.

   c. a memory bias.

   d. defensive attribution.

3. The idea that the Irish drink too much is an example of

   a. stereotyping.

   b. ethnocentrism.

   c. discrimination.

   d. all of the above.

4. The idea that actresses get jobs because of their sexuality (the "casting couch") is an example of

   a. biased attribution.

   b. proximity effects.

   c. selectivity in person perception.

   d. the repulsion hypothesis.

5. The idea that many blacks have poor academic records because they are less intelligent than whites is an example of

    a. selectivity in person perception.

    b. observational learning.

    c. effects of dissimilarity.

    d. the fundamental attribution error.

Short Answer

List the three components of prejudice.

6. _____

7. _____

8. _____

9. Give an example of prejudice without discrimination.

    _____

    _____

10. Give an example of discrimination without prejudice.

    _____

    _____

Essay

Explain where, according to the reading, prejudice comes from. Use a separate sheet of paper.

Vocabulary Check

Write the best word from the following list in the blank in each of the sentences below.

components   affective   selectivity   subjective   bias

attribution   defensive   proximity   repulsion   ethnocentrism

1. _____ is the opposite of attraction.

2. Believing that your religion is favored by God over others is an example of _____.

3. If you feel criticized when someone disagrees with you, you are being _____.

4. If you think that Jews tend to make money because they are dishonest, you are making an _____ error.

5. Psychologists are supposed to be more aware of feelings, or the _____ area, than are other scientists.

6. Facts can be agreed upon by everyone, but opinions are always _____.

7. All attitudes have three _____.

8. If you have a _____ against national health coverage, you will pay more attention to the arguments opposing it than to the arguments in its favor.

9. People are likely to marry people they meet at school, at work, or in their neighborhoods because of the _____ effect.

10. If you have a prejudice against a group, _____ of person perception means that you are likely to see what you expect to see when you come into contact with members of that group.

21   The All-American Male

Comprehension Check

True–False

Mark T or F.

_____ 1. We can infer that one reason men talk so much about sports is that they don't want to talk about their feelings.

_____ 2. We can infer that traditional men are like "powder kegs" or "steam kettles" that could explode into violent behavior.

_____ 3. Black men are less likely to conform to male stereotypes than are white men.

_____ 4. According to the authors, if a man can succeed at the stereotypical male role, he will be happy.

Multiple Choice

Circle the letter preceding the best answer to each of the following questions.

5. The authors imply that healthy women
   a. cannot love the "all-American" male.
   b. are attracted to men who have money and power.
   c. follow gender stereotypes.
   d. reject weak men.

6. The authors imply that being aware of your feelings
   a. is necessary in order to give and receive love.
   b. is necessary in order to live a happy life.
   c. reduces stress.
   d. does all of the above.

7. The authors imply that "all-American" males tend to be
   a. engaged in a fruitless search for the perfect house, job, and mate.
   b. susceptible to stress-related disorders.
   c. potentially dangerous to themselves and others.
   d. all of the above.

8. The authors imply that

    a. the only way to have love and happiness is to "be yourself."

    b. people should try to improve themselves.

    c. women are better than men.

    d. all of the above are true.

Short Answer

Fill in the blanks.

9. What do the authors mean by "emotional unavailability"?

_____

_____

_____

10. What do the authors mean by "protection of his inner self"?

_____

_____

_____

Essay

Briefly define the "all-American" male and discuss the price he pays for remaining in a traditional role. Use a separate sheet of paper.

Vocabulary Check

Write the best word from the following list in the blank in each of the sentences below.

Part A

conform   objective   rational   nurturing   distorted

disclose   façade   impoverished   compassion   submissive

1. If people had _____ for each other, there would be no crime, poverty, wars, or capital punishment.

2. Every generation has a group that refuses to _____ to the norms of the time—from beatniks in your grandparents' day, to hippies in your parents' day, to Goths now.

3. A judge must always be _____, deciding on the merits of the case alone.

4. Nondominant dogs will display _____ postures, such as crouching low or rolling over.

5. You need to plan for your retirement so you won't be _____ in your old age.

6. You should not _____ your Internet access password, or other people might be able to use your account.

7. If you are in a rage, you should wait until you are calm and _____ before discussing the problem.

8. When people tease you, you have to keep up a _____ of not being upset or they will tease you more.

9. People with some kinds of eating disorders have a _____ image of themselves, thinking they are fat when they are really skeletal.

10. Foster parents have to be very _____ to care for needy children.

Part B

deviate	obsession	intuitive	affront	bravado
psyche	lethal	contended	vigilant	susceptible

11. The deadly puffer fish, a delicacy served in some of the finest Japanese restaurants, contains a _____ poison in the skin, muscles, and internal organs that must be carefully removed before eating.

12. The Pacific rim is the area of the world most _____ to volcanic explosions.

13. One way in which cartoon characters _____ from regular humans is that they are almost always drawn with three fingers and a thumb to save time.

14. Sigmund Freud _____ that many powerful human motives are unconscious.

15. The ancient Roman god, Janus, is portrayed with two faces, one on the front and the other on the back of his head, so he can be extra _____.

16. Both psychologists and clergy say that the only way your _____ can be strong and healthy is if you have nothing to hide.

17. My Chihuahua displays great _____ by barking at huge dogs, but if they come toward him, he runs.

18. Whistling at a woman you don't know and making sexual comments is not a compliment; it's an _____.

19. Fortune-tellers have to be _____.

20. Having a passionate interest in something is good, but calling it an _____ gives it a negative spin.

22 Sexual Abuse and Harassment

Comprehension Check

True–False

Mark T or F.

_____ 1. Incest, date or acquaintance rape, and sexual harassment are all abuses of power.

_____ 2. Sometimes the responsibility for the abuse falls on the victim.

_____ 3. Some sexual harassers do not understand that their behavior is offensive.

_____ 4. Sexual crimes are typically underreported.

Multiple Choice

Circle the letter preceding the best answer to each of the following questions.

5. The number of children who have been molested is at least

   a. 1 out of 5.

   b. 1 out of 10.

   c. 15 out of 20.

   d. 3 out of 100.

6. Incest is

   a. not a crime in every state.

   b. a misdemeanor in all fifty states.

   c. a misdemeanor in some states, a felony in others.

   d. a felony in all fifty states.

7. Implied goals of counseling for sexual abuse victims include

   a. improving the ability to enjoy sex.

   b. learning to trust others.

   c. raising self-esteem.

   d. all of the above.

8. Prevention of date rape includes

   a. communicating clearly.

   b. avoiding alcohol and drugs.

   c. learning how to protect oneself.

   d. all of the above.

Short Answer

Fill in the blanks.

9. What do incest, date and acquaintance rape, and sexual harassment have in common?

_____

_____

_____

10. Why do the authors advise not using drugs and alcohol excessively?

_____

_____

_____

Essay

Define incest, date and acquaintance rape, and sexual harassment. Discuss the responsibility of the perpetrators and the victims, and the effects on the victims. Use a separate sheet of paper.

Vocabulary Check

Write the best word from the following list in the blank in each of the sentences below.

Part A

incest   syndrome   therapeutic   molestation   perpetrators

conservative   coercion   metaphorically   recurring   dysfunctional

1. "Megan's law" allows neighbors to be notified when someone convicted of child _____ moves in.

2. We had _____ arguments about money until we finally worked out an agreement that was fair to everyone.

3. When the United States ended the draft, they had to make military service attractive instead of using _____ to get people to join up.

4. Shakespeare's Hamlet accused his mother of _____ after she married his uncle.

5. Many children go into foster care because their families became _____.

6. Physical assault of a wife by a husband (or vice versa) occurs in an estimated 16 percent of families, but this estimate is probably _____, because some families won't admit to domestic violence that has occurred.

7. Every year some 8,000 infants in the United States die from Sudden Infant Death _____ (SIDS), also known as crib death, the cause of which is still unknown.

8. Although it is not clear why it works, Prozac seems to have a _____ effect on depression, with many patients reporting improvement.

9. When I call my daughter "Princess" I am speaking _____.

10. In ancient China the punishment for minor crimes, such as shoplifting or breaking a curfew, was to brand the _____ on the forehead with a hot iron.

Part B

| self-esteem | vacillate | resolution | dynamics | trauma |
| equate | explicitly | demeaning | innuendoes | reprisals |

11. The _____ of his work group help him keep focused on the task.

12. It's common for college students to _____ for a few years before deciding on a career goal.

13. If there are _____ for telling the truth, people are likely to lie.

14. The breakup of his marriage was such a _____ that he has avoided women ever since.

15. Many women feel that being asked to make coffee for their male coworkers is _____.

16. Sexual _____ in the workplace can be considered harassment.

17. There will never be a _____ to conflict in places like the Middle East so long as the majority dominates the minorities, instead of letting them participate in decisions that affect them.

18. Low _____ may cause people to marry spouses who mistreat them.

19. Pro-life supporters _____ abortion with murder.

20. I _____ told you to clean your room before school, so why is it still dirty?

Ethical Considerations in Psychology Experiments

23

Comprehension Check

True–False

Mark T or F.

_____ 1. Informed consent means agreeing to something only after you know exactly what it is.

_____ 2. A Human Subjects Committee gives ethical guidelines but does not have the right to stop an experiment from taking place.

_____ 3. Experimenters are never permitted to conceal information about the experiment from the subjects.

_____ 4. The APA has no authority to punish members who violate ethical guidelines.

_____ 5. Laboratory Animal Care Committees ask researchers to look for other ways to do research before they use animals.

Multiple Choice

Circle the letter preceding the best answer to each of the following questions.

6. The most effective way to study the effects of an unknown drug on cancer is to use

   a. tissue cultures.

   b. animal subjects.

   c. vegetable subjects.

   d. computer simulation.

7. Experiments with human subjects must

   a. require subjects to give informed consent.

   b. be approved by the Human Subjects Committee.

   c. follow APA guidelines.

   d. do all of the above.

8. Psychologists use animals in what percent of their studies?

    a. 0 to 5 percent

    b. 5 to 10 percent

    c. 10 to 15 percent

    d. 15 to 20 percent

Short Answer

9. Give at least one argument opposing animal research.

    _____

    _____

    _____

10. Give at least two arguments in favor of animal research.

    _____

    _____

    _____

    _____

    _____

    _____

    _____

Essay

Discuss the ethical considerations in psychology experiments with humans and with animals. Use a separate sheet of paper.

Vocabulary Check

Write the best word from the following list in the blank in each of the sentences below.

subjects   guidelines   censure   expelled   simulation

1. You can be _____ from the Army for disciplinary problems.

2. Professional associations prefer to _____ their own members instead of encouraging the public to take legal action for malpractice.

3. _____ in some experiments are paid for participating; others receive course credit.

4. Virtual reality is a _____ of experience.

5. The APA's *Publication Manual* offers _____ not only for published articles but also for term papers.

24 Textbooks Distort History

Comprehension Check

True–False

Mark T or F.

_____ 1. The author thinks junior high school history texts are less honest than elementary texts.

_____ 2. The author thinks history texts have become less accurate in recent years.

_____ 3. The author implies that American history texts omit important facts.

_____ 4. The author implies that a Russian history text would give quite a different account of World War II than American ones do.

Multiple Choice

Circle the letter preceding the best answer to each of the following questions.

5. The war against the Philippines was mentioned as an example of

   a. controlling the emphasis given to embarrassing events.

   b. omitting historical facts.

   c. the exaggeration of the importance of U.S. involvement.

   d. sanitizing a flawed leader.

6. The bombing of German civilians was given as an example of historical fact which is treated in history textbooks

   a. accurately now, although not in the past.

   b. in a distorted manner to hide America's shameful behavior.

   c. by omitting mention of it entirely.

   d. in an exaggerated way, making it seem more important than it was.

7. In history texts, the role of the Soviets in World War II has been

   a. exaggerated.

   b. accurately reported.

   c. minimized.

   d. omitted.

8. The author thinks that textbook descriptions of Theodore Roosevelt are usually

   a. accurate.

   b. one-sided.

   c. completely false.

   d. overly critical.

Short Answer

9. What devices are used in textbooks to distort history?

   _____

   _____

   _____

10. What reason does the author give for the distortion of U.S. history in textbooks?

   _____

   _____

Essay

How does the author describe history textbooks? Use a separate sheet of paper.

Vocabulary Check

Write the best word from the following list in the blank in each of the sentences below.

sanitize   spruce up   exuberant   trust-buster   progressive

bigots   squalid   puffed up   unsophisticated   guerrilla

1. The government functions as a _____ when a company or group of companies gets large enough to strangle the competition.

2. The tiny North Vietnamese army fought a _____ war against the giant United States and eventually won.

3. People who live in other parts of the country tend to think most Southerners are racial _____.

4. It is wise to _____ your house with a coat of paint and a few flowers before you try to sell it.

5. Liberal political views are about the same as _____ones.

6. People from places like Kansas and Missouri are sometimes considered _____ compared to people from the East and West coasts.

7. Children are often disappointed when they get the toys they see advertised on TV; they believe the ads because they don't understand that products are _____.

8. Some people wake up _____; others barely manage to drag themselves out of bed.

9. Native Americans often had to put up with poverty and _____ living conditions on the reservations.

10. All nations _____ their history to increase patriotism.

Progress Chart

Record your score in each column on the next page as a percent by dividing the number correct by the number of questions. The Comprehension Checks each have 10 questions, so you can use the 10-question column below. The Vocabulary Checks have either 5, 10, 15, or 20 questions. The percentages are given below.

5 Questions	10 Questions	15 Questions	20 Questions
5/5 = 100%	10/10 = 100%	15/15 = 100%	20/20 = 100%
		14/15 = 93%	19/20 = 95%
	9/10 = 90%		18/20 = 90%
		13/15 = 87%	17/20 = 85%
4/5 = 80%	8/10 = 80%	12/15 = 80%	16/20 = 80%
		11/15 = 73%	15/20 = 75%
	7/10 = 70%		14/20 = 70%
		10/15 = 67%	13/20 = 65%
3/5 = 60%	6/10 = 60%	9/15 = 60%	12/20 = 60%
		8/15 = 53%	11/20 = 55%
	5/10 = 50%		10/20 = 50%
		7/15 = 47%	9/20 = 45%
2/5 = 40%	4/10 = 40%	6/15 = 40%	8/20 = 40%
		5/15 = 33%	7/20 = 35%
	3/10 = 30%		6/20 = 30%
		4/15 = 27%	5/20 = 25%
1/5 = 20%	2/10 = 20%	3/15 = 20%	4/20 = 20%
		2/15 = 13%	3/20 = 15%
	1/10 = 10%		2/20 = 10%
		1/15 = 7%	1/20 = 5%

Comprehension Checks	Vocabulary Checks
1.	1.
2.	2.
3.	3.
4.	4.
5.	5.
6.	6.
7.	7.
8.	8.
9.	9.
10.	10.
11.	11.
12.	12.
13.	13.
14.	14.
15.	15.
16.	16.
17.	17.
18.	18.
19.	19.
20.	20.
21.	21.
22.	22.
23.	23.
24.	24.

Evaluation Checklist

1. Score on total test _____

2. Which section was your weakest: objective, essay, application, or problem solving? _____

3. Objective section:

    a. Do you understand why your wrong answers were wrong? _____

    b. Did your underlining and marginal notes cover the correct information? _____

    c. Did you review them enough to remember them?_____

    d. Other problem: _____

    _____

4. Essay/application:

    a. Do you understand why you got the score you did? _____

    b. Did your graphic organizer(s) cover the correct information? _____

    c. Did you review them enough to remember them?_____

    d. Other problem: _____

    _____

5. Problem solving:

    a. Did you provide the right kind of practice problems?_____

    b. Did you provide enough practice problems so that you could understand and remember the information?_____

    c. Other problem: _____

6. Test-taking skills:

    a. Did you use the time available to maximize your score?_____

    b. Did you follow the directions?_____

    c. Did you answer the easy questions first?_____

    d. If you changed any answers, did it improve your score? _____

    e. Did you leave anything blank? _____

    f. Other problems: _____

    _____

Reading Efficiency

Increasing Reading Flexibility

Because they have to read so much, efficient reading is crucial for college students. But if your response is to say "I read _____ words per minute," you do not understand a basic principle of efficient reading. Good readers are flexible; they adjust their reading speeds. They read a textbook more slowly than a newspaper. They read Shakespeare more slowly than *Newsweek*.

The most important thing to keep in mind is the purpose of your reading. If you are trying to read and memorize textbook material for a test, you read much more slowly than if you are relaxing with a detective story or looking through a newspaper.

Types of Reading

There are four basic types of reading: study reading, rapid reading, skimming, and scanning. Each type is suited to a particular type of reading material and reading purpose, and each should be practiced at different speeds.

Use **study reading** on difficult textbook or technical material when your purpose is thorough understanding and/or memorization. Study reading rates usually do not exceed 250 words per minute.

Rapid reading should be used when your purpose is to get a general idea of what you read and when the material is not extremely complicated. Types of materials suitable for rapid reading include newspapers, magazines, novels, and light nonfiction.

	Study reading	**Rapid reading**	**Skimming**	**Scanning**
Speed	Up to 250 wpm	250–800 wpm	Up to thousands of wpm	Up to thousands of wmp
Purpose	Thorough under-standing and recall	Recreation, information, light reading	Survey, overview, review	Locating specific information
Types of material	Textbooks, tech-nical materials	Newspapers, magazines, novels	Any type	Any type

Skimming is quickly looking over a selection to get the general idea rather than reading every word. It is used (1) when surveying a chapter or article, (2) when all you need is a general overview, and (3) when reviewing something you once read to refresh your memory. To give you an example of skimming, we have emphasized some words in the following article. Read the bold print only; then, without looking back, answer the questions that follow the article.

If you are seriously interested in a **car,** you should **haggle with the dealer** over the price. The sticker price on the window of a car is there because the law says it must be, but only a naive buyer accepts the sticker price as anything but a starting point for negotiations. Shop around, shop carefully, and **never pay the asking price.**

You can easily **learn the dealer's cost for a new car** (invoice price) by buying an inexpensive guide titled **Edmund's New Car Prices,** available at bookstores and newsstands. Total the dealer's cost including options, and then **offer $125 to $200 above** this cost. You should aim to settle for **no more than $200 to $500 over** the dealer's cost for an **American** car, **or $500 for a foreign** car.

A **good time to close** a deal is often **late Sunday night** (or the last night of the week the dealer is open) **or at the end of the month.** (Many dealerships offer bonuses to the person who has the best sales record at the end of the week or month.) It is good **to deal directly with the sales manager or assistant** manager, because this person is authorized to agree on a price.

When you have settled on the car you want and have agreed with the salesperson on a price, you should **have the dealer put the agreement in writing before** you make a **deposit.** The order form for this agreement should **include a statement of the precise car** being bought, the **accessories** agreed on (if any), the **sales tax, registration fee,** and the **value of the trade-in** (if any). In addition, an **officer of the firm must sign** the order form or it has no legal value. The salesperson's signature means nothing; you may find that when the time comes to close the deal, you have been low-balled (promised a better deal than you are actually able to get) or high-balled (offered more on your trade-in than you will actually get). A person might be both high-balled and low-balled during the course of the negotiations. Both practices are very common among car dealers.

1. What is the article about? _____

2. What is the main idea?_____

3. How much should you pay for a new foreign car? _____

4. Who should you try to deal with? _____

The answers are (1) buying a car (2) you can get a better deal if you know what you're doing, (3) no more than $500 over the dealer's cost, and (4) manager or assistant manager.

 Scanning is locating specific information, such as a name, a place, or a date. For example, when you look up something in the dictionary or in the telephone book, you are scanning. You run your eyes over the page and read only the information surrounding what you are looking for. You may also use scanning in textbooks—for example, when you are looking for a particular name or date in a chapter.

Factors in the Reader

In addition to your purpose and the type of material you are reading, factors in yourself also affect the rate at which you read.

 One cause of slow reading is a small vocabulary. If you encounter many unfamiliar words, your thought processes will be interrupted. This will interfere with both speed and comprehension.

 Another factor that influences reading rate is your comprehension skills. The ability to quickly identify the author's organization (subject, main ideas, and support) is essential to grasping the overall picture that he or she is trying to present.

 Your speed and comprehension will also increase if you have some familiarity with the concepts you will be reading about. Your background knowledge also affects your level of interest and, therefore, your ability to concentrate.

 Finally, the way you read affects your speed and comprehension. Phrase reading—grouping words into meaningful phrases—allows you to read faster. Poor readers read word by word.

 Poor | readers | read | like | this.

 Good readers | read like this.

 One way of overcoming word-by-word reading is to practice drawing lines between thought units, as in the second example above. After you have drawn lines, you can practice reading by looking at each unit rather than each word. Phrase reading also reduces some other common bad reading habits, such as habitually looking back at what you have just read.

Rate Chart

To find your reading rate, first look in the left-hand column of the chart on page 422 to find the time it took you to read the article. Then look along that line until you come to the column headed by the number of words you read. Where the two lines cross, you will find a number indicating how many words per minute you have read. For example, if you read 1200 words in five minutes, you have read 240 WPM.

To find your reading rate for timings that do not appear on the chart, first compute your time in seconds. (Multiply the number of minutes by 60 and add the number of remaining seconds.) Then divide the number of words read by your time in seconds. Multiply the result by 60 to get back to minutes and seconds.

Rate Chart

$$\text{WPM} = \frac{\text{Words read}}{\text{Time in minutes}} \quad \text{OR} \quad \frac{\text{Words read}}{\text{Time in seconds}} \times 60$$

Reading Time / **Number of Words Read**

Min.	Sec.	550	650	700	800	900	1000	1100	1200	1300	1500	1600	2100	2200	2400	2600	3500	4000
1	30	367	433	467	533	600	667	733	800	867	1000	1067						
1	40	330	390	420	480	590	600	660	720	780	900	960						
1	50	300	355	382	436	492	545	600	655	769	818	873	1145					
2	00	275	325	350	400	450	500	550	600	650	750	800	1050	1100	1200			
2	10	254	300	323	369	415	462	508	554	600	692	738	969	1015	1108	1200		
2	20	236	279	300	343	386	429	477	574	557	643	686	900	943	1028	1114		
2	30	220	260	280	320	360	400	440	480	520	600	640	840	880	960	1040		
2	40	206	244	263	300	338	375	413	450	487	563	600	788	825	900	975		
2	50	194	229	247	282	318	353	388	424	459	529	565	741	776	847	918		
3	00	183	217	233	267	300	333	367	400	433	500	533	700	733	800	867	1333	1500
3	20	165	195	210	240	270	300	330	360	390	450	480	630	660	720	780	1050	1200
3	40	150	177	191	218	245	273	300	327	355	409	436	573	600	655	709	955	1091
4	00	137	163	175	200	225	250	275	300	325	375	400	525	550	600	650	875	1000
4	30	122	144	156	178	200	222	244	267	289	333	356	467	489	533	578	778	889
5	00	110	130	140	160	180	200	220	240	260	300	320	420	440	480	520	700	800
5	30	100	118	127	145	164	182	200	218	236	273	291	382	400	436	473	636	727
6	00		108	116	133	150	167	183	200	217	250	267	360	367	400	433	583	667
7	00		93	100	114	129	143	157	171	186	214	229	300	314	343	371	500	571
8	00				100	113	125	138	150	162	187	200	263	275	300	325	437	500
9	00					100	111	122	133	144	167	178	233	244	267	289	389	444
10	00						100	110	120	130	150	160	210	220	240	260	350	400
11	00							100	109	118	136	145	191	210	218	236	318	364
12	00								100	108	125	133	175	200	200	217	292	333
13	00									104	115	123	162	183	185	200	269	308
14	00										107	114	150	169	171	186	250	286
15	00										107	140	157	160	173	233	267	
16	00											100	131	147	150	163	219	250
17	00												124	137	141	153	206	235
18	00												117	122	133	144	194	222
19	00												111	116	126	137	184	211
20	00												105	110	120	130	175	200
21	00													105	114	124	167	190
22	00														109	118	159	182
23	00														104	113	152	174
24	00															108	146	167
25	00															140	160	

Word Parts

Most of the difficult words in English come from Latin, or from Greek through Latin. Following are 60 common prefixes and 150 common roots. You already know many of them, and learning the rest will greatly improve your vocabulary.

Here are some suggested ways to learn them:

As you look at each word part, read the meaning and the examples. Then try to think of another word that comes from the same word part. If you can think of another word, check it in a dictionary that gives the etymology of each word, to make sure that it does come from the same word part. Some pocket-size dictionaries save space by omitting the etymology. If your dictionary doesn't have etymologies, you can use a dictionary in a library. If you can't think of another word, try to find one by looking in the dictionary.

To memorize the word parts you don't already know, you can put them on flash cards. Put the word part on the front. Put the meaning and some examples on the back. Examples that you have made up yourself will be easier to memorize than ones that have come from our list or from the dictionary. Then test yourself until you have memorized the word part. The average person takes seven self-testing sessions to learn a new word part. Following is a sample flash card:

Front	Back
mem (men, mn, min)	mind, memory, remind, memoria, demented, remember, memento, reminisce, mnemonic

60 Common Prefixes

Prefix	Meaning	Examples
a (an)	not	anonymous, atypical
ab (a)	away, from, down	absence, amoral
ad (ac, af, ag, an, ap, ar, as, at)	to	admit, accept, affect, aggravate, annex, appeal, arrange, assess, attract
ambi (amphi)	both	ambidextrous, amphibian
ante (ant)	before	antecedent, anterior

Prefix	Meaning	Examples
anti (ant)	against	antisocial, antonym
auto	self	autobiography, autocrat
bene	good	benediction, benefit
con (com, co, col, cor)	with, together	concurrent, communicate, cooperate, collate, correspond
contra	against	contradict, contraband
de	from, away, down	derail, descend
dia	through, across	diameter, diaphanous
dis (dif)	apart, not	discontinue, different
epi	on, over, among	epidermis, epidemic
eu (ev)	good	eulogy, evangelical
ex (extra, e, ec, ef)	out, former, beyond	exit, ex-wife, extraordinary, emit, eccentric, effect
hetero	different	heterogeneous, heterosexual
homo	same	homogenize, homosexual
hyper	over, beyond	hyperactive, hypersensitive
hypo	under	hypodermic, hypoallergenic
in (il, im, ir, en, em)	not, into, very	inaction, insight, invaluable, illogical, immobile, implicit, irregular, encompass, embrace
inter	between	interrupt, intercollegiate
intra (intro)	into, within	intramural, introduce
mal	bad, wrong, ill	malicious, malfunction
mega	big	megaphone, megalopolis
micro	small	micrometer, microbe
mis	wrong	misspell, misgivings
multi	many	multiply, multimillionaire
non (n)	not	nonprofit, neither
ob (oc, of, op, o)	against	obstruct, occasion, offend, oppose, omit
omni	all	omnivorous, omnipotent
pan	all	pan-African, panacea
para	alongside, beyond	paragraph, paraphrase
per	through, by, thorough	per annum, perspective
peri	around	perimeter, peripheral
poly	many	polygon, polyester
post	after	posterity, posterior
pre	before	preliminary, prevent
pro (pur)	before, forward, for	prospect, pursuit

WORD PARTS

Prefix	Meaning	Examples
re (retro)	again, back	reenter, retroactive
se	apart	secede, secret
sub (suc, suf, sup, sus)	under, below	submarine, succumb, suffer, suppress, suspect
super (sur)	above, beyond	superior, surpass
tele	distance	telegraph, telepathy
trans	across	transatlantic, transfer
ultra	beyond, extremely	ultrasonic, ultraviolet
un	not, reverse of an action	unwise, undo

Numbers

Prefix	Meaning	Examples
uni, mono	one	unison, unit, monotone
du (di), bi	two	duo, dioxide, biennial
tri	three	tripod, triple, trilogy
quarter (quadr), tetra	four	quartet, quadrangle, tetrahedron
quint, penta	five	quintuplet, pentagon
sex (hex)	six	sexagenarian, hexagon
sept (hept)	seven	September,* heptagon
oct	eight	octopus, October*
nov (non)	nine	November,* nonagenarian
dec	ten	decade, December*
hemi (semi, demi)	half, partial	hemisphere, semicircle, demigod
kilo, mil	thousand	kilowatt, milligram, mile
cent	hundred	century, bicentennial

*Note that prefixes for the months are based on their places in the Roman calendar.

150 Common Roots

Root	Meaning	Examples
act (agi)	drive, do	activate, agitate
aer (aero)	air	aerial, aerodynamics
al (alt)	other	alien, altruist
am (amat, amour)	love	amicable, amateur, paramour
anim	mind, soul	inanimate, animal
ann (enn)	year	annual, biennial
anthro (anthrop)	man, human	anthropology, misanthrope
aqu	water	aquatic, aqueduct
arch	chief, ruler	monarchy, anarchist

Root	Meaning	Examples
aster (astr)	star	asterisk, astronomy
aud (audit)	hear	audible, audition
biblio, bibl	book	bibliography, bible
bio	life	biology, biography
cad (cas, cid)	fall	cadence, cascade, coincidence
cap (cep, ceive)	hold, seize	capacity, reception, deceive
capit (cap, chap, chief)	head	capitulate, captain, chapter, chief
cav	hollow	cavity, cavern
cede (ceed, cess)	go	secede, succeed, process
chrom(e)	color	chromatic, monochrome
chron	time	chronicle, anachronism
cide (cis)	cut, kill	matricide, scissors
cir, cycl	round	circular, cyclone
cit (civ)	government	citizen, civil
claus (close, clus, clude)	shut	claustrophobia, foreclose, cluster, exclude
cline (clim)	slope	incline, climax
corp	body	corporate, corpulent
crat (cracy)	rule	democratic, aristocracy
cre (crease, cres)	grow	increment, increase, crescent
cred	believe	credible, credit
cult	develop	cultivate, acculturate
cur (cour)	run	recurrent, recourse
cur (sur)	care	manicure, curator, insure
dem	people	democratic, epidemic
dent (dont)	teeth	denture, orthodontist
derm	skin	dermatologist, hypodermic
dic (dict, dit)	say, speak	indicate, dictate, edit
doc (dox)	opinion, belief	doctrine, orthodox
duc	lead	conductive, aqueduct
dynam	power	dynamic, dynamo
ego	self	egotistical, egocentric
equa (equi)	equal	equanimity, equilibrium
fac (fec, fic)	make, do	facilitate, effect, fiction
fal (fals)	deceive	fallacy, falsify
fend (fens)	against, from	defendant, offensive
fer	carry	prefer, ferry
fic (fig)	form	fiction, figure
fid	faith	confidant, infidel

Root	Meaning	Examples
fin	limit	infinite, finish
fix	stationary	prefix, fixate
flect (flex)	bend	inflection, reflex
flu	flow	fluid, influential
fort (forc)	strong	fortress, reinforce
fract (frag)	break	fraction, fragment
fund (fuse, found)	pour or melt	refund, fusion, profound
gamy	marriage	bigamy, misogamy
gen (gin)	birth, origin, race	genetic, origin, genocide
geo	earth	geology, geography
grad (gress)	go, walk, step	graduate, progress
gram (graph)	write	telegram, graphics
grat (grac)	pleasing, thanks, favor	gratis, gracious
her (hes)	stick	inherent, adhesive
hydr (hydro)	water	dehydrate, hydroelectric
jac (ject)	throw	jacket, reject
jud (jus, jur)	right	judicial, justice, injure
jug (junc, just)	join	conjugate, juncture, adjust
kine (cine)	move	kinetic, cinema
labor	work	collaborate, laboratory
lect (leg)	gather, read, law	collect, legal
libr (liber)	book, free	library, liberal
lic	permit, allure	license, elicit
liter	letter	literate, literature
loc	place	location, allocate
log (logy)	word, speech, study of	logo, logic, geology
luc (lum, lus, lun, lux)	light	lucid, luminous, illustrate, lunar, luxury
magn (max)	great	magnify, maximum
man	hand	manual, emancipate
mania	madness	kleptomania, manic
mater (matr)	mother	alma mater, matriarch
mem (men, mn, min)	mind, memory	memo, mental, amnesia, remind
meter (metr)	measure	thermometer, metric
mis (mit)	send	emissary, emit
mob (mot, mov)	move	mobile, motivate, remote, remove
mort	die	mortal, mortuary
nat (nai, neo, nov)	new, born	prenatal, naive, neoclassic, novel
naut, nav	water	astronaut, navigate

Root	Meaning	Examples
nom, onym	name	nomenclature, synonym
ocle (ocul, opt)	eye	monocle, binocular, optical
pac (pact)	peace	pacify, pact
par (part)	equal, share	disparity, compartment
pass (path)	feel, disease	passion, antipathy, pathology
pater (patr)	father	paternal, patriotic
ped	child	pediatrician, pedagogy
ped (pod)	foot	pedal, podiatrist
pel (puls)	drive	compel, repulsive
pend (pens, pond)	hang, weight, pay	pending, expense, ponder
pet (peat)	seek, request	perpetual, repeat
phil	love	philanthropy, philologist
phobia	fear	claustrophobia, hydrophobia
phon	sound	phonograph, symphony
photo (phos)	light	photographic, phosphorus
pict (pig)	paint	depict, pigment
plac (plea)	please, calm	placate, implacable, please
plic (plex, ply)	bend, fold	implicate, perplex, reply
polis (polit)	city, citizen	metropolis, politician
port	carry	porter, opportune
pose (posit, pound)	put	dispose, deposit, impound
press (prim, print)	squeeze, press	pressure, reprimand, imprint
psych	mind, soul	psyche, parapsychology
punct (pung, point, pug)	prick	punctuate, pungent, appoint, pugnacious
quer (ques, quir, quis)	ask, seek	query, question, inquiry, inquisition
reg (rect, right)	straight, direct	irregular, erect, forthright
rog	ask, seek	derogatory, interrogate
rupt	break	interrupt, rupture
scope	see	telescope, microscope
scrib (script)	write	inscribe, manuscript
sens (sent)	feel, think	sensitive, sentiment
sequ (secut, suit)	follow	sequence, persecute, pursuit
sid (sed, sess)	sit	reside, sediment, session
sign	mark, signal	insignia, designate
sim (sym, syn, syl)	together, same	simulate, sympathy, synonym, syllable
sol	alone	solo, solitude
solv (solu)	loosen, explain	solvent, solution

Root	Meaning	Examples
son (sound)	sound	sonar, resound
spec (spect, spic, spis)	see, look	speculate, inspect, despicable, despise
spir	breathe	respiration, expire
stat (stan, sist, stit)	stand	static, stand, resist, constitute
struct	build	construct, structure
tact (tag, tang, ting)	touch	contact, contagious, tangible, tinge
temp	time, heat	contemporary, tempo, temperature
ten (tain, tin)	hold	contain, retention, pertinent
tend (ten)	stretch	tendon, extensive
ter (terr)	earth	interment, terrestrial
text	weave, construct	textile, texture
theo (the)	god	theology, atheist
therm	hot, warm	thermos, thermometer
thesis	put, place	synthesis, hypothesis
tom (tomy)	cut	atom, tonsillectomy
torq (tort)	twist, wind	torque, contort
tract	draw, pull	subtract, traction
urb	city	urbane, suburban
vac (void)	empty	vacuum, evacuate, void
val (valu)	worth, strength	ambivalent, evaluate
ven (vent)	come	intervene, adventure
verb	word	adverb, verbatim
vers (vert, verg)	turn	versus, avert, verge
vic (van, vinc)	conquer, change	vicarious, vanquish, invincible
vid (vis, view)	see	video, visual, review
vita (viv)	life	vital, vivacious
voc (vok)	call	vocal, revoke
volv (volu)	roll, will	revolve, voluntary

Pronunciation and Phonics

Practice for Pronunciation

Vowel Sounds

Long and Short a: The key word for short a is *cat*. The key word for long a is *ate* (pronounced āt). These sounds can be spelled in many different ways. Don't be confused by the spellings; just pay attention to the sounds. Pronounce the words below to yourself. If you hear the vowel sound that's in *cat*, write a. If you hear the vowel sound that's in *ate*, write ā.

_____ 1. weigh   _____ 6. rain

_____ 2. great   _____ 7. calf

_____ 3. hatch   _____ 8. they

_____ 4. game   _____ 9. trace

_____ 5. have   _____ 10. laugh

Long and Short e: The key word for short e is *pen*. The key word for long e is *evil* (pronounced ē'vəl). Pronounce the words below to yourself. If you hear the vowel sound that's in *pen*, write e. If you hear the vowel sound that's in *evil*, write ē.

_____ 1. bread   _____ 6. ski

_____ 2. piece   _____ 7. guest

_____ 3. real   _____ 8. key

_____ 4. friend   _____ 9. bean

_____ 5. said   _____ 10. leaf

Long and Short i: The key word for short i is *if* (pronounced if). The key word for long i is *kite* (pronounced kīt). Pronounce the words below to yourself. If you hear the vowel sound that's in *if*, write i. If you hear the vowel sound that's in *kite*, write ī.

_____ 1. give   _____ 4. eye

_____ 2. fly   _____ 5. build

_____ 3. gym   _____ 6. buy

_____ 7. light   _____ 9. pie

_____ 8. lived   _____ 10. aisle

Long and Short o: The key word for short o is *hot.* In the dictionary, short o is written ä (hät). The key word for long o is *no* (nō). Pronounce the words below to yourself. If you hear the vowel sound that's in *hot,* write ä. If you hear the vowel sound that's in *no,* write ō.

_____ 1. calm   _____ 6. hold

_____ 2. know   _____ 7. odd

_____ 3. both   _____ 8. soul

_____ 4. stop   _____ 9. toe

_____ 5. dough   _____ 10. don't

Long and Short u: The key word for short u is *up.* The key word for long u is *mule.* Long u is written in the dictionary as yōō (myōōl). If you hear the vowel sound that's in *up,* write u. If you hear the vowel sound that's in *mule,* write yōō.

_____ 1. few   _____ 6. huge

_____ 2. love   _____ 7. once

_____ 3. does   _____ 8. use

_____ 4. view   _____ 9. rough

_____ 5. tongue   _____ 10. was

Long and Short oo: The key word for short oo is *book.* The key word for long oo is *food.* In the dictionary, short oo is written oo (book) and long oo is written ōō (fōōd). If you hear the vowel sound that's in *book,* write oo. If you hear the vowel sound that's in *food,* write ōō.

_____ 1. proof   _____ 6. fruit

_____ 2. put   _____ 7. could

_____ 3. do   _____ 8. wood

_____ 4. wolf   _____ 9. move

_____ 5. shoe   _____ 10. grew

PRONUNCIATION

Review of Long and Short Vowels: The key words are listed below.

Vowel	Short	Long
a	cat	ate
e	pen	evil
i	if	kite
o	hot	no
u	up	mule
oo	book	food

If the vowel sound in the following words is short, write S. If the vowel sound is long, write L. In the second space, write the key word for each vowel sound.

_____ 1. young _____   _____ 6. mop _____

_____ 2. hate _____   _____ 7. high _____

_____ 3. eight _____   _____ 8. head _____

_____ 4. some _____   _____ 9. swam _____

_____ 5. pull _____   _____ 10. chief _____

The following words have long vowel sounds. Write ā, ē, ī, ō, yo͞o, or o͞o to show which long vowel you hear.

_____ 1. glue   _____ 6. pain

_____ 2. steak   _____ 7. suit

_____ 3. height   _____ 8. meat

_____ 4. glow   _____ 9. though

_____ 5. cute   _____ 10. my

R-Controlled Vowels är and er: Some vowels are neither long nor short. They have a special sound because they are followed by the letter r. The key word for the är sound is *car* (kär). The key word for the er sound is *there* (ther). Pronounce each word to yourself. Again, don't be fooled by the spelling. If you hear the vowel sound that's in *car*, write är. If you hear the vowel sound that's in *there,* write er.

PRONUNCIATION

_____ 1. spare   _____ 6. guard

_____ 2. sharp   _____ 7. bear

_____ 3. star   _____ 8. arm

_____ 4. where   _____ 9. air

_____ 5. chair   _____ 10. prayer

R-Controlled Vowels ir, ôr, ur: There are three more R-controlled vowels: ir as in _here_ (hir), ôr as in _or_ (ôr), and ur as in _turn_ (turn). Pronounce each word to yourself, compare it with the key word, and write ir, ôr, or ur.

_____ 1. near   _____ 6. bird

_____ 2. four   _____ 7. year

_____ 3. verse   _____ 8. door

_____ 4. word   _____ 9. her

_____ 5. store   _____ 10. beer

Review of R-Controlled Vowels: Write är, er, ir, ôr, or ur to show which vowel sound you hear in each word below.

_____ 1. world   _____ 6. glare

_____ 2. fair   _____ 7. serve

_____ 3. weird   _____ 8. hard

_____ 4. park   _____ 9. fear

_____ 5. sport   _____ 10. swear

Vowel Sounds ô, oi, ou: The key word for ô is _gone_ (gôn). The key word for oi is _boil_. The key word for ou is _house_. Write ô if you hear the sound that's in _gone_. Write oi if you hear the sound that's in _boil_. Write ou if you hear the sound that's in _house_.

_____ 1. toy   _____ 6. pause

_____ 2. soft   _____ 7. cough

_____ 3. plow   _____ 8. blouse

_____ 4. voice   _____ 9. spoil

_____ 5. ounce   _____ 10. crawl

Schwa—Unaccented Syllables: The schwa sound is pronounced uh, similar to the short u, and it is written ə. It occurs in syllables that do *not* have the accent or stress. For example, in the word *ago,* the accent is on the second syllable (ə gō′). In the word *healthy,* the accent is on the first syllable (hel′thē). For each word below, write 1 if the accent is on the first syllable and 2 if the accent is on the second syllable.

_____ 1. above

_____ 2. onion

_____ 3. kitchen

_____ 4. unfold

_____ 5. honest

_____ 6. water

_____ 7. hotel

_____ 8. purpose

_____ 9. describe

_____ 10. music

Schwa Sound: The schwa sound can be spelled with any vowel letter and many vowel combinations.

a   ago (ə gō′)

e   oven (uv′ən)

i   April (ā′prəl)

o   collect (kə lekt′)

u   circus (sʉr′kəs)

ou   famous (fā′məs)

In the words below, if you hear the schwa in an unaccented syllable, write ə. If you do not hear a schwa, write 0.

_____ 1. upon

_____ 2. icy

_____ 3. allow

_____ 4. jealous

_____ 5. monkey

_____ 6. locate

_____ 7. precious

_____ 8. lemon

_____ 9. friendly

_____ 10. silly

Review of Vowel Sounds: Your key words are listed below.

Vowel	Pronunciation	Key word	Pronunciation
short a	a	cat	kat
long a	ā	ate	āt
short e	e	pen	pen
long e	ē	evil	ē′vəl
short i	i	if	if
long i	ī	kite	kīt

Vowel	Pronunciation	Key word	Pronunciation
short o	ä	hot	hät
long o	ō	no	nō
short u	u	up	up
long u	yo͞o	mule	myo͞ol
short oo	oo	book	book
long oo	o͞o	food	fo͞od
ar	är	car	kär
er	er	there	ther
ir	ir	here	hir
or	ôr	or	ôr
ur	ʉr	turn	turn
o	ô	gone	gôn
oi	oi	boil	boil
ou	ou	house	hous
schwa	ə	about	ə bout′

Match the following words with their pronunciation by writing the appropriate letter from the second column in the blanks next to the first column. In the second blank, write the key word from the list above.

_____ 1. full   a. fo͞ol   _____

_____ 2. fool   b. fôl   _____

_____ 3. fall   c. fyo͞ol   _____

_____ 4. fuel   d. fāl   _____

_____ 5. fail   e. fool   _____

Match the following words with the correct pronunciation and fill in the key word.

_____ 1. soil   a. sēl   _____

_____ 2. soul   b. sōl   _____

_____ 3. sail   c. soil   _____

_____ 4. seal   d. sel   _____

_____ 5. sell   e. sāl   _____

Use the key words at the beginning of this review to match the following words with the correct pronunciation and fill in the correct key word.

_____	1. fair	a. fär	_____
_____	2. fire	b. fer	_____
_____	3. far	c. fir	_____
_____	4. fear	d. fôr	_____
_____	5. for	e. fīr	_____

Match the following words with the correct pronunciation and fill in the correct key word.

_____	1. where	a. wʉr	_____
_____	2. were	b. wôr	_____
_____	3. war	c. wīr	_____
_____	4. wire	d. wer	_____
_____	5. we're	e. wir	_____

Match the following words with the correct pronunciation.

_____	1. button	a. bēt'ən
_____	2. baton	b. bit'ən
_____	3. bottom	c. bə tän'
_____	4. beaten	d. but'ən
_____	5. bitten	e. bät'əm

Irregular Consonant Sounds

You have seen that vowels in English often have sounds that differ from their spellings. Some of the consonants have different sounds, too. This review introduces you to the most common irregular consonant sounds.

Sounds of c: The letter _c_ can sound like s as in _city_ (sit'ē), like k as in _cat_ (kat), or like sh as in _ocean_ (ō'shən). In the following words, write s if the c sounds like the c that's in _city_. Write k if the c sounds like the c that's in _cat_. Write sh if the c sounds like the c that's in _ocean_.

_____ 1. center   _____ 6. coffee

_____ 2. cold   _____ 7. social

_____ 3. crazy   _____ 8. cigar

_____ 4. special   _____ 9. cent

_____ 5. candy   _____ 10. count

Sounds of g: The letter *g* can sound like j as in *gym* (jim), or it can sound like g as in *goat* (gōt). For the following words, write j if the g sounds like the g that's in *gym*. Write g if it sounds like the g that's in *goat*.

_____ 1. large   _____ 6. giant

_____ 2. get   _____ 7. give

_____ 3. edge   _____ 8. gem

_____ 4. gentle   _____ 9. generous

_____ 5. guess   _____ 10. gutter

Sounds of d: The letter *d* usually has three sounds. It can sound like d as in *dog* (dôg), like t as in *walked* (wôkt), or like j as in *graduate* (graj′ o͞o wāt). Listen for the sound of d in the words below. Write d, t, or j.

_____ 1. add   _____ 6. educate

_____ 2. looked   _____ 7. would

_____ 3. filled   _____ 8. asked

_____ 4. soldier   _____ 9. worked

_____ 5. draw   _____ 10. played

Sounds of s: The letter *s* usually makes four sounds. It can sound like s as in *sat* (sat), like z as in *his* (hiz), like sh as in *sugar* (sho͞og′ ər), or like zh as in *treasure* (trezh′ ər). Listen for the sounds of s in the words below. Write s, z, sh, or zh.

_____ 1. desert   _____ 6. is

_____ 2. tissue   _____ 7. fasten

_____ 3. measure   _____ 8. yes

_____ 4. sleep   _____ 9. television

_____ 5. sure   _____ 10. desire

Sounds of ch: The letters *ch* usually make three sounds: ch as in *chart* (chärt), k as in *school* (sko͞ol), and sh as in *machine* (mə shēn'). Listen for the sounds of ch in the words below. Write ch, k, or sh.

_____ 1. Chicago

_____ 2. touch

_____ 3. Christmas

_____ 4. chef

_____ 5. chorus

_____ 6. speech

_____ 7. parachute

_____ 8. echo

_____ 9. child

_____ 10. stomach

Sounds of th: The letters *th* usually make two sounds: th as in *thick* (thik) and th as in *the* (thə). You can tell the difference between th and *th* if you put your hand on your throat and say the key words out loud. When you say *thick*, you cannot feel any vibration on the th sound. When you say *the*, you can feel your voice box vibrate on the th. Listen for the two sounds of th in the words below. If you hear the sound that's in *thick*, write u for *unvoiced*. If you hear the sound that's in *the*, write v for *voiced*.

_____ 1. thirty

_____ 2. father

_____ 3. thank

_____ 4. smooth

_____ 5. tooth

_____ 6. three

_____ 7. month

_____ 8. they

_____ 9. thing

_____ 10. throw

Silent Letters: Many words have silent letters. For example, in the word *caught*, gh is silent (côt). In the word *hour*, the h is silent (our). Write the letter or letters that are silent in the words below.

_____ 1. whole

_____ 2. sign

_____ 3. debt

_____ 4. handsome

_____ 5. autumn

_____ 6. cupboard

_____ 7. island

_____ 8. talk

_____ 9. often

_____ 10. two

Review of Irregular Consonant Sounds: Look at the underlined letters in each word in the first column and then write the letter for the matching sound.

_____	1. pre<u>c</u>ious	a. g
_____	2. colle<u>g</u>e	b. zh
_____	3. <u>k</u>nife	c. sh
_____	4. <u>th</u>ick	d. silent
_____	5. <u>ch</u>emical	e. *th*
_____	6. talke<u>d</u>	f. s
_____	7. <u>th</u>e	g. k
_____	8. plea<u>s</u>ure	h. j
_____	9. ex<u>c</u>ept	i. t
_____	10. <u>g</u>ive	j. th

Posttest: Vowels and Consonants

cat, āte, fäther; pen, ēvil; if, kīte; nō, ôr, fōōd, book; boil, house; up, tʉrn; chief, shell; thick, *the*; zh, treasure; ŋ, sing; ə for *a* in *about*; ' as in *able* (ā'b'l)

Using the pronunciation guide above, translate the following paragraph into English spelling.

> ə mer'ə kənz spend siks hun'drid mil'yən däl'ərz ə yir än hät dôgz. *th*ā ēt i nuf' uv *th*em ēch yir tōō fôrm ə chān strech'iŋ frum *th*ə ʉrth tōō *th*ə mōōn and bak ə gen'. *th*ə av'rij ə mer'ə kən ēts fôr'tē hät dôgz ə yir. but *th*ə hät dôg wuz nät in ven'tid in *th*ə yōō nīt'id stāts; it wuz fʉrst mād bī ə grōōp uv bōōch'ərz in fraŋk'fərt, jʉr'mə nē in 1852.

_____

_____

_____

_____

_____

_____

Credits

These pages constitute an extension of the copyright page.

Page 36. Exerpts from *Webster's New World Dictionary*, Pocket Star Books Edition. Copyright © 1990, 1995 by Simon & Schuster.

Page 70. From HOUGHTON MIFFLIN ENGLISH, Level 8 by Haley-James, et al. Copyright © 1988 by Houghton Mifflin Company. Reprinted by permission of Houghton Mifflin Company. All rights reserved.

Page 78. Excerpt titled "A League of Her Own" from WNBA: A CELEBRATION by WNBA ENTERPRISE, L.L.C. Copyright © 1998 by WNBA Enterprises, L.L.C. Reprinted by permission of HarperCollins Publishers, Inc.

Page 87. Malcom Forbes, "How to Write a Business Letter," from *Power of the Printed Word Program*, 1979. Reprinted by permission of International Publishing Co.

Page 98. Bill Cosby, "How to Read Faster," from *Power of the Printed Word Program*, 1979. Reprinted by permission of International Publishing Co.

Page 117. Walter Cronkite, "How to Read a Newspaper," reprinted by permission of International Paper Co.

Page 128. Reprinted from *Better Investing* magazine, June, 1998, p. 78–82, and with permission from The Motley Fool (www.fool.com).

Page 143. "Improve Your Memory in 7 Easy Steps." Copyright © 1986 by Morton Hunt. Reprinted by permission of Georges Borchardt, Inc. for the author. Originally appeared in *Parade* magazine.

Page 152. From *Healthy for Life: Wellness and the Art of Living (also: Health Information Update 1994-95), 1st Edition*, by B. Williams and S. Knight. © 1994. Reprinted with permission of Wadsworth Publishing, a division of Thomson Learning. Fax 800 730-2215.

Page 164. From *Business Communication, 4th Edition*, by A. Krizan, P. Merrier, C. L. Jones, and J. Harcourt. © 1999. Reprinted with permission of South-Western College Publishing, a division of Thomson Learning. Fax 800 730-2215.

Page 180. From *The Challenge of Effective Speaking, 10th Edition*, by R. F. Verderber. © 1997. Reprinted with permission of Wadsworth Publishing, a division of Thomson Learning. Fax 800 730-2215.

Page 189. From *The Challenge of Effective Speaking, 10th Edition*, by R. F. Verderber. © 1997. Reprinted with permission of Wadsworth Publishing, a division of Thomson Learning. Fax 800 730-2215.

Page 211. Photo courtesy of Corbis.

Page 214. From *Essentials of Oceanography, 1st edition*, by T. Garrison. © 1995. Reprinted with permission of Brooks/Cole Publishing, a division of Thomson Learning.

Page 216. Jamestown Publishers, 1978. Reprinted by permission.

Page 217. From *Biology: Concepts and Applications (Hardcover Version), 3rd edition*, by C. Starr. © 1997. Reprinted with permission of Brooks/Cole Publishing, a division of Thomson Learning.

Page 220. From *Communicating for Success, 1st edition*, by J. S. Hyden, et al. © 1994. Reprinted with permission of South-Western Publishing Co., a division of Thomson Learning.

Page 222. Cindy Krunnesky, timeline from "It's in the E-Mail," from *PC Novice*, Sept. 1995, p. 31. Reprinted by permission of the publisher.

Index